MW01389129

Table of Contents

Introduction	6
Home	9
Code 1019	15
This Old House	22
Rachel Hollingsworth	30
Visitors	35
Dr. Cook	40
Hell's Hole	46
Camille Carmichael	49
Rachel's Visit	60
Ray Phillips	68
Rainman Elementary School	72
Another Visit	76
Travel Plans	80
Micah's Visit	83
Leap And The Net Will Appear	89
A Change In Direction	97
Here Here!	108
Forgiven	116
What The ...	121
God Be With Us	127
The Dinner Party	134
Betty Bishop	141
Good News Bad News	148
Bear Hunt	152

You Never Know	160
A Glimpse Of Heaven	167
"It"	174
Focus on Me	181
A Good Day	188
Ho! Ho! Ho!	204
Christmas Eve Eve	212
Reparation	222
Farewell	230
Full House	236
The Commission Piece	243
The Stillmore's Christmas	264
What A Gal	275
The Kiss, The Letter	292
The Woes Of Wine	296
Tommy	306
April	321
Adam	340
Rosewood	344
For Lease	351
Seafood Festival	360
Epilogue	369

*I wish I could take language
And fold it like warm, moist rags.
I would lay words on your forehead.
I would wrap words on your wrists.
"There, there," my words would say—
Or something better.*

*I would ask them to murmur,
"Hush" and "Shh,shhh, it's all right."
I would ask them to hold you all night.*

*I wish I could take language
And daub and soothe and cool
Where fever blisters and burns,
Where pain turns yourself against you.*

*I wish I could take language
And heal the words
that were the wounds
you have no names for.*

Julia Cameron
The Artist's Way

Introduction

It amazes me how fast earth travels through space. The little blue ball we call home not only rotates on it's axis at about 1000 miles per hour, but it's also whizzing around the sun at about 155 miles per second! But we have no sense of this speed. We barely notice the changes that all this whirling through space causes. But everything is always changing. Life sometimes seems like an airport terminal with people on the move, constantly coming and going. Just in the short span of 3 years, while I was writing this book, my son Vince had his first grandchild. Then he died after a long illness. His granddaughter was just arriving as he was departing (and way too soon.)

It was my son Vince that came over almost daily during his illness and wanted to hear any new words I had written about Rainman Island. He applauded, smiled, and shouted "encore!" It encouraged me so, I wrote on, stopping here and there to be mad at what was happening to him, and to me. It was Vince that wanted me to add the bear attack (if you read on, you'll understand). He said my story needed the impact of something completely unexpected. Since my story is about faith and redemption, I immediately saw the metaphor. I hope you will, too.

But the character I heard most from in writing this story was my sister Camille. Parts of her personality are on every page, in every conversation, in every character. In real life Camille is my one and only sister, my true friend, and the most profound person I have ever met. And it is in my character Camille Carmichael that I let her identity surface--one aspect of it at least.

My sister Camille is an artist extraordinaire. But as I write this, her hands, back and feet are so crippled by Rheumatoid Arthritis that she can barely function. She is plagued by other health problems also. She spends many hours each day in the bed. Rheumatoid Arthritis has devoured both of her hands to the degree that she only has one finger and a thumb on her right hand that she can (sometimes) press into service enough to paint, or open a can, or hold a coffee cup.

But she has a force of spirit—a will so intense that I think sometimes her spirit is going to pop right out of her diseased body and go off on it's own! And she continues to turn out masterpieces in watercolor and oils still worthy of the blue ribbon she won at the fair over 60 years ago.

I could name hundreds of times I have needed her and she has been there for me. I likewise have tried to be there for her, though often without the grace she extends to me and to others. Camille writes those crazy letters and covers them with bright, funny stickers. Inside her letters she embellishes the ridiculous -- making me laugh, which is almost always her intention.

I dedicate this book to Camille.

I fashioned the character of Ray after the love of my

life, my dear husband, Carroll. While it is true that I killed him off in the bear attack! Oops! It is also true that no matter what surprises life has thrown at us, we have muddled through—together. He is my biggest fan, my chief supporter and the one I point to when asked who loves me most. After twenty years of marriage I can honestly say his love is as close to unconditional as human love gets.

Home

Once my life was full of fools and strangers. Now, only one fool, stranger than them all, remains.

Nancy Hogan drove her green Volvo off the ferry ramp onto Peterson Point Road then turned right onto Honey Bear Lane. The slanting rays of the late afternoon sun filtered through what remained of the leaves and cast small, moving splotches of pale yellow light on the road. Nancy's tires crunched in the fallen acorns. She drove slowly down the familiar road noticing that some industrious neighbors had piled leaves neatly here and there along the side of the road.

As she drove past the old Victorian house at 14 Honey Bear Lane she noticed the sudden movement of a squirrel. He returned her glance, seemingly frozen with his tail curled into a question mark. Nancy smiled and thought how the squirrel's gesture seemed to emphasize the mystery of the woman that lived there. She recalled her one and only visit. It happened right after she and her husband moved to the island, 15 years earlier.

A large manila envelope had been left in Nancy's mailbox by mistake. It was labeled: Camille of Rosewood, 14 Honey Bear Lane, Rainman Island, BC. Nancy drove past the short, gravel driveway and thought about the black metal mailbox attached to what appeared to be the front door, although the door was on the side of the house. The house had several porches and exterior doors. Nancy had been confused as to which door to knock on. That's when she had spotted the mailbox, attached to a side door. She recalled stepping silently onto the porch intending to leave the misguided package. That's when she had discovered the sign that informed her to "USE REAR ENTRANCE - DO NOT LEAVE PACKAGES HERE!" The sign was hand made in bright red letters. Nancy thought it sounded angry or at least annoyed.

Rosewood. That was the name of the house on the package. *Not much Rosewood around here.*

She remembered going around to the back of the house and onto a large screened porch. She assumed it must be the rear entrance referred to on the sign. She had tapped lightly on the door and waited.

The older woman who finally opened the door had gotten there by the aid of a cane. She was wearing stage length false eyelashes! She had flashed Nancy a dazzling smile and offered her some bit of humor about the postal service. Nancy even remembered what the woman had been wearing; a brightly colored muumuu. *You don't see many of those now days.*

Nancy drove on. Honey Bear Lane curved gently up a slight incline and away from Rosewood but her thoughts of the house and its owner lingered. Through the intervening years, Nancy had come to know Camille as a gifted artist and active in many aspects of the cultural life of the island community.

Little did she know it then but their paths would cross again, and soon.

A few minutes later Nancy parked in her own driveway. From force of habit she glanced at the little clock on the dash of her car. 6:11 p.m. She scooped up her purse and the small empty container that had held her lunch and stepped out into the early evening glamour of mid October. The air was cool and tinged with the smoke of burning leaves, mingled with the sweet aroma of something cooking somewhere and the acrid smell of chrysanthemums that lined her driveway. Her neighbor's dog started barking. *He was doing his job*, *alerting anyone that cared that she was now home.*

Her dog Bernie was the first to welcome her. In fact he had his chin in her lap as soon as the car door swung open. Claude, the cat, came slinking up. He licked a paw and watched nonchalantly at all the 'hoorah' the dog was making over the human getting out of the car. The cat's golden-eyed stare conveyed his total disinterest. Nancy smiled and thought about a saying she had seen recently on a plaque in the hospital's gift shop: "Dogs have masters, cats have staff!" *How true.* She watched the cat glide away.

It was an evening to cherish. One of those mild fall days that you wish you could conjure back on demand. Nancy stood in her driveway and stretched her arms up over her head. She had been sitting in her car for a while, her body felt stiff. She glanced up at the familiar sight of her home.

She did not, in fact could not have seen the eyes that watched her.

Nancy's home at 354 Honey Bear Lane was a large, two story cape cod she'd had painted a creamy yellow last year. When she'd moved into this house, both she and her husband thought they wanted to live the island life. It was an escape for both of them. They had remained married through forty-one loveless years and one disappointing son.

She often wondered why people said that she and Frank were the lucky ones. If they only knew. Nancy's husband had been a banker and made what she later found out to be shrewd investments. When he turned 55, there was cash enough to purchase this place and live a lifestyle that Frank thought would somehow fulfill him. It never did. In truth, Frank had been a self-absorbed man and shamelessly spoiled their only child. They had been arguing, once again, about their son, Frank Jr. the night Frank died. He'd been seized with a heart attack in the middle of a rant about Frank Jr. and BAM! He was gone. Just like that.

Frank Jr. was nearly 35 when his father died. But he had continued to live with his mother on and off after his dad's death for nearly 5 years. Nancy never saw him drugging or drinking but she knew he did. Frank Jr.'s life was in chaos. It struck Nancy that her son was one of those people that never does anything with their life, no matter how much she urged or threatened. And then, one day, Frank Jr. had simply disappeared. He'd been staying on the main island with one of his friends for several months so she had not missed him immediately. A phone call had tipped her off, then the search had started. No one had seen him leave. He seemed to have simply dropped off the face of the earth. A private investigator was hired but found no trace of Frank Jr. There wasn't even a paper trail, the PI had told her. The police searched, friends made inquiries, but nothing ever turned up. Nothing. He'd been gone for almost 5 years now.

The warm evening air seemed to beckon her, convincing her there was nothing at all waiting inside the big empty house, except the laundry and a few breakfast dishes. For a moment she considered calling her friend Claudia to see if she could be lured out for a walk. Then she decided she really didn't want to wait on Claudia to drive from the other side of the island.

She shoved her purse and lunch container into a small cabinet near the back door, grabbed the dog's leash and clipped it on Bernie's collar. Bernie immediately started tugging her toward the road. The cat watched in stunned silence, seemingly shocked that he was not the center of Nancy's universe.

Honey Bear Lane runs exactly 2.6 miles West to Northeast in gentle curves that skirt around ancient trees and over two creeks. At one end Honey Bear Lane dead ends into Peterson Point Road, the main road connecting the ferry to Peterson Point, near Tribune Bay. At the other end Honey Bear Lane intersects Peterson Point Road again but on the opposite side of the island. There are no sidewalks on Honey Bear Lane so Bernie and Nancy walked along the right side of the road so as to face any oncoming cars, although there weren't many of those on the island in mid-October.

It was her favorite time of day. As she walked along through the last golden light of day she felt a bit tired but wonderfully alive and free. Nancy thought of the challenging comment she had read that morning: *Hallowed be Thy Name...reminds us that our life and work are without significance, except in so far as they glorify that God to whom nothing is adequate though everything is dear.* "Have I glorified You today, Father?" she said out loud. "Were the things I did and thought today somehow dear to an awesome God that lacks nothing, needs nothing?

The single headlight that loomed up directly in front of her startled her. Nancy tugged at Bernie's leash, dragging him out of the road. It was Rachel Hollingsworth driving her blasted motorbike at top speed!

"Damn it!" Nancy shouted. Rachel flew past them without even noticing the two figures standing by the side of the road in the growing darkness. "Better get you home, Bernie, before that damn fool woman kills us both!"

Code 1019

The lights in the small clinic on Rainman Island had just come on via the automatic timer. There was only one patient in the clinic tonight. The clinic was not, in fact, designed for patients requiring more than primary care. Dr. Alice was the only medical doctor on Rainman Island. Her practice these days consisted of the usual supply of cuts and sprains, especially for the spring and summer vacationers. But tonight, things were quiet. Ray Phillips was staying in the small wardroom of the clinic after a nasty bout with pneumonia. Ray was nearing his 75th birthday. He had lived on the island most of his life and wanted to die there. His parents and his wife were buried in the small Methodist cemetery on the North side of the island. So was his young daughter.

At 53, Dr. Alice Mitchell's hair was still an amazing auburn color, thick and bouncy and of absolutely no interest to Alice. She kept it clean and pulled back in a ponytail. No one remembers ever seeing Dr. Alice (as she is known on the island) without her ponytail. It is a preference she formed more than 40 years ago. She wears no makeup, never has, but the years have been kind to her. Her eyes wrinkle up into little slits when she smiles and her open mouth grin reveals large white teeth, a little too big for her small mouth.

Dr. Alice peeked around the curtain that sectioned off Ray's bed from the front door. "How's it going?" she asked brightly. She once again noticed Ray's full head of dazzling white hair.

"Lousy, rotten, no good!" Ray said grinning back at her. He had to bend his knees a little so that his long, Abe Lincoln body fit into the hospital bed.

"Yea, that's what you always say, Ray. I can count on it. Let's have a listen to that old chest of yours." Dr. Alice warmed the stethoscope in her hand for a moment before she put it down on Ray's bare chest. She wore half glasses over her grey-blue eyes.

After a moment of moving the stethoscope around on his chest she frowned down at Ray and said, "that old clock of yours sounds like it needs winding."

He shot her a half smile. "Well what did you have in mind?" he asked playfully.

"I was thinking maybe a little game of Scrabble. That's about as racy as you or I can handle."

"Oh shucks!" Ray mimicked a complaint. "I thought I was finally getting somewhere with you, Doc!"

The banter between old friends continued for a few moments. Neither of them noticed as Rachel Hollingsworth slammed her scooter to a stop outside the clinic. She dug both feet into the loose gravel of the parking lot trying to bring her speeding scooter to a stop.

Rachel kicked the scooter's stand down and took

long, quick steps toward the front door of the clinic. She started shouting for Dr. Alice the minute she pushed opened the door.

Startled by the suddenness of Rachel's entrance, Dr. Alice stood up and pulled the curtain around Ray's bed back so she had a view of the front door.

"Rachel! What's wrong?"

"It's my mother!" Rachel said. "Can you come right away? I just found her on the kitchen floor, unconscious!"

"Be right with you, Rachel," she said and turned back to Ray.

"Will you be alright here by yourself for awhile? Pam had to run home and do something for her kids. Micah isn't home yet." Pam was Dr. Alice's nurse, the only other medical person on the island. She lived about ½ mile from the clinic.

"I'll leave Pam's phone number with you Ray, in case you need something before she comes back."

"That'll be OK. I'm quite use to being by myself since my Linda died." Ray said as he waved her toward the door.

Alice Mitchell didn't need any directions to Rachel's mother's house. She passed it every day. Betty Bishop lived at 64 Honey Bear Lane. In the growing darkness they made a strange little caravan up Honey Bear Lane, Rachel leading the way on her ancient Allstate motor scooter and Alice right behind her in her Army surplus Jeep.

They both whizzed by Nancy and Bernie without so much as a wave. Nancy's open jacket fluttered in the breeze of their wake. She pushed a lock of hair back into place. *That's strange. Rachel's mother again, I guess,* Nancy thought.

Dr. Alice followed Rachel into the dark kitchen. Alice noticed that the back door was standing wide open when they came up in the yard. Betty's house was like a square box containing 4 small rooms. It had been built cheaply in '50's as someone's summer vacation cottage. Cooking smells like stale bacon grease mixed with the earthy smell of mold filled Alice's senses. Instantly another smell assaulted her senses. It was overwhelming – *what was that*?

"Gas! Rachel! Turn off the stove!" Dr. Alice shouted.

Rachel raced over to the stove and noticed that all 4 jets had been turned wide open. The oven door was also open and the gas turned on.

"Open all the windows and doors" Dr. Alice shouted again as if Rachel were far away. "And then get out of here. Quick!" She picked up Betty's feet and dragged her unconscious body through the open back door onto the small back porch of the house.

"For God's sake! Rachel, don't light a match in there!" Dr. Alice bellowed from the porch.

One look at Betty Bishop's face and you know she has suffered. The lines in her face make her look much older than her 56 years. Life for Betty had been a series of mostly bad choices followed by years of family reminding her of her bad choices. Dr. Alice knew that Betty slipped in and out of depression and thought she was probably bi-polar but undiagnosed and untreated.

"Is it too late?" Rachel asked in a shrill voice as Dr. Alice pulled Betty's eyelids back and shined a small flash light into them. Dr. Alice quickly took Betty's pulse and listened to her heart.

"She's alive, barely," she said. "Good thing you left that back door open when you came to get me. If you hadn't she might not have made it this far. Call Big John and see if he can come over with the stretcher. We'll need to get her over to Memorial on the big Island as soon as possible."

Big John Parker was the owner of the local ferry and could be counted on to help in emergencies. In fact, after his wife died, Big John had trained as an EMT. But after a few years of ambulance work, he had burned out. That's when he had moved to Rainman Island and started the ferry business.

Dr. Alice raced to her car and grabbed box off the back seat that contained a portable oxygen concentrator. She kept it there in case of emergencies.

"Damn, I forgot the batteries, she said under her breath."

With fluid motions she worked efficiently, with little or no emotion. She hooked up the portable oxygen concentrator with an extension cord ran it into a kitchen receptacle. She then placed the oxygen mask over Betty's face and switched the machine on.

With forced air going, Alice began to massage Betty's heart and lungs. "Breathe, Betty, breathe!"

Meanwhile, Rachel stood in the yard and dialed Big John's Ferry Service. "No answer", she screamed. "I'm just getting a message."

"Call over to the restaurant, see if anyone has seen him." Dr. Alice said. "If not, ask for anybody else with a boat that's ready to go. Tell them to get up here, stat!"

Rachel did as she was told, wondering all the while who might have opened the back door and all the windows in the kitchen. She knew she had not done it. She had panicked when she found her mother lying on the floor. She hadn't even smelled the gas.

Sandy answered the phone at The Sleeping Pig restaurant. The Sleeping Pig was a barbecue joint open 6 days a week for lunch and dinner and a gathering spot for the locals.

"Do you know where Big John is?" Rachel was screaming. "I have an emergency--it's my mother! She's unconscious! She's at home. I need to get her over to the Big Hospital on Vancouver Island quick!"

"Hey John!" Sandy turned to the crowd of noisy customers, and held up her hand trying to make her voice heard over the noise.

"Big John said he'd be right there," Sandy said when she came back on the line. "He said hang on he'd be there in about 15 minutes or less. He's already gassed up with his small boat in the water at the ferry. Said he doesn't have a stretcher though."

"We'll manage - just get him coming out here as quickly as possible." Rachel struggled to keep her balance as she ended the call.

This Old House

Much is required from those to whom much is given, and much more is required from those to whom much more is given. Jesus

It was completely dark by the time Nancy and Bernie returned home from their walk. A pale moon had started its climb. Nancy took a final deep breath of the fragrant October night before she opened her kitchen door with the key she kept on top of the doorsill. *With the key in such an obvious place, why bother to lock doors?* Frank had always insisted on locking things up.

She flicked on the light and sat her purse and lunch bag down on the kitchen island. On her way in she had stopped by the mailbox and collected a small stack of envelopes, which she now shuffled through aimlessly: one bill and several advertisements. The last one in the stack was a letter from her sister. She received a letter from her sister several times a week. *I wish I had that kind of discipline or love or whatever it takes.* The envelopes containing her sister's letters were often decorated with one or more brightly colored stickers or some quirky artwork. Nancy often amused herself trying to guess what the tone of the message inside would be based on the type of stickers or art on the outside of the envelope. For example, if the stickers were little yellow smiley faces, or happy bunny rabbits, then the letter inside might be funny. Sometimes the stickers had a religious theme like angels or a cross.

In that case the message inside might be reporting on some spiritual experience or "God-thing," as Laura called it. As often as not, letters from Laura on the subject of religion or God were negative and angry.

Laura was Nancy's identical twin sister. However, they are total opposites in both values and temperament. Laura is as artistic as she is outspoken and a confirmed agnostic. Nancy is a gentle and kind believer and doesn't have an artistic bone in her body. But other than Claudia, Laura is Nancy's best friend.

As Bernie lapped water from his bowl in the kitchen floor, Nancy sank down on a tall upholstered bar stool near the kitchen island and tore open her sister's latest letter. A picture of a bed fell out. Something unusual was often enclosed in Laura's letters. Nancy smiled when she remembered Laura once sending her a pair of red high heel shoes in a Corn Flakes box!

October 5 (Tuesday)
Dear Sisterwoman,
Here is a new idea for you. Brison Home Catalogue is where I ordered the current bedspread and taffeta dust ruffle, years ago. Also the sewing machine I gave you came from Brison's. Idea: Could you take the photo of this spread and ruffle, send it to them over the NET and ask if they could find another one in their closet? Newer catalogues don't offer anything even close to this set. Or I'd have done it sooner. Sick hope! Again. If I want it – it's gone, discontinued, or destroyed.

Also, while you are on the NET see if you can find a local curse remover. They may want a lot of $ to remove all my curses! Find a cheap one! Latinos will do.

My friend, Steve, called and came by my house last night with a big bucket of apples. He's got Fall Fever and spent all of Sunday picking

apples up in North Georgia. It was late (after 9 p.m.) and I asked if he'd come during daylight next time so I could show him where to dig some holes for me. He's done with his work in India and back in the states. I told him it had been so long since I heard from him; I thought he'd been curried to death!! Steve's passion is food. After all that liposuction he went through, he's now double the body weight he was before. Other passions are antique frames and old art. He was my oldest and best customer back when I owned the framing shop and gallery. He's the one that brought me all the jobs to restore from Barrington Hall. Oh! I did tell him about my birthday plan for us, which includes a lobster and a tour of Barrington Hall. He responded to the lobster with a yummm. Nothing at all on Barrington Hall (teehee). What ideas do you have for your birthday? Or should I ask someone else?
Happy Thanksgiving you Canadian you!
Laura

Nancy glanced at the envelope to see if the stickers had in fact heralded the enclosed subject matter. There was a sticker with a little string of musical notes being played and bright yellow stars. *Guess the envelope theory has a few flaws.*

Laura hated computers. She said they were blight to society. She had never seen an Internet Browser and if she had it her way, she never would. *Guess that's why she wants me to get on the "net" as she calls it. She has no idea what the Internet is.*

I must answer her back soon. Our birthday is next month. I probably need to make reservations tonight to get to Atlanta. Nancy held the letter in her hand as she walked into her office. The room was filled with overloaded bookshelves on three walls. Her desk was centered under a bank of windows that covered the fourth wall.

The view from this small room adjacent to the kitchen was spectacular. Through these windows she could see the creek, rushing tirelessly over layers of sandstone forming small waterfalls here and there. Across the creek was open farmland that was lined horizontally with low stone hedges spaced about 5 acres apart.

A small white farmhouse sat deserted on the hill above the stone hedges. On the horizon beyond the little white house were the snow-capped mountains of Vancouver Island. Even in spring and summer the low lying white clouds often hovered on the mountain peaks making them appear snow covered. Sunrises and sunsets were spectacular from this window. It was a picture post card perfect scene as far as Nancy was concerned.

The computer buzzed to life as Nancy pulled up Google. Bernie followed her into the office and lay his head down in her lap hoping for a little more petting as she started searching through airline rates. She had been concentrating on her task for several minutes when Bernie suddenly snapped his head off her lap and started growling. The sudden movement startled Nancy.

"What did you hear boy?" Nancy said to the dog. She sat perfectly still, trying to hear what he had heard.

"Go see." She whispered softly to Bernie. He trotted toward the hallway leading upstairs. The hair on his neck was raised. Nancy had lived alone in this large house for more than 5 years, ever since Frank Jr. had disappeared. It was a quiet life, nothing remotely threatening about it, except maybe the weather sometimes. She had taken cover a few times when the weatherman warned about a strong wind blowing through. *Back in the states, they call them tornadoes. Here they call it a "wind".*

Nancy followed Bernie and they both stood at the foot of the steps. She flipped the lights on. Bernie sat beside her feet, his head cocked to one side listening. Again he growled and glanced up at her.

"Well, boy, you better go see." Bernie weighed about 30 pounds. His usefulness as an attack dog was limited, but he was a superb alarm system. Many times she had been alerted to something on the property by his frenzied barking. Usually it turned out to be a deer or wild turkeys he spotted strolling across the backyard. Stray cats and dogs that wandered over would also produce a round of barking and door clawing. He would chase after them until they turned and looked him in the eye and then he would make friends.

"Some watch dog." Nancy said.

Tonight, Bernie sat frozen gazing up the steps. His behavior made Nancy feel uneasy. Her imagination was traveling at warp speed. *What if someone did break in? What if some crazed murderer was waiting upstairs ready to strangle her, shoot her, then knife her to death?* Her mind went stupid with fear.

I'll call Big John next door and see if he'll come over and check it out for me. He's offered before. She quickly walked back to the kitchen, picked up the phone and dialed her next-door neighbor.

His son answered. "Dad's not home yet," Danny said. Nancy explained the reason for her call. "Do you want me to come over and take a look?" Danny was 14, a big boy for his age. Big like his Dad.

Nancy did not know Danny very well. He kept to himself. She remembered when he had been born. His mother died that night. Dr. Alice, working alone and in their home, had not been able to save her. It had all been such a horrible tragedy. Nancy had seen more of Danny as a baby than she had since he turned into a teen. His dad said he spent most of his time behind a computer. Sort of a geek Nancy guessed.

"Well if you don't mind...do you think your dad would mind?"

"No Mam, I don't mind. I'll come right over." And he did. Nancy smiled shyly as Danny came into the kitchen. Bernie started barking the minute he heard the sound of Danny in the driveway. He continued to bark furiously until Nancy grabbed his collar and said, "be quiet Bernie, its just Danny."

"Bernie seems to have heard something upstairs and well, it frightened me." She stumbled with the words." Danny had the body of a man. He was already 6'2" and overweight. *I bet he wears Big John's clothes.*

"Have you got a hammer or something like a weapon I can carry, Ms. Hogan?" Danny asked smiling nervously.

"Sure." She went over to the kitchen drawer and pulled out a small hammer. Danny looked at it and smiled. It was almost a toy in his big hand. Nancy giggled like a young girl.

Danny left the kitchen. She heard him walk quickly

up the stairs to the second floor. The stairs were hardwood and more than one of them creaked. She listened and heard him flip the switch in the upstairs hall. Light flooded down the stairs.

She suddenly wondered why she was standing safely in her kitchen and letting a 14-year-old kid that she didn't know very well do her dirty work. She suddenly felt ridiculous.

She started up the steps at the same time that Danny started back down.

"I think I found the problem Ms. Hogan." His comment startled her. She wasn't expecting him to find anything.

"There was a window open up there. It goes out on the roof. I guess Bernie heard the blinds over that open window blowing and hitting the window sill."

"Oh." Nancy didn't remember any windows being left open upstairs. Her bedroom was downstairs. She hardly ever went up there.

"Well close it then, please, Danny, and lock it for me."

"Oh, I did Ms. H."

"Thank you Danny," Nancy said, and meant it.

"Please let your dad know that you came over and helped me out." Danny smiled down at his feet and was gone as suddenly as he had come in.

Alone again in the big house, Nancy still felt a little

uneasy. She couldn't put her finger on the reason. She noticed that Danny had left the lights on upstairs, so she decided to go up and have a look around herself. She glanced into each room, first turning on the lights and then turning them off again.

She did not notice the damp towels folded neatly back into place in the hall bathroom or the little drops of water still clinging to the rim of the sink.

Without warning a feeling of loneliness came over her. She stood there in the upstairs hall, clicking the light switch on then off then on again. She felt very small as if the house were about to swallow her up.

Silently she began to pray. *Dear Lord, how do You want to use this big old house You have given me? It seems foolish to have four bedrooms and two baths up here that are never used, never touched except when I clean them. Can You use them Father?* No answer came to her, only silence.

As she went back down the steps to her office and busied herself booking the flight to Atlanta, feelings of peace and safety returned to her without her even noticing.

Rachel Hollingsworth

Life shrinks or expands in proportion to one's courage. Anais Nin

They had used a blanket from the back of Dr. Alice's Jeep to wrap Betty in. It took all three of them to lift Betty into Big John's van, then into his boat for the 15-minute ride to Vancouver Island. Dr. Alice had called ahead. An ambulance would be standing by at Buckley Bay on the big island.

Betty was such a small person it seemed odd to her daughter that it took three people to pick her up. *Dead weight, I guess.* Rachel had never picked her mother up before.

The whole episode felt like she was watching someone else going through the motions and delivering her mother to the waiting ambulance while she watched, mutely. Betty had rallied a little while Dr. Alice worked on her. She was breathing on her own by the time they reached Big John's boat. Betty's slow response confused Dr. Alice a little. Rather, it left her curious as to what else might be going on. This was obviously an attempted suicide, which she dutifully communicated to the ambulance driver. Attempted suicide cases required special handling; they are referred to as code 1019 meaning someone has to watch the patient at all times. They can have nothing in their hospital rooms except what the hospital provides. Visitors are also restricted from bringing anything into the room that patients could use to injure themselves.

Dr. Alice phoned the attending physician in the ER at Comox Memorial Hospital. She suggested some tests to run on Betty. Dr. Alice knew that Betty had been a chain smoker all her adult life. She also remembered Betty's husband had been dead for about 6 years. He was a small engine mechanic. On the island his services were in constant demand. His death was a loss to everyone but no one more than Betty.

"Kenneth," Betty moaned.

Rachel was making the crossing with Big John and Betty. She was a little startled to hear her mother call her step dad's name. Rachel bent over Betty to make sure she was warm and to try and comfort her a little. It was the first time Rachel noticed what her mother had been wearing when she tried to kill herself. She was wearing Kenneth's pajamas.

Two days later Rachel had the full diagnosis. Lung Cancer, stage 4. The cancer had metastasized into her lymph nodes. Depression. Prognosis: she was at the end of life with somewhere between 4-6 months left. A rapid decline was anticipated. It was all described to Rachel in detail.

Once Betty had come out of the effects of the gas, she had seemed meek, rather ashamed of what she had tried to do. Betty wanted to know who had come to get her and how they had gotten her to Vancouver Island. Rainman Island is a small community; she knew everyone would be talking about her. She dreaded going back to "face the music" but she also dreaded not going back to her home. Rainman Island was where she had lived for most of her adult life. It's where she was living when she met Kenneth. It's where she wanted to die.

Betty had spent most of the last two days trying to come up with a plan she thought Rachel would go for regarding her return home. She felt vulnerable to Rachel, like she was now the child and Rachel was the mother. She knew she must be clever. She figured Rachel would raise some sort of protest and want to put her in a nursing home--be *done* with her. *And she had the power to do it--now*. There were no nursing homes on Rainman Island. Betty knew Rachel did not want to be bothered with other people's problems, especially hers.

Betty only had one friend on the Island, if you want to call her a friend. Fern. Fern was a self-proclaimed, born again Christian who had been coming by to visit Betty each Tuesday at 10 a.m. ever since Kenneth's death six years earlier.

Betty put up with these weekly visits because, at first, she had been lonely and needed someone to talk to. She didn't know how to even start to grieve the loss of Kenneth.

Rachel seldom came by unless something was wrong, or broken. The relationship between Rachel and Betty was tense and strained. Betty knew why. The bad choices she had made when her children were young and vulnerable was surely to blame for the distance she now experienced with Rachel. Rachel had been eight years old; her brother Robert was ten when Betty left them. No word, no warning, just gone when they came home from school one day. Robert had called their dad crying after waiting two days for their mother to return. She never did. They had moved in with their dad in Seattle and lived with him until they both finished high school.

Then one day Betty showed up again. She breezed in like she'd simply been out shopping. She told them she had bought a little house on Rainman Island and would love to have the kids visit. No explanation at all about the 8-year absence.

Rachel remembered being dumbfounded but totally delighted to see her mother again. She always felt that it was somehow her fault that her mother had left. Rachel had never been able to forgive herself for making "it" happen. She had wanted her mother so many times, cried herself to sleep so many nights. Rachel didn't really care where her mother had been. She didn't ever want to lose her again. Rachel's brother Robert felt a little differently. He was already dating steady when Betty came back and showed no interest whatsoever in Betty's mysterious return.

"Mother!" Rachel said louder than she meant to. Betty jumped. She had been staring out the window of her hospital room for over an hour. She did not hear Rachel come in.

"I need to talk to you about going home." Betty hurled the words at Rachel like she was trying to beat her to the punch. Rachel nodded slowly.

"Yes, we do need to talk, Mother" Rachel said almost in a whisper.

"Do you remember my friend Fern?" Betty asked as brightly as she could manage.

"Yeaaasss" Rachel drew the word out making a hissing sound. Instantly she knew where her mother was taking the conversation. She was stalling, trying to think.

"Well, she has offered to check on me a little more often than once a week. You know, to see if I need anything. She phoned me a little while ago. I think that will work out well, don't you?" Betty risked making eye contact with Rachel. She expected Rachel's head to be swinging into a "no."

But Rachel didn't say anything. She looked at her mother. In fact Rachel tried to take it all in: the cancer, her attempted suicide, her loneliness, and her age. She noticed how small her mother looked sitting there by the window. She was less than 90 pounds now. She noticed the deep wrinkles on her face and throat, probably from all the years of smoking. She remembered the years when her mother had not been there and how much she had wanted a mother like her friends had.

The pain was still there, always there…just below the surface. She thought about how Betty had lived alone after Kenneth died and how seldom she got by to check on her, even though she lived on the same small island. She thought that now the roles had switched. She was the mother and her mother was the vulnerable child.

Rachel finally nodded her head and acknowledged what Betty was saying.

Visitors

We cannot do great things on this earth, only small things with great love. Mother Teresa

"It's your turn" Pam said, as she wheeled the Scrabble board around for Ray. "Still feel like playing a little while?"

"Yeah. I sure don't have anything better to do today," Ray said. The phone rang in the small front office of the clinic. Pam bounced up and ran for it. Ray watched her move. She was cute, she was young and she was certainly full of life. Pam and her young family had come to Rainman Island on a vacation 4 years earlier and fell in love with the place. It is a neat place to raise kids, she and Micah had agreed. The small elementary school on the Island was perfect for their needs then. High school would require a daily ferry ride for the children. But they were young, seeking an adventure and it all seemed to add to the island's allure.

Pam and her husband Micah had sold their home in Iowa, loaded up and moved their two children to Rainman Island, BC before school started that fall. Micah had quickly purchased a boat and started a small charter and whale watching business. Since then, Micah had persuaded his brother and family into joining them on the island.

Micah was one of those fortunate individuals that

could do many things well. He volunteered as one of the island's firemen and served as the island's electrician when there was a problem with the power lines. And there was often a problem with the power lines. Permanent Island residents were few and most of them wore many hats. That's one thing both Pam and Micah loved about Rainman Island.

If you ever wanted to run for Mayor and be sure of getting the job, Rainman Island is the place for you. Micah had used that line to persuade his brother into moving to the Island.

Micah was also a gifted musician and enjoyed entertaining. He could frequently be found at the Sleeping Pig restaurant on Friday nights taking requests, strumming his guitar and singing. Micah and Pam rented one of Dr. Alice's houses when they first arrived. When Alice Mitchell found out that Pam was a registered nurse, she was delighted.

Soon after Pam's arrival she and Dr. Alice started a community drive to build a medical clinic on the island. Together they worked on their mission statement for the clinic and after several days finally came up with their, rather grandiose objective for the clinic: *to maintain optimum function, socially, emotionally and physically, minimizing complications in illness, stress in crisis, and physical and emotional deterioration in aging.*

"Pretty lofty stuff" Pam had said, grinning at Dr. Alice. But they needed a mission statement to help raise the funds that were needed to build the clinic. And as it worked out, the clinic had been a labor of love by most of the local residents. The clinic had been in operation for almost 3 years now and both

Pam and Dr. Alice said they wouldn't change a thing. They had even been able to get a retired dentist to move to the island. The locals kept him fairly busy during the off-season, but the summer crowd was always coming up with some dental emergencies. Dr. Gregg took it all in stride.

"She's not in today, could I take a message." Ray heard Pam on the phone. He knew Alice wouldn't be in today, it was Tuesday. She always went to Vancouver Island on Tuesday to work at the free clinic in Parksville.

Pam walked back into the ward. "What 'cha want for lunch Ray?"

"Got any more of that turkey you brought me yesterday? That was good. I don't cook turkey at home; too much for one person to deal with."

"Sounds like you're feeling better to me," Pam said. "Giving such specific orders about lunch and all."
Ray smiled weakly at her joke.

"I'll run over and fix us a couple of sandwiches. I'll be back in a few. Call me on my cell if you need something before I get back." Ray nodded and smiled. Pam banged the screen door as she left.

Ray lay there for a few minutes enjoying the silence. The sun had moved and now streamed in across his bed through a bank of high windows on the east side of the ward. He looked at his hands in the strong October sunlight. They were old hands, wrinkled and spotted. They were slightly twisted now with arthritis. His fingernails were clean but uneven.

He let his mind wander, thinking about all the things his hands had touched -- the face of his precious wife, Linda. He remembered the first time he actually touched her hair, how luxurious and thick it felt in his calloused hands. He thought about holding his baby daughter for the first time, how close to perfect innocence the newborn child was. He thought about how his hands had carried her lifeless body ten years later. His mind drifted to the days and years he had spent as a fisherman using his hands to haul in the large nets and traps; how bruised and beat up they often were.

Ray heard someone come in the front door. The unexpected sound startled him. Intuitively he lay perfectly still listening for a voice or some indication of who might have come in so abruptly. He knew almost everyone on the island, had heard their voices many times. No one spoke. He was keenly aware that someone had shuffled into the wardroom and was standing on the other side of the curtain that draped around his bed, blocking his view.

Whoever it was did not move. They just stood there. The hair on Ray's arms rose up in goose flesh. He couldn't reach the curtain around his bed to pull it back. As a precaution, Pam had left the side rails up on his bed. She didn't want him to fall, not on her watch! This made it impossible for him to get up and move the curtain. Whoever this was made no sound at all. Ray was a little groggy. He'd been sick for two weeks before he'd come in to see Dr. Alice. She'd ordered him to bed in the clinic three days earlier. He felt drugged and thick minded. He couldn't think what to do. He knew the visitor wasn't Pam or Alice. Pam had only been gone a few minutes. Alice was off the island for the day. He glanced at the clock on the wall. 12:35 p.m.

He lay there quietly for what seemed like a long time wondering whether or not to call out...then..."Hello...who's there?" Ray's voice was shaky and weak. Ray heard movement then the door open and close with a bang as the screen door slammed shut. Then nothing.

At almost the same moment a large bird flew past the windows in Ray's room momentarily throwing a moving dark shadow across his bed. Ray's eyes automatically looked toward the movement. Then he noticed an eagle perched up high on a branch outside the window.

Dr. Cook

To accept the responsibility of being a child of God is to accept the best that life has to offer you.
                                        Stella Terrill Mann

Halloween. *Everyone at the Comox Memorial Hospital on Vancouver Island will be dressed up in their Halloween get-ups today,* Nancy thought as she bent over the sink and rinsed the toothpaste from her mouth. Glancing up she saw her reflection in the mirror and quickly appraised the damage that sleeping 6 hours had done.

Nancy Hogan and her twin sister Laura had been born last to exhausted parents. They had three older brothers and by the time Nancy and Laura were born, life had pretty much been sucked out of their parents. Neither of their parents had invested much in the way of time or energy in the girls' early childhoods. The kids sort of raised each other. Her older brothers were often left in charge while both of their parents worked at farming a small place in North Georgia.

Nancy's once glamorous good looks had morphed into gently sagging skin around her mouth and eyes that gave her the general appearance of being tired, even first thing in the morning. Her 5'5" frame and now graying brunette hair classified her, she thought, into that nebulous, nondescript group of sixty something women that you see everywhere.

But she was, in fact, a poised, self-confident older woman with short hair, spreading hips, and glasses. However, there was one thing that Nancy regarded about herself as exceptional. By her own initiative she had managed to obtain her PhD. She was technically, she mused this Halloween morning, Dr. Nancy Hogan. She had studied religion as her undergraduate then worked her way through a masters then a doctorate in Health Sciences. This had helped fill her time while her only child, Frank Jr. was young. Secretly through those years, Nancy was preparing herself for the single life and perhaps a career. It never happened. Frank Sr. had seemed more or less uninterested in her educational pursuits and in fact had not attended two of her graduations.

Oh, well, she thought as she smeared liquid makeup across her small, straight nose and under her eyes, *his loss.* Nancy had always been intellectually curious and was blessed with an agile, quick mind. Since her early childhood she had simply loved to learn anything. By the time she was entering the 2nd grade, she could typically be found with her nose in a book. Lately she found that she was quite good at growing things. In the spring she had herb and vegetable gardening books arriving almost daily. Until, that is, she noticed they were stacking up unopened in her office. She reluctantly stopped ordering them. However, she had grown some lovely tomatoes, peppers and even some broccoli in her small backyard garden. Her love of nature and growing things was evident everywhere around her home. Seasonal flowers filled the large beds in her front yard. The soil on the island would grow just about anything. The fact that Rainman Island received so much rainfall each year meant that the berry bushes and fruit trees dotting her property were laden with seasonal fruit; berries in the spring and summer and apples and pears in the fall. It was not at all unusual for her to pick berries the size of her thumb or apples and pears the size of Bernie's head!

"Wonder what I should dress up like today," she asked her dog as she hugged the softness of a cashmere sweater to her bare skin then zipped into her slacks. Her closet was full of cashmere for winter and linen for summer. Frank had insisted that she dress in the finest of everything. He certainly did. *Image was his greatest concern.* Over the years she had replaced some of her wardrobe with island clothes, sturdy cotton shorts and sweat shirts. But today, with a wet chill in the air, cashmere would work fine. Bernie ran ahead of her to the kitchen and sat wagging his tail, anticipating his first treat of the day.

The kitchen was Nancy's throne room. Nancy loved to cook. It did not matter that she lived alone. Her motto was that living alone was no excuse for not eating a gourmet meal, if you were so inclined. Her home cooked meals were quite popular with the island folks. *I need to have a dinner party-- soon,* she thought as she poured herself a cup of freshly brewed coffee. Years earlier Nancy had formed the habit of grinding her coffee beans and programming the coffee maker to be ready for her arrival around 6 a.m. The fragrance of freshly brewed coffee hugged her nose and lifted her spirits. She loved the luxury of having a fragrant cup of coffee ready and waiting when she arrived in her kitchen.

Frank spared no expense during the remodeling of the kitchen. He'd brought in a kitchen designer from Vancouver (against Nancy's will) but Frank wanted to manage every aspect of the project. Nancy thought at the time that it gave him someone to boss around. The appliances were high end, stainless steel. The cabinets were oak, hand finished to a creamy, satin finish. The counter tops were a mixture of tile and granite except for the large center island. After several arguments with Frank, Nancy had finally gotten her way and the kitchen island had been topped with a slab of ancient butcher block she had retrieved from an estate sale.
She ran her hand over the surface. She did not notice the little dips in the wood worn down from use. The island remained Nancy's favorite place in the whole house. The wood had a history and no doubt outlived many previous owners. If the kitchen was her throne room, the butcher-block island was her throne. From here she commanded potatoes and ham to turn into delicious soup and eggs to blend with sugar and cream into all sorts of sweet delicacies. With the herb garden window box and the copper pots hanging from a rack over the island, the overall feel of the kitchen was welcoming luxury. This was the room people migrated to when Nancy invited them over for one of her 'specials.'

"Bernie, what would a *PhD'ed* cook dress up like for Halloween?" Bernie cocked his head and looked at her seriously with large brown eyes.

"Hummm, Dr. Cook you say?"

She heard a thump on the kitchen door and knew it was the local newspaper being delivered. The paperboy had an uncanny ability of hitting her kitchen door while his father drove slowly down Honey Bear Lane in his pickup truck. "I sure couldn't do that," she said out loud to no one.

The dim morning light revealed low clouds and a rain slick street. Mid-September started the wet season on the island. It also started the salmon runs and for a moment, as she stepped outside to retrieve the newspaper, she thought of all the anglers that would be out in their rain slickers today, fly fishing until they caught their limits. When she first moved to the Island someone told her that the salmon used to be so thick in the Little English River that a person could walk across the river on their backs and not get their feet wet! *I'd like to have seen that,* she thought. She tossed the paper onto the kitchen island. It plopped open enough to reveal a headline about the Fall Festival at the elementary school. She glanced at it and thought of her recipe for caramel corn.

I might have time to make some tonight-- have it ready in case I do get some trick or treaters, which is unlikely. If the trick or treaters didn't eat it, the hospital staff sure would.

The small local newspaper was delivered twice a week. Nancy didn't notice the article, front page, below the fold about a break-in at the co-op. Constable Roberts had investigated but no one had been arrested yet. 'The only thing reported missing was food so far as they could tell at news time.'

'Dr. Cook' left 354 Honey Bear Lane that morning wearing a chef's hat, a white lab jacket and carrying a large metal spatula. She had tucked a copy of Julia Childs 'the Joy of French Cooking' into her pocket for effect. As she backed her car out of the driveway, she made a mental note to call Claudia, her best friend, for lunch.

Wonder if she dressed today for Halloween. It might boost business at her consignment shop.

As she pulled forward onto Honey Bear Lane she did not notice the remains of a single muddy footprint on her driveway, quickly disappearing in the morning rain. If she had inspected it she would have seen that it was human and that it had been made a short time earlier, and in haste.

Nancy volunteered three days a week at the large hospital in Comox on Vancouver Island. She had made the trip there so many times over the past 10 years that she thought she could have done it blind folded. Nancy knew who would probably be on the ferry and for the most part she knew why they were going to the big island. That's the way it was during the fall and winter months, only the island's permanent residents were out and about. When she reached the ferry she was a little surprised to see Rachel Hollingsworth's car lined up waiting to board.

Wonder if her mother is in the hospital. That might be why the damn fool woman was speeding down Honey Bear Lane the other night. I'll check when I get there.

Hell's Hole

Every autumn nature disrobes herself, showing first the previously hidden spectacle of her undergarments, then later the fierce beauty of her bare form.
Miriam Peterson

A long, rusting chain hangs from a tree limb. The chain has a big knot at the bottom and sways slowly back and forth when a breeze stirs it, which is often. Behind the tree and to the right, the ground gradually rises up about 6 feet. From Peterson Point Road, this appears to be a tree that some child might have tried to make a swing in. But there has never been a house there. The tree stands at the entrance of a 2600 hectares area that was donated more than 50 years ago to the people of Canada as a Provincial Park. This track of land is important because of the many old growth Douglas fir and Garry oak meadows. The Park culminates in the stunning high cliffs that guard the northern entrance to Tribune Bay.

The change in the topography of the ground nearby is not noticed from the road since the entire Island undulates with hills, ridges and valleys. If you walk around behind the tree with the chain to the far side of the hill, the side opposite the road, you will find an entrance to a cave. Caves are common on Rainman

Island. But almost everyone who lives on the island knows about this one. In fact someone had the good sense years ago to put a heavy iron gate across the entrance and lock it. This has worked well to keep out curious spelunkers. But before the gate was placed there, several times every summer, island volunteers would be called out to rescue some camper or island visitor who ventured into the cave. It has been estimated that the cave runs underground for almost a mile, along the base of a ridge with many forks and dead ends. It is very easy to get lost and disoriented in the cave. Old-timers on the Island tell of a child who was lost in the cave in 1932 and never found. A more often repeated story, and probably true, is that the cave was a gathering spot for the early island settlers. Cabin weary men who loved to drink and play a little poker would meet there on a winter evening. Mentioning that the chain in the tree was put there to mark the spot completes the tale.

Ray said he first heard tales of the cave when he was a teenager, over 60 years ago. Ray had been hired at the Tribune Bay Summer Camp as a cook's helper. After the evening meal was finished he was allowed to join the other campers around the campfires for a ghost story or two. He remembered that no one told stories about "the cave" better than ole' man Waters. Stories dropped out of him like ripe fruit falls from a tree. It was old man Waters that came up with the name for the cave – Hell's Hole, he called it in one of his stories. It stuck.

Some hikers had been on the trails in the Park recently and noticed numerous fresh claw marks on the ground--lots of them. They realized the park trails would be deserted in November. The thought of becoming someone's dinner that night grew in them until they literally were running by the time they reached their car. They immediately headed to the co-op. The hikers had seen notices posted on the Hikers Board -- if some dangerous animal was on the loose, someone should have posted it.

When they got to the co-op they saw warnings about feeding bears and what to do for snakebite. There were lots of old posters about poison ivy and even one about bee stings, but nothing at all about a dangerous animal alert.
There should have been. About the time the Hikers left the Park, a huge bear came lumbering out of the brush and stood on his hind legs, boxing the air with huge paws.
He stood right in front of Hell's Hole.

Camille Carmichael

Art is an attempt to come to terms with life. There are as many solutions as there are human beings. George Tooker

Ray was going home today. He felt better but Dr. Alice had warned him to take it easy, keep up with the meds and of course call if things didn't improve quickly. Ray didn't drive anymore. He went to the co-op a couple of times a week in his golf cart. Today, Dr. Alice told him she'd take him home, 'special delivery.' She drove him to his small home on Honey Bear Lane in her jeep. Along the way they stopped at the co-op so Ray could pick up some milk and bread. A person could pick up about anything needed at the co-op. It provided residents and visitors with a wide range of both products and services including groceries, produce, meats and deli goods. You could also buy hardware, fuel, propane and liquor there. The co-op housed a Post Office and an Internet cafe and of course a place to rent videos. You could even buy a car or a boat there, if you advertised.

The bulletin board at the co-op is 'communication central." People left notes about anything they wanted to buy, sell or have someone pick up for them on the main island. The large board was located next to the red double doors of the co-op and typically supplied with thumbtacks, pencils and paper. All one had to do was write out who you are, what you wanted and someone would pick it up for you or give you a call.

Community co-operation is fundamental on Rainman Island. Most permanent residents take their commitment to this place seriously. Through them the island has prospered both culturally and economically. There are not less than 20 associations, organizations, councils and societies, made up mostly of volunteers on the island. They maintain every aspect of community life on the island. And the co-op contributes financial support to all of them.

It was into this vibrant, self-governing community that Camille Carmichael landed like a meteor shower in the fall of 1992. The Rainman Island Arts Council did not exist before Camille Carmichael arrived on the island. She could not have created for herself a more perfect place to live and work. To begin with over 60 percent of the full time residents on the island are artists. So, like Julius Caesar, 'she came, she saw, she conquered.'

With typical decisiveness, she walked through the old, run-down Victorian house at 14 Honey Bear Lane and said, "I'll take it." She immediately named the house *Rosewood* and placed a small brass plaque on the front lawn bearing the name. Camille gives almost everything a name, from each piece of art to the stuffed birds that sit in her kitchen. She named her favorite soup pot as well as the old Lincoln that sits in her driveway. 'Lola the Lincoln' actually has two names. The second one only gets used when it won't start.

In 1992 she moved lock, stock and barrel from

Barnesville, Georgia, USA, to Rainman Island, BC. Camille quickly established herself as a volunteer extraordinaire. She started by spearheading a drive to raise funds for a new Community Center. Camille, along with a small battalion of other artists she enlisted, raised money by offering such things as summer art festivals, workshops and winter concerts. The results were amazing, even to Camille. The Art Council was eventually able to fund the building of a rustic community center to house a permanent art exhibit by local artists, as well as provide a small auditorium that would seat up to 75 people. The auditorium quickly became used for all sorts of community activities. But each summer the Rainman Island Little Theater group held their productions there. This hardworking, award-winning theater company brought the magic of the stage to the tiny island, and Camille cheered them on. They aimed at professionalism in spite of their limited resources and were always looking for new talent - and not just acting talent. They needed the skills of set construction, costume design, directors, producers and promoters, etc. Camille filled many of these slots and recruited for the others. She was simply adored by all the Island Thespians.

During the tourist season these productions attracted a packed house almost every evening. In fact, there was such a demand for the performances that they frequently had two seatings per night. The co-op, which is located next door to the community center, added an ice cream and coffee bar and featured live entertainment, before and after each seating. It was a win-win situation for everyone.

The house Camille purchased and uses as her headquarters is often referred to as low Victorian, meaning that it has only one story (plus an enormous attic). It was designed to imitate those homes built during the reign of Queen Victoria, (1837-1901). With its dark green shutters and soaring roofline, the house still holds her head high. Camille lives there alone. She was overheard to say that by her best estimates parts of her house are over 140 years old. She also says that the creek on the back of her property was the site of an unsolved murder involving the beautiful wife of a farmer and a lumber tycoon back in the 30's. This story seems to work on most of her visitors (who don't have a clue). They usually respond with a wide-eyed "r-e-a-l-l-y?" which of course doesn't require Camille to come forth with any troubling details.

Camille Carmichael has never been one to let facts get in the way of a good story. Take, for example, the child size, marble tombstone in her back yard. It rests peacefully beside an ancient pear tree. The marble head stone is pitted from age and splotched with dark mossy spots. A small, sleeping lamb has been carefully carved on the top and the stone itself is in the shape of a heart. The engraving in the stone contains the name of a little girl named Gracie who lived only one day in 1933. The stone sits almost hidden at the base of the pear tree. When visitors spot it with Lily of the Valley growing profusely all around, the obvious conclusion would be that it is, in fact, a grave. Camille has told and retold the fabricated details of little Gracie's demise until she has honed a story that has at least three very tragic, very believable versions (depending on Camille's mood - or whether she likes the visitor or not). None of these stories even remotely touch on truth. The truth is one of Camille's friends found the tombstone in an abandoned headstone factory on the main island and lugged it over to Rainman Island and put it in Camille's yard as joke. Whatever it's original purpose was intended to be, it was abandoned. Anyone can see how boring that story is.

Camille takes the attitude of *drama queen* to new heights. She was born Camilia (ke mēl' ya) Myron Brock in the summer of 1942 when the entire world was at war. Maybe that's why she has always been discontented with leaving things as they are. For starters, she was never satisfied with her name. Over the years she has revised it several times.

When she was 6 years old (while her name was still Camilia) she discovered that she had been born an artist. The first of her many artistic accolades was a blue ribbon won at the county fair for a small watercolor portrait of a woman's face. As far back as she could remember she had always loved to draw, paint, sculpt and create art. But her confidence as an artist unfolded slowly. In her early years she would have benefited from art lessons and some encouragement but her parents did not comprehend her giftedness and did not bother to help her develop it. But her art demanded release and eventually came to define who she is.

If giftedness and talent come rubber stamped into our DNA like blue eyes and blonde hair, Camille Carmichael came to know of her encoding the day she won that blue ribbon.

It was during the high school years when she shortened her name from Camilia to Cam. The 1958 version of Cam can still be seen in her High School album. With short, light brown hair swept back into *duck tails* she grins at you with a wide mouth punctuated with deep dimples. Her straight white teeth have a small gap in the middle. Braces were out of reach for a child being raised by a mother who sold Avon to make ends meet and a father who couldn't stay with any job very long.

As a teenager Camille tried all sorts of hairstyles in an attempt to conceal the unyielding cowlick that ran the entire width of her forehead and dipped into a sharp widow's peak in the middle. Her large, almond shaped, blue grey eyes were her best feature and even when the rest of her face was smiling, her eyes remained steady and focused. As a budding artist she was voted *Most Talented* of her senior class but spent her high school years learning to smoke, drink and have sex. She broke many hearts.

Her high school years were definitely not characterized by academic achievements. Instead she will forever be remembered by her classmates as having introduced the mini-skirt to a shocked, small town audience. She was athletic, beautiful and gifted artistically, and she knew it. As a parting gift to her High School Alma Mater, she created a mural that covered most of a wall in the school cafeteria. A masterpiece in pastel chalk was preserved under glass for nearly three decades, until the school was razed to make way for a new K-Mart Superstore. She named the piece *The last fight of the Gladiators*, referring to the name of the high school athletic team, Gladiators. No one seemed to pick up on the irony of the mural's name.

She was still Cam in 1963 when at the invincible age of 21 she left adolescence behind forever and joined Hugh Hefner's Playboy Club in Miami Florida. That's when the serious drinking started. This addiction would flame across her life scorching everything in its path until she finally arrived at the bottom. But not before giving up several fortunes, three husbands, her health and a child.

In 1984 she began the slow process of healing and restoration. To distance herself from what she now refers to as her 'drinking career', she changed her name again in 1992 -- this time to Camille. Her move to Rainman Island began the years of both her personal enlightenment and her physical decline. She took an existing old house and created *Rosewood* with artistic attention to every detail. The house was like a blank canvas to her. As she restored the house, she recreated herself, one last time. And the result? The old Victorian house holds her spirit like a sarcophagus. Her wit, her love of art, and her attraction to the dramatic cascades like a waterfall over everyone who enters.

"You'll have to do better than that Mr. Wilkins!" Camille raised her voice as she spoke into the phone. The first year she lived on the island she had jumped into organizing the Annual Art and Seafood Festival. This event had been her brainchild and was now in it's 8th year. In the beginning she told anyone that would listen "the money we raise will help get the Art Association going," and she had been right.

The idea for a festival came to her when she was invited to the annual Blessing of the Fleet party. The Fleet Party started out simple enough. A few of the islanders got together each Spring, brought some beer and casseroles and said a prayer over the fleet of Whale Watching Tour and fishing boats. Camille persuaded the newspapers on the main island to publicize it as the "best thing going on Rainman Island all year." The first year the crowds were small but they grew steadily year after year as word spread. And it turned out to be a great moneymaker. To get things rolling that first year Camille had charmed two of the local fishermen into providing enough fish, crab and shrimp to feed about 300 people. She then turned her charm to convincing the ladies of the Rainman Episcopal Church, one of the three island churches, to set up booths and sell homemade food and handmade crafts. The deal was that they split the profits with the Art Association, right down the middle. To her surprise they had gone for it. Sandy Blackstead at the Sleeping Pig was an easy sell. She said she'd put up a tent and sell beer and barbecue. Camille told her, in no uncertain terms, "Sell beer and soft drinks only! This is a *^&%%!! Seafood Festival for God's sake!" Sandy had obeyed. Camille had that effect on people.

The second year of the festival Camille enlisted the help of convicts from the main island jail to do the cooking and help Mr. Wilkins set up the tents, toilets and clean up. The inmates loved to get sent over to the island for this duty. They ironed their shirts and put a crease in their pants, the white ones with a blue strip down the side. They always had plenty of pretty girls to stare at during the festival. No one seemed to notice the armed guard that kept strolling around keeping a close eye on the prisoners.

Finding art and artists for the festival was Camille's forte. She sent out letters inviting artists from far and near. And she knew people, who knew people, who knew people. That first year, of the 26 artists who committed to have a booth at the festival, only

6 of them lived off the Island. Each year during the festival days Camille ran sort of a B&B for the traveling artists. Six extra people at Rosewood for three nights, with only two bedrooms and one bath caused a good deal of 'togetherness' for everyone. But Camille loved it and rose to the occasion with her typical *tour de force.*

"We'll need 7 tents this year, Mr. Wilkins. We'll need to seat a minimum of 100 people in each tent and they must be installed by May 21st. We'll need tables and chairs for that many also. You can remove everything on May 26th. The festival dates are May 23-25th." Camille paused. She had made numerous lists in her day planner and now with the ever present, black horn rimmed glasses propped on the end of her nose, she read Mr. Wilkins his portion of a list. There was a force in Camille's words, a command in the way she spoke, which let people know she was in control. You either loved this about her or you hated it. Camille entirely lacked mediocrity. She was forthright and honest and Mr. Wilkins liked her. For years he had received this phone call each November, giving him plenty of time to acquire everything he would need per her instructions. Each year the number of tents, tables and chairs had gone up as more and more people made Rainman's Art and Seafood Festival part of their Spring vacation. Last year estimates were that well over 1000 people attended.

"That's right, Mr. Wilkins. Yes, 7 tents plus tables and chairs for 700. This year we're expecting over 1000 people to attend. Got to have a place for 'em to sit down or get out of the rain, God forbid!"

She hung up the phone and made a note to call Big

John and make sure he had the dates so he could add additional Ferry times and boats to his schedule. She then turned her attention to the brochure she had started. She stopped again. Another thought surfaced. She made a note to let Pat Roberts, the island constable, know the final dates of the festival so he could contact the aviation control towers in the area. Last year, seaplanes owned by people attending the festival had inundated the island's three public docks. This was a twist she'd rather let Pat handle.

Camille opened the brochure on her laptop:

This year's festival will again include a sail-past procession to bless this season's whale watching boats and community fleet. A demonstration by the Canadian Coastguard will be a highlight of the activities.

May 24th at 2 p.m. *head on down to the docks and watch the various local vessels of all shapes, sizes and styles kick off another safe season on the water.*

Camille smiled. For a moment she wondered where the tradition of Blessing the Fleet had come from. She had little interest in God's *blessings* and assumed He felt the same way about hers. But she gave wide berth to people who enjoyed celebrating religious holidays. This of course included blessing the fleet, Christmas and Thanksgiving.

Having finished the brochure she hit save and headed through the double French doors, across the back porch and into her kitchen. A large stuffed black raven sat perched on the kitchen table and stared menacingly at everyone who entered the kitchen, including Camille.

"Hi Little Joe" she said in greeting to the permanently muted bird.

Rachel's Visit

Accept the value of problems in this life. Count them as pure joy.
                                    James, the brother of Jesus.

Rachel hurried across the rain soaked asphalt of the hospital parking lot, side stepping as many puddles as she could. Betty was being transferred today and Rachel was feeling far from adequate to handle what lay ahead for both of them. She had no experience in dealing with an aging, estranged mother, diagnosed with cancer who had only months to live, maybe less. She pressed the button in the elevator and looked down at her wet shoes.

How long had she run after this woman? Didn't her own life matter? Why hadn't her brother Robert come to help with their mother? Rachel felt tired and depressed. She hadn't slept well since the 'gas incident.' She kept thinking about how life ends. She had concluded that most of the time it's ugly. *A person can work their fingers to the bone and what do they get? Bony fingers!* Where had she heard that? Probably some country song. Rachel loved country western music. The dial on her car radio as well as the one in her kitchen was permanently set to WLAC Country.

The elevator stopped. A lab tech got on pushing a cart of blood specimen paraphernalia. Right behind her was an older woman carrying a young child. Rachel looked at the child and tried to smile as the elevator doors closed softly. The child smiled back. *Was my mother ever a young child in someone's arms, smiling, feeling safe? Was I?* Rachel had never known her mother's parents, only her dad's. She had always imagined that her mother's parents were ashamed of the way Betty had deserted her family. *If they weren't they should have been!* Rachel felt her face heat up, her emotions taking control of her thoughts as the old anger came bubbling up. It was a familiar feeling. She came to believe that her dad blocked her maternal grandparents from visiting them when she was a kid. She saw a movie like that once. Since she had no other explanation, and she needed one, Rachel had arranged the movie version into her memory as fact. Her dad made no attempt to explain her absent mother or her absent grandparents. Looking back she realized she was always making up excuses for people who should have loved her...but didn't. Betty's parents lived in Texas. She knew that much. They just were never part of Rachel's life. *Gone now*, she supposed as the elevator doors opened on the 4th floor.

She steadied herself. She dreaded the scene that lay ahead. She wasn't sure if Betty knew she was not going home. She was being transferred to a psychiatric clinic for seven days. It was the law: mandatory for all code 1019s, attempted suicide. Required -- even for cases that no one in their right mind would have questioned, like Betty's.

Rachel stood outside her mother's hospital room for a moment and wished she knew how to pray. No one had ever taught her. She remembered trying once, right after her mother left them. She stood in front of a mirror in her bedroom and prayed like she had heard the man on the radio pray.

Looking back now she thought it sounded like someone reading from a Thesaurus – *lead, guide, direct – don't they all mean the same thing?* She thought she could never trust a God that would allow her mother to -- *vanish*. Was God even good? The idea of a loving God simply had not penetrated her reality or the anguish of abandonment. *Lead, guide, and direct* she said to herself as she pushed open the door to Betty's hospital room.

"Good morning." Rachel forced the words out with a false smile. Betty looked up at her with a blank stare. "How are you today?" Rachel's tone still sounded false. Betty did not speak. She looked down at the folded hands in her lap. Rachel looked at them too.

"How did you sleep?" Betty looked up at Rachel. For a split second she thought Betty looked like a tiny animal that had been trapped, sterilized, wrapped in a white sheet and ready to be processed by a *medical machine*. The silence in the room became awkward. Rachel felt like an intruder.

"I should have told you before today, Mother, that you aren't going home just yet." Betty looked up at Rachel. Emotions pulled at the corners of her mouth.

Funny thing Rachel thought as she studied her mother's face. *You can never tell what someone else is feeling.*

Rachel didn't have any plans for her mother beyond the next 7 days just a lot of questions. "Someone from the Community Services Department of the hospital dropped by," Betty said. "They want to see you as soon as possible." Rachel felt relieved. She had no idea where to take this. Maybe they would help.

Rachel sat in the small waiting room of the Community Services Department chewing on a broken fingernail. It was a nasty habit she'd tried to break a few times. She was startled when Nancy Hogan came walking into the room wearing a tall, pleated chef's hat and carrying a large metal spatula. Rachel had completely forgotten it was Halloween. Nancy had stuck a piece of duck tape on the lapel of her lab coat and scribbled the name "Dr. Cook" on it with a black felt tip pen. Nancy had to smile when she saw the expression on Rachel's face.

"Sorry Rachel" she said. "It's meant to be funny, not scare the wits out of your neighbors."

"Oh," was all Rachel could think to say.

"Is your Mom back in the hospital?" Nancy asked Rachel. Rachel's face registered surprise. She didn't know her mother had been in the hospital before.

"Has she been here recently, before this time I mean?" Rachel blurted it out.

Nancy picked up the surprise in Rachel's tone and immediately tried to retract what she had just said. The hospital had a policy on confidentiality and then there's the privacy act and good Lord! *Dr. Cook* had just violated at least 50 rules and more than a few laws and she knew it! She had no idea that Rachel did not know her mother had been a frequent visitor to the hospital in the past few months.

"It was a slip of the tongue, Rachel. How have you been? You'd think we'd see more of each other, living on the same small island and all." Nancy tried to change the subject. Her attempt to chat Rachel up fell flat. Rachel glared at her.

"Are you here to see one of the counselors?" Nancy straightened to her full 5'5" height.

"I suppose so," said Rachel. "I was told to see Mrs. Lacey as soon as possible about Mother"

Nancy walked over to a book lying open on the desk near a closed door. Rachel assumed the door led into the counselors' office.

"Could you sign this book, please Rachel?" Nancy was using her professional voice.

"Put your Mom's name here under the column for patient and her address and birth date. Your name goes here," Nancy pointed, "as next of kin or responsible party." Rachel did as she was instructed and took a seat facing Nancy.

Nancy wasn't sure why she didn't like Rachel Hollingsworth, but she did not. Maybe it had to do with her kamikaze scooter driving on the island, or the way she glared at people. Maybe it was her mousy brown hair or the way she chewed her fingernails. Nancy looked down at what Rachel had written trying to avoid more eye contact. It was the first time she realized Betty Bishop had the same birthday as she and her twin sister.

When Rachel left, Nancy went up to Betty's room. After all, she was sort of a neighbor though Nancy had never actually spoken to her. She found Betty sitting quietly staring out the window, waiting for the ambulance drivers to come and take her to the psychiatric hospital. When she looked up at Nancy, Nancy could tell that she had been crying. Nancy sank down in a chair near her and smiled. She didn't speak. She couldn't think of anything to say. Life has hard places and this was one of them. Nancy dropped her eyes to her hands and studied them for a minute, hoping Betty would say something to open the conversation.

Finally Betty spoke. "You like to cook, don't you?"

"I sure do! Love it!" *Bingo*, thought Nancy. "What are your favorite foods?" Nancy looked at Betty hoping to get a response that would carry the conversation for a few minutes.

Betty shrugged her shoulders and said, "I don't eat much, cook even less. I don't remember what good food tastes like anymore."

"Well when you get home, I'll make sure I fix that," said Nancy. And at that moment she meant it.

As she left the hospital that afternoon, heading to the ferry and home, the conversation with Betty kept running through Nancy's mind. She had glanced over Jennifer Lacey's notes about Betty's case. Jennifer had made a brief note referring to Betty's 'dilemma.' As naturally as she would speak to her closest friend sitting next to her in the car, Nancy prayed, if you want to call it that. Her conversation with God went something like this: *Lord! Is this what*

You want me to do with that big old house? Turn it into some kind of home for dying, dysfunctional, bi-polar, chain smokers with no visible means of support that have a nasty looking, screwed up, hellacious driving daughter? Well not me, Lord! You must have me mixed up with somebody else!

Her rant ended in a small apology to God.

Nancy turned her green Volvo into the parking lot of the supermarket near the hospital. She pulled the recipe for Caramel Corn out of her purse where she'd stuck it that morning and studied it for a moment.

Oven preheated to 250 degrees
Melt together:
2 cups brown sugar
2 sticks margarine
1 tsp. salt
½ cup light Karo Syrup
Simmer for 5 minutes (stir occasionally)
Add:
1 tsp REAL vanilla
½ tsp baking soda
Pre-pop 3 pkgs. Light buttered

Layout popcorn in large aluminum roast pan (sprayed with Pam)
Stir in Caramel coating all the popcorn. Stir well.
Place in oven for 15 minutes, remove and stir.
Stir every 15 minutes for 1 hour and 15 minute. Cool on wax paper.
Store in Airtight container after cooled.

She remembered adding the note about REAL vanilla – that's the good stuff she made from vanilla beans and vodka (home brew she called it). Once she'd found out how much difference it made in her recipes, she'd never purchased 'store bought' vanilla again. As she pushed her shopping cart down one of the isles, she picked up a small jar of mayonnaise and winced at the price...$6.00. In the states this would be about $1.50 she thought. Living on an island was certainly more costly than life in the states. Nancy immersed herself in her shopping and pushed the situation of Betty Bishop out of her mind completely.

On the short drive to the ferry, Nancy wondered if she would see her friend Claudia there. They often managed to be on the same ferry home.

Ray Phillips

October left mad. Halloween night had truly been a dark and stormy night. High winds had kicked down power lines and two sections of Rainman Island went dark. At 6:30 a.m. Ray was startled awake. He had clearly heard someone call his name! Had he been dreaming? Maybe but it seemed so real! He looked over at his dog Sally. She was sleeping on her little bed in the corner. Obviously Sally hadn't heard anything.

"Who called me?" he said out loud to a dark room. *Do angels call out to you and wake you up. They did in the Bible!* He was thinking about Gabriel. *That guy was busy! Why he almost scared ole' Zechariah to death, not to mention Elizabeth, Joseph and sweet little Mary.* Ray knew his Bible well. In fact he excelled in Bible knowledge. *If angels can call your name, can Satan? Satan was an angel.* Ray moved his legs slowly under the heavy blankets, enjoying the warmth and the feel of the rough sheets on his bare legs. For more than half of his life his first clear thought each day was prayer. *Father help me to be Your man today in all that I say, in all that I do, and in all that I think. Amen*.

Ray slowly sat up and swung his feet onto the cold floor. A little shiver went through him. It was only a few steps to the bathroom from his bed, but sitting there at that moment it seemed like a mile. He stood up resolutely and reached for his housecoat. He kept it on a hook beside his bed. *No telling when I might need to cover up quick these days* he thought. *These days* meant there were no warm hands to give it to him, or to give him a little pat on the back as a bonus. He missed Linda every day but never more than the first five minutes after he woke up. That's when he realized once again that she was gone. Linda had been Ray's 'true North', his compass. She had observed Ray closely, questioned his choices occasionally. She knew his habits and even helped him change a few of them. *A wife is a good thing* Ray thought as he moved toward the bathroom and bladder relief. *If she saw things she didn't like, she'd find ways to let me know. Was that her calling my name just now?* Sally nosed the bathroom door open and walked in.

"Hey girl" Ray said. "Ready to go outside?"

He opened the front door and Sally trotted out. He still felt sleepy as thoughts rolled gently in and out of his mind like slow, lapping waves. He'd spent a good bit of his life on a fishing boat. His mind often returned to the feel of it. *One life rolls in and then out, another takes its place. Just like the ocean's waves, each new life brings a kind of destiny. One life touches another and both lives are forever changed. I bet the water is up over at Yellow Point today* he mused as he closed the door behind Sally.

Ray sat down in his kitchen at the small dining table he had built for Linda over 50 years earlier. He had taken down a large red cedar from his own land and worked a thick slab of it into a smooth disk. He'd used another section of the trunk to form a pedestal. The table fit perfectly into the bay window he'd added to their kitchen the first summer they lived together. Linda had scrubbed the table clean so many times that the varnish Ray had so carefully applied was now completely gone.

He stretched his neck and shoulders and let the steam from the mug of coffee he was holding warm his face. He picked up the Bible he kept on the table and opened it reverently. He'd been reading through the gospels again but today he decided to read wherever the Bible opened. The well-worn Bible fell open to Isaiah. Ray smiled. He loved Isaiah, the second half in particular. He had made lots of notes in the margins in the second half of Isaiah. There were almost none in chapters 1-39. Over the years, as he had learned to trust God more and more, he sometimes wrote the word *tested* and a date in the margin beside one of God's promises. On some of these entries he had gone back and entered the word *proven* and a date. When he came across these little notes it reminded him that he had indeed tested and proved a specific promise from God in his own life. On some of the notes he had added, *proven many times*.

And God had surely proven Himself to Ray. It was all part of his journey of faith, one that had begun when a teenage driver had killed his only child, a daughter, while she was walking down the road near their home. The driver said he hadn't seen her. She was gone just like that. She had been ten on her last birthday. The pain and shock of those terrible days that followed her death were gone now, but not the empty place she had left in his life. *We don't get over losing those we love, we learn to live with the loss.* Ray thought about how people are always coming and going in this life - *sort of like at a bus station, people arriving, people leaving. This life is just a temporary assignment,* he reminded himself. *But I know where she is and I'll see her someday. Maybe even soon -- Linda, too.*

He smiled as he touched the note he'd written in the margin near Isaiah 43. His Bible was old now. He had other Bibles but this one was his favorite. It was held together with duck tape. He didn't want to replace it because he knew he'd never be able to transfer all his notes. He hoped it would last as long as he did.

His eyes fell on a verse he had underlined with a black pen: 'If you do these things, your salvation will come like the dawn. Yes, your healing will come quickly. Your godliness will lead you forward, and the glory of the Lord will protect you from behind. Then when you call, the Lord will answer, Yes, I am here, he will quickly reply.'

His concordance referred to Psalm 85 and Ray turned to it. Vs. 12: 'Yes, the Lord pours down His blessings, our land will yield its bountiful crops.' He looked up through the window near the kitchen table, through the white café curtains. He saw the rain dripping slowing from the eave of the house that overhung the kitchen window. His eyes lingered there watching the drops of water slowly drip, drip, drip...enjoying the thought of how God waters His garden, a garden he was privileged to live in.

He could almost feel his health returning.

Rainman Elementary School

Micah Stillmore had held many jobs for a man only 35 years old. One of those jobs came in handy to the local residents of Rainman Island. Back in Iowa he had worked two years with the Iowa Power Company as a lineman. Once that had become known on the island, he was more or less drafted into the island's Volunteer Fire and Power Association. When you live on an island, all resources are limited, including human ones. It was more or less understood that every able-bodied resident of Rainman Island had a civic obligation to donate some time to the community. Micah was glad to do it, especially if it kept the lights on for the kids in the island's elementary school. And this morning, it did. Once he'd finished cutting away the huge tree limb that the storm had thrown on the power line, he repaired the broken connection and the lights in the school blazed on. Right on time, too, as the island's one and only school bus arrived shortly after 8 a.m.

A retired English School Master named Brian Newberg and his wife Deidra had started Rainman Island Elementary School. They had discovered Rainman Island one summer while visiting Deidra's parents on Vancouver Island and quickly purchased 200 acres at Yellow Point. They were both prolific writers and the lure of isolated island life for writing had drawn them both. In 1952, within days of their arrival on Vancouver Island, both Deidra's parents were killed in a boating accident. Deidra had inherited their large estate, which funded the construction of their new home at Yellow Point on Rainman Island. They called it Newberg Gardens and it was fashioned it after the stone cottages of Cotswold, England.

It had taken almost a year to complete their home. Skilled workers were scarce on the small island so Brian resorted to contracting workers from the mainland. Finally completed in 1953, the ever restless and energetic Brian began to alter the main house almost immediately. First he had added a second floor then a guest cottage. Later that same year he added a tower very near the cliffs of Yellow Point. He said he enjoyed the view and often wrote there. A few years later, he added another wing to the house to hold his ever-growing collection of antique furniture. A gardener's cottage was added sometime after 1957 and so by 1960, the sprawling 200-acre estate was far and away the largest private estate on Rainman Island, maybe on any of the more than 6000 small islands in the Strait of Georgia.

At first the couple had taken little notice of the fact that young island children had to be bused three hours round trip every day to attend public school. When his interest in building projects had finally petered out, Mr. Newberg had announced to his wife one day, "not having a school on Rainman Island simply won't do!" He had proceeded to build a large 6-room rock cottage on the property near the main road to serve as the island's school. And serve it had. Brian and Deidra both taught at the school for the first 4 years, establishing both the curriculum and the school's recognition as an independently operated charter school. At Brian's death in 1977, Deidra donated the entire estate to the island. It was specifically set aside for educational uses. Deidra, then in poor health, had moved back to England for her final days. Over the years the estate's executors, a law firm in London, had employed various property managers whose primary goal was to keep the property clear of debt and maintain it for 'educational pursuits.' In 1995 the main house had been opened as a special event/bed and breakfast establishment with all profits going to enhance and maintain the gardens and school.

Rachel Hollingsworth was in her usual place this first day in November, opening car doors for the kids that were being driven to school and making sure things ran smoothly during student arrival time. She worked as a teacher's aid for Ms. Kennedy in the combined 3rd and 4th grades. Each school year, different grades were combined, based on the latest crop of kids and their ages and abilities. Like most everyone else at the island's only elementary school, Rachel was frequently called upon to fill in where needed. Last year she had worked in the kitchen fixing lunches for the schools 62 students while Eva Mae Burton was out having a baby.

Rachel had followed her mother to Rainman Island that first summer after Betty mysteriously re-appeared in her life after an 8-year absence. That was more than 23 years ago now. Rachel remained on the island that first summer, staying with her mother. She was 18 years old then and full of the notion that her mother could or would somehow want to make up for the devastation she had caused in her life. But it didn't happen that summer, or the next or the one after that.

A disillusioned Rachel went to school and obtained a beautician's license. But cutting hair all day, having to interact with people that were sometimes pleased and sometimes not, was unsettling to Rachel. That same year Rachel married a young man she had known in high school. She had unexpectedly run into Mike Hollingsworth at a party she attended while visiting her brother in Seattle. They started dating right away. It had been a little girl's dream. She thought marriage would fill the emptiness inside her. It did not. After three years of trying, Mike was the one to call it quits. Rachel was the one to call it abandonment. Feeling victimized again, a 24-year-old Rachel returned to the island, got the job at the elementary school and rented a small house on the opposite side of the island from her mother.

Except for her contact with the children and teachers during the school year and the occasional drop by visit to her mother, Rachel Hollingsworth was *alone*.

Another Visit

The sun was shining brightly by the time Ray finally made his way outside. He'd spent the earlier part of the morning catching up on his reading. Micah had collected his mail and papers while he had been confined in the clinic and stacked them neatly on the kitchen table.

When he pulled the barn door open, a blast of cold air carried the fragrance of cedar sawdust past his nose and stirred his white hair. He breathed the smell in deeply and was suddenly seized by a fit of coughing. *Guess this stuff isn't ready to let go of me just yet,* he thought as he leaned against the door jam, bent double to catch his breath. He'd had plenty of time lately to think about the lazy susan he wanted to make Pam for Christmas. He'd never made one before but thought oak would work fine.

Ray's barn sat about 400 yards behind the house. From the outside no one would have suspected that it was filled with state-of-the-art woodworking equipment. An almost new table saw dominated the center of the workspace and to it's right, Ray had installed a long workbench. Sanders and routers sat in a neat row on the shelf below the workbench. Above the workbench, Ray had installed a 4 x 8 sheet of pegboard. He had stuck over a hundred little hooks in the pegboard to hold his small power and hand tools. At a glance he could put his hand on almost any tool a woodworker might need. Several cabinets stood around the perimeter of the room, filled with chisels, clamps, screwdrivers and gadgets of every conceivable shape and size. And more power tools.

He glanced at the large white dust bag that stood silently in one corner of his workspace. Once while he had been in the middle of a project, Linda had slipped in to bring his lunch. She had been shocked at how much dust he had stirred up and was obviously breathing. For Christmas that year she had given him a dust collection system. She had ordered it from one of her catalogs. Linda had a catalog for just about anything. Long before online ordering replaced the need for catalogs, Linda kept them filed by category in a small cabinet Ray had built. The dust collection system stood there silently in the corner, fully installed but these days, rarely used.

Although fishing had been the way Ray made a living, woodworking was Ray's calling. He caught the love of woodworking from his father who had been a carpenter and built several dozen of the homes on the island, many of which were still standing. Ray flipped on the overhead lights and walked toward the back of his shop. He had built shelves back there that ran from the floor up into the open rafters. He used these shelves to sort out the pieces of wood he kept for projects -- short and long, pine, cedar and oak. There was even a little mahogany and teak he'd gotten somewhere, but he didn't remember where. He began to rummage around for some oak boards.

A memory dropped into Ray's mind as he ran his hand over a pine board sticking out of one of the lower shelves. *I want you to go over to that trailer and build Mrs. Rhodes a set of steps.* It was his father's voice. He heard it clear and strong. *I have no idea how to build steps, dad!* The 15-year-old Ray had protested. *Well, it's high time you began to see in yourself what others see in you. I see something like a carpenter. You'd best get out there and see for yourself.*

Ray smiled. He had built those steps from a pencil sketch his dad had handed him. He had loved the smell of the wood, the feel of the sun on his back while he worked and when he had finished, he had loved the smile on Mrs. Rhodes' face. He was hooked.

Ray took down a disk of maple he'd saved from a tree that toppled over during a storm. Micah cut the tree up and hauled it to the recycle, all except for this piece. *Maybe this will work better than oak*, he thought as he laid it out on the table. He turned to gather some tools he'd need to get started. He'd left the big barn door open to catch the light and fresh air. He was startled when saw the outline of someone standing near the doorway. He held up his hand to shade his eyes from the glare of the sunlight and said, "who's there?" No one answered. Sally, who had sprawled out on the coolness of the concrete floor, shot to her feet and started barking furiously. Ray walked quickly to the door and looked out toward his back yard. Nothing moved. He was sure someone had been standing there. He walked over to the right side of the barn where the path led down to the creek. No one was on the path. "What tha heck?" he said out loud. *What ever it was, looked huge.* Returning to his shop, he decided his mind must be playing tricks on him. *Maybe it was just a shadow; maybe another eagle flew over like the other day in the clinic.* He tried to dismiss it but Sally's bark had gone to an urgent 'yipping' sound. Finally he had to wag his finger in her face and command her to "hush, girl!"

Travel Plans

November 2,

Dear Laura,
I have booked my flight for our annual birthday bash. I'll arrive November 14 at 4:30 p.m. and return home November 28, 8:30 a.m. Both of those dates are Sundays, hoping to miss some of Atlanta's finest traffic. But Laura! I sure wish our birthday was not so close to Thanksgiving. People get crazy in airports around Thanksgiving! Thank the Lord, Canada's Thanksgiving is already finished and done with. If I didn't love my annual return to the home of my ancestors so much, I'd make you come here!

What are you getting me for my birthday? I'd like something tall, dark and reasonably handsome... or maybe just tall, dark and intelligent. Oh well, forget the tall and dark part, let's just go with intelligent. Ok, Ok, just make sure he can walk with a cane and speaks English!

Barrington Hall sounds like an interesting stop. Make sure they have handicap ramps (ha ha). I'm sure I'll talk to you before I leave for Atlanta.

Love, your better half (the left brained one)

Nancy rummaged through her desk drawers for some kind of absurd sticker to put on the envelope to her sister, but found nothing. Instead she decided to draw a little stick man bent over and holding a cane. Laura had gotten all that right brain, creative stuff. Nancy had gotten all the left-brain, linear stuff. Yin and yang, polar opposites, black and white; the hell raiser and Miss compliant! The twins had often said that together, they made one complete human being. Nancy wrote Laura's address on the envelope, placed a stamp on it and laid it on the kitchen counter for mailing on her next outing.

The weather front that moved through on Halloween had been followed by three days of rain, limiting her afternoon walks with Bernie. She looked down at Bernie. She needed to make plans for him while she was gone to Atlanta. She also needed to figure out how to get to the Vancouver airport, that was her departure and return point for the Atlanta trip. She had tried flying in and out of Seattle a few times, but she didn't like it as much. Either way was a hassle. It took a full day and a half or more of traveling, each way. *Come on, you can handle anything one time a year,* she thought.

She picked up her cell phone and pressed Pam Stillmore's name on her contacts list. She had nearly every permanent resident of Rainman Island in her contact list. Pam answered almost immediately.

"Hi Pam, it's Nancy" she said, smiling into the phone.

"Oh Hi." Pam always sounded happy. Nancy wondered if she was.

"I have a little vagabond dog to leave with you and the kids again while I visit my sister in Atlanta. Are you up for it?"

"Yep!" she said without hesitation. "The kids just love Bernie and so does Sam. When are you leaving?"

Nancy gave Pam the dates and they hung up. Sam was Pam and Micah's dog and pals with Bernie. He would be a happy dog while she was gone. That done, she turned her attention to the other details of her trip, like getting to the ferries, then to the airport and back. Each leg of the trip needed to be prearranged as soon as possible. Booking the flight was the easy part. Getting to and from the airport was the hard part.

Nancy was fully involved in her task of making travel plans when she heard Bernie growl. It was a low growl as if he heard something that he was uncertain about. Nancy froze. She was listening too. She looked at Bernie to see where his eyes and ears were directed. He was looking up, directly past her head, out of the darkened window. *What on earth?* She looked at the darkened window and strained to hear any sound. She couldn't hear or see anything except her own reflection in the dark window. Bernie stopped growling, looked up at her and wagged his tail.

"What did you hear, boy? What was it?"

Once again, she wished her companion could speak.

Micah's Visit

Micah pulled his truck into the long dirt driveway leading to Ray's house. The only indication there might be a house down the little dirt track was the rusting metal mailbox sitting on a low post near Honey Bear Lane. The mailbox had been smashed so many times that it wouldn't close right. But you could still read the crinkled numbers on it. 91. The driveway wound past several old growth Douglas firs then down a gentle slope for almost ¼ mile. The driveway was full of potholes and grass. Ray only drove his golf cart back and forth to the co-op a couple of times a week now. It wasn't enough traffic to keep the grass down.

The small frame house was almost hidden in an orchard of mature apple trees. About half way down the driveway, on the right side lays a three-acre patch that Ray worked into a grape vineyard years ago. The sweet fruit from these vines had been used to make enough homemade wine to supply half the island. "Best wine on the island," some said.

Ray took some to the co-op one year, just to see if it would sell to the summer tourists. "Them American's will buy anything", he said laughing with the co-op manager. And he was right. Linda had hand written on each bottle with labels she had ordered from one of her catalogs: 'Rainman Island

Wine [+year].' No frills, no fuss. That was Linda's style.

The following year, Ray was in the co-op one day and overheard a man asking the manager if he could get some more of that Rainman Island Wine. The manager told him they sold out within the first week of getting it on the shelf each summer. Ray listened quietly as the man described the wine as being so good it tasted like an angel pissed on his tongue! Ray came home and asked Linda to order 'Angel Piss' on her next batch of wine labels. They had laughed together until they cried.

Micah glanced over at the vineyard as he slowly drove down the driveway, avoiding as many mud holes as possible. The tall grass made scraping sounds on the oil pan under his truck. The wooden braces Ray had used to support the heavy grape vines were all rotted and broken down now. Moss covered what Micah could see of the fence. The unkempt vines sprawled along the ground, covering everything in their path, like a giant weed out of control. The vines headed down a hill toward the creek and a distant tree line. Near the driveway, a newer fence restrained vines. Micah could see white scars hacked into the vines along the fence line. He smiled when he thought of Ray out there cutting them back. *Looks like he used a machete.* Micah grinned as he pictured Ray wildly slashing his way along the driveway with a machete.

Micah pulled into Ray's yard, directly in front of the porch. He cut the engine, opened the door and swung himself out in one fluid motion. The air was crisp and smelled like a Christmas tree. *After all the rain for the last few days, this was shaping up to be a good-looking fall day,* Micah thought.

"Hey! My man!" said Micah smiling as Ray threw open the door. "How you doing? Heard you been a little under the weather!"

"Aw, just a little," Ray responded as he stuck out his hand in greeting. Micah grabbed his hand and pulled the tall, lanky man into a warm embrace. A waitress at the Sleeping Pig had introduced them right after Micah and Pam moved to the island. She heard that Micah wanted to start a whale watching tour/fishing business and Ray had just retired from one.

"Sounds like you two need to meet," she had told Micah. And they did. Micah was drawn to Ray's quiet ways, his respect of people and his willingness to teach him the fishing business. Ray told Micah where to get the best deal on a boat and even what kind of boat he'd need to start out. He introduced him to some of the other men on the island that were still fishing or running charter boat services. After a time, Ray had invited Micah to come by his house one day. That's when Ray had taken Micah back to the barn behind his house and loaded him up with nets and traps and all sorts of things he had used in his fishing business - things that Micah still used everyday. Ray had given Micah something else too. Ray had given Micah a desire to know his God.

"Come in! Come in!" Ray stepped back to let him enter. Micah came into the familiar room. He noticed the old TV that sat on a metal table and the low bookcase that ran along one side of the room. He noticed the yellow blanket thrown over the back of the red leather couch, worn shiny in spots from use. He wondered if Ray had been napping there.

An over-sized leather recliner sat directly in front of the TV. The floor was covered in dark brown, wood parquet. Everything was neat and clean. Micah had never seen it any other way. Micah smelled coffee.

"Got a cup of coffee for me?" Micah asked.

"You bet I do. Sure good to see you" he said as they took the 8 or 10 steps needed to reach the kitchen.

"What brings you out my way?"

It was just small talk. They both knew that Micah had come to make sure Ray had everything he needed after being in the clinic for several days.

"Got to check on my best friend" Micah grinned as Ray plowed around in the small cupboard above the stove for another cup.

"Say, did you hear about the break-in over at the co-op?" Micah asked Ray.

"No, I missed that bit of news." Ray sounded surprised. "Any idea who it was *this* time?" Break-ins at the co-op were not unusual, especially during the summer months, when all the tourists hit the island. But this was November, the rainy season. Not many tourists these days.

"No," said Micah slowly. "Constable Roberts was telling me yesterday that the unusual part about this break-in was they only took staple food, like flour, salt, coffee and a few canned goods. Stuff like that. Oh and he said there was a 5 gallon can of fuel oil taken and some of those tablets used to purify drinking water."

" Sounds like somebody is planning a camp out, don't it?" said Ray as he filled up Micah's cup with the strong black coffee.

As they sipped coffee, a comfortable silence drifted into the room. Ray wondered who on the island might be in need of food, maybe in need of shelter. He knew of no one. Micah's thoughts turned toward his children. He had last seen them as they hurriedly finished their breakfast and Pam herded them into the small school bus that stopped near their house. The friends sat in silence for several minutes, both feeling blessed.

As Micah was leaving about an hour later he said, "you wanna go over to the "Pig" tonight, I'm doing my usual Friday night *gig-at-the-pig*."

Ray smiled at the familiar reference to Micah's guitar strumming and singing sessions at the local watering hole.

"I could come by and pick you up."

"Sounds like a plan" Ray smiled.

 As Micah drove away, Ray turned back into the empty house and thanked God for Micah, the son he always wanted.

A little while later, Ray's white hair caught the late morning sun as he carried a pan of stale bread and corn across his back yard to feed the ducks gathered down by the creek at the back of his barn. He knew they'd be there, waiting and hungry.

Most of the seats were filled at The Sleeping Pig by 7 p.m. that night. Micah and Ray had gotten there about 6:30 so Micah could get setup. The restaurant was nothing fancy; a square concrete block building with a dining room on the front and a commercial kitchen on the back. Brown vinyl booths had been installed along three sides of the room and a bar with extra seating ran along the back wall. The four red dinette sets that usually filled in the middle of the room had been moved out and a few card tables with folding chairs set up for the Friday night crowd.

Through the week Sandy Blackstead, the owner of the Sleeping Pig, worked the front. Sarah and Nora, her teen aged daughters took turns helping out. However, on Friday nights, since Micah had started playing, Sandy had hired two extra waitresses to work the front. She also added an extra cook. Besides pork barbecue sandwiches and barbecue plates, Sandy served a daily special along with five different bottled beers. She had added potato skins and nachos to her Friday night menu once she saw how well the locals responded to Micah's music.

The amplifiers on Micah's electric guitar were cranked up full blast by 9 p.m. for Micah's closing song. John Denver's *Thank God I'm a Country Boy!* hammered the walls of the small restaurant and floated out into the cool damp night.

No one noticed the shadowy figure passing by the restaurant on the deserted street outside. The form moved silently through the misty moon lit night in the direction of the empty ferry dock. The last ferry of the day had pushed off promptly at 8:35 p.m.

Leap And The Net Will Appear

November 5th

Dear Sisterwoman,

Did you see the big, red Harvest Moon last night? It was a glorious thing. Jupiter is visible at the 5:00 o'clock position, a rare and spectacular sight.

Whatever happened to the boxes of greeting cards you were going to send me? You know the ones by that artist on the island I like so much. I could use a few more (hint, hint).

I'm going to try and make a peach cobbler today as practice for your visit. I don't want any complaints about my cooking while you are here. I forced my 'earthsuit' (code name for my body) to the grocery store today and bought kale and small things I needed to make that recipe you sent me for 'Italian Wedding Soup.'

I discovered a large quantity of canned beans in my cupboard. I don't know how they got there.

I had a call from Dr. Rob today. I haven't heard much from him since lightening struck my house and he had to come over and help hook up the new TV and air conditioner. Three hours later, about the time I finished making the soup, Aunt Mary called to say she was on her way over with her 4-cheese lasagna, a spinach-mushroom combo. (Aunt Mary is Steve's Aunt, not ours. I know you forget these things.) Anyway, I'm now stocked up with food and I thought I'd be living on bean soup all week! All this happened out of the blue. I haven't heard from Aunt Mary in over a year. She's had spine surgery, is fully recovered and looks great. I'll call her when the figs come in next summer. She's the only person I know who eats them. Got to run and break up the squirrel wars in the back yard. November 14 is coming soooooonnnnn!
                                   Much love to you. Laura

Wonder what the weather will be like in Atlanta while I'm down there? Nancy thought as she slowly walked toward her bedroom reading the latest letter from her sister. She flipped on the light and put the letter on her bed then moved to her closet. The door on the closet was standing open about 6 inches but Nancy didn't notice it. She slid the closet doors fully open with a bang and stood there a minute looking at the double row of neatly hanging slacks and jackets. To the right of the jackets was a line of silk shirts in every conceivable color. "Well, if you don't wear slacks, a silk shirt and a jacket, kid, you'll go naked!" she said out loud in her John Wayne voice. Bernie came to investigate. *Better check the weather forecast before I make any decisions,* she thought and headed back down the hall to her office. *High 60's low 30's, rain several days starting Wednesday…sounds like the same stuff I get here, except with traffic!* She frowned.

****

She was just finishing her dinner, a roast pork Panini on homemade sesame French bread and some apple slices, when the phone ran. It was Rachel Hollingsworth. *Oh no,* thought Nancy, *hope this is not about her mother.* "Good evening Ms. Hogan, this is Rachel Hollingsworth" the voice said, like Nancy didn't have caller ID. "Oh, Hi." Nancy's voice lacked any trace of enthusiasm.

Nancy braced herself. She wasn't sure why. "It's about mother," Rachel said. "Uh huh" Nancy managed. Rachel pushed ahead in a singsong, little girl voice. "Dr. Alice said you might be a good one to talk to about mother coming back home, to the island I mean, since you work over at the hospital with the counselors and all." Nancy slid the last slice of apple into her mouth and chewed it slowly, recalling the tree in her back yard that had produced the sweet fruit, and wishing she had not taken the call.

"What's your plan, Rachel?" Nancy asked authoritatively, without wanting to know. "She'll need a good bit of help, the doctors told me," Rachel started. "You know with the cancer and all. She's going to be taking a lot of meds and stuff. They say she'll need to be watched—you know—so she don't try to kill herself again--I guess."

"She tried to kill herself?" Nancy said, louder than she meant to. She honestly did not know.

"Oh, I thought you knew why she was in *your* hospital. I thought all you counselors knew everything."

"Rachel I just keep the appointment book for the counselors and do a little of their paper work. I really did not know your mother tried to kill herself. I am sorry," she said and meant it.

Rachel must have noticed the change in Nancy's voice because she, in turn, changed hers. It had sounded staccato and high-pitched before. Now she sounded almost pleading. "I wondered if you know anybody on the island that would be willing to help me look after mother." There, she had said it. It was her last hope. Nancy could not have known, but Rachel had spent the last 2 hours calling almost everyone in the island's tiny phone book. She had started with Betty's "friend" Fern. Fern had kept Rachel on the phone for almost 30 minutes complaining about all she had to do every week for the church. Fern finished her remarks by saying "I'm not a young person myself anymore. I can't help you Rachel," then abruptly hung up.

Rachel waited. There was a long pause on the other end of the phone. Nancy instantly remembered her conversation with God a few days earlier. She also remembered the night she prayed rather flippantly, asking God what she should do with the big house she occupied *alone*. And right now it seemed that God was giving her an answer. An answer she definitely did not like. She thought of the perfect excuse and blurted it out.

 "Rachel, I'm leaving to visit my sister in Atlanta in a few days and plan to be gone most of the month." Rachel wondered why Nancy mentioned her trip. Nancy seemed to be answering a question that Rachel had not asked.

"Uh huh," Rachel said. Rachel didn't know Nancy very well, so she figured she was about to hang up on her like the rest of the island had that night.

Then Nancy suddenly said..."Rachel, let me pray about it and get back to you tomorrow."

"Uh huh - OK" Rachel said, surprised.

****

"Great God in Heaven!" This was NOT a reverent beginning to her prayer. "Why have you answered me this way? And at this time!" She was screaming. She spat the words out in anger. Bernie looked at her and rolled over on his back. That's what he did when he thought Nancy was scolding him. Bernie's reaction did not escape Nancy's attention.

She knew she had entered God's classroom mad. *When you're ready for the lesson the Teacher shows up.* Nancy walked down the hall toward her bedroom. Once there, she knelt beside her bed as the tears welled up in her eyes. She cradled her head in her hands. Her prayer this time started with a heart-felt apology. Was she ready for this lesson?

I said I would trust You Lord -- follow wherever You lead. Remember Lord? He did.

Later that evening, Nancy tried to sleep, but couldn't. Finally she gave up and switched on the reading lamp beside her bed, pushing the pillows up under her neck and shoulders. She lay there in the stillness and listened. She heard the wind chime in the back yard tinkling as the wind moved through the tops of the ancient red cedars near her house. She heard Bernie snoring softly in his bed in the corner. Her thoughts drifted backward in time.

September 1962. She was 18 and had been dropped off at college. She was waving good-bye to her parents who lived 4 hours away. For the first time in her life she realized she was among twenty-five thousand strangers. She had never felt so alone. Laura, always a constant in her life had chosen an art college out west. It had all been hashed out a hundred times, each sister wanting independence from the other. She remembered she had turned to God in prayer. That's when she had memorized Psalm 139. The words were still there, in her mind and heart:
    "O Lord, you have examined my heart and know

everything about me.
You know when I sit down and stand up.
You know my every thought when far away.
You chart the path ahead of me and tell me where to stop and rest.
Every moment you know where I am.
You know what I am going to say even before I say it, Lord.
You both precede and follow me.
You place your hand of blessing on my head.
Such knowledge is too wonderful for me, too great for me to know!

March 1966 She was 22, single, pregnant and scared. She had met Frank at an office party for the bank in Atlanta where she worked as a teller. Nancy lay there and tried to remember her feelings from those years. She had transgressed her own moral code when she started dating Frank. Was it ever love she had felt for him or just lust. She remembered telling him about the baby and his less than enthusiastic response. His parents had insisted that they get married. He demanded that she quit her job and stay home with the baby. If it hadn't been for Laura's constant love and frequent contact, she thought she might have gone crazy those first couple of years.

Laura's life had taken an entirely different path. After Art College, she had started her own business, an art gallery and framing shop in Roswell, Georgia, a suburb of Atlanta. She was always telling Nancy about meeting dazzling people or quirky artists and decorators. Nancy remembered that during those years she had clung to God's word and read with new understanding the words of Ecclesiastes "For everything there is a season, and a time for every matter under heaven: a time to be born, a time to die." The scriptures had brought her hope and courage.

When Frank Jr. started school, so did she. She took every sort of course she could work into her schedule. She didn't know where she was going with an education, but she sensed God's presence in her life.

She grew accustomed to the world she and Frank had created: the stylish home, the lavish parties with his friends. The prestige of being married to the youngest *ever* Vice President of First National Bank. Her mind lingered for a moment on little snap shots of her husband. She saw him walking away from her on the beach in Hawaii after a fight. She saw him laughing with Frank Jr. as they tried to fly an expensive remote control toy airplane.

December 1990 Frank Jr. was a 24-year-old dropout. By the time he was 16, he'd dropped out of school. By the time he was 20 he'd dropped out of a brief marriage. He'd dropped out of so many jobs Nancy lost count. How many times had she taken him to God in prayer, pleading for God to change him? How many arguments had she had with Frank about how to handle him? Frank just threw money at him, what ever he said he needed, whenever he asked. Finally, Frank grew discouraged and disconnected from both of them. That was his way. What he couldn't figure out he got mad at and went silent, emotionally disconnecting. On weekends he would find reasons to be gone from the house. He immersed himself in bank projects that took him away from home for months at a time. Nancy tried tough love on her son, reading everything she could get her hands on. But nothing seemed to work.

She remembered a Christmas Even candle light service and her pastor's creative reading from Luke. Mary's troubled response to Gabriel's news that she was to be the Mother of the Son of God. "How can this be?" Mary said.

Mary's question echoed down through the halls of Nancy's memories.

How can this be? That was also the question Nancy faced as she waited before God.

On that Christmas Eve many years ago, she had let the light of acceptance seep into her resistant heart.

She lay still now, listening to the silence around her. "Let it be" Mary had said. "Thy will be done," Nancy whispered as she reached up and switched off the light. "Thy will be done."

The Light of His presence had thrown a shadow over her past, hiding all the trouble and sorrow, fear and disappointment. Gentle sleep came to her swiftly now. It was 4:15 a.m.

A Change In Direction

Figuring out God's ways isn't any of my business. Following Him is.
Kay Warren

Nancy dialed her sister's number bracing herself against the kitchen counter. Without realizing it, her left hand was clenched into a fist. She felt tense all over when her sister answered on the second ring. "Well hello there!" Laura said, in a low, sultry voice. "Laura, brace yourself for bad news. I'm not coming." After a long pause Laura said quietly "Go on...tell me why." It wasn't what Nancy had expected. "I thought you'd at least scream at me!" Nancy said. "I was ready for that. I'm not sure I'm ready for you to sound, well, like it's OK!" Nancy didn't realize how loud her voice had gotten. "Peter's here Nancy. He's just come in. He's standing here looking at me like a deer in headlights. Can I call you back?" "Well...sure..." Nancy's voice trailed off. She was disappointed. She had wanted to get this over with.

Thirty minutes later Laura called back. "You had better be dying," Laura said coolly.

"Not me, but someone I know is and I feel like helping her is more important than... I mean...not more important than...just, well it's real important and..." Nancy had lost her way. She'd made up a little speech to give to Laura but had left God's name out of it completely. She knew Laura was not a believer. Laura had often told Nancy she didn't want to hear any of that "God talk." Nancy suddenly realized that without God's name in it, her actions could not be explained. "God has changed my plans, Laura." She blurted it out. It was the truth.

"I see," said Laura after a long pause. "Well, who am I to argue with God?" Laura sounded angry. "Who is anyone to argue with God?" Nancy said it slowly, hoping Laura would at least give her the chance to explain what had led her to her decision.

Laura sounded distracted again then said "Hell! it's Peter again! Damn fool boy can't even cut my grass without a million questions! I gotta go, Nancy. Talk to you later," and abruptly hung up.

She's mad all right Nancy thought as she headed to her office to cancel her trip. *And who could blame her?* Nancy started taking Laura's side. They had spent every birthday together for the past 56 years, except one or two. One was the year Frank had died. She couldn't remember the other one.

Five minutes later she was on hold with the airline agent trying to get her money back.

"Hello Rachel." Laura's angry reaction on the phone had thrown Nancy off kilter all day. She hated to disappoint people, and especially Laura. "I wondered if you'd come by my house this afternoon. I want to talk with you about your mother." She'd left a message at the school for Rachel at 9:30 a.m. It was 3:30 p.m. when Rachel finally called her back. "I guess so," said Rachel. "What's it about?" "I have a room here in my home for your mother. And I will make sure she has the care that she needs." Nancy spoke plainly, almost matter-of-factly.

"Huh?" It was all Rachel could think to say. Nancy hesitated picturing whom she was talking to: *a stringy haired, overweight girl who glared at everyone before she tried to run him or her over on her motor scooter. The word "huh" was probably at the top of her vocabulary preferences.* "Could you come by on your way home?" Nancy tried to get control of her thoughts. "Well, OK, I guess." Rachel didn't sound thrilled, Nancy thought. Just stupid. Nancy instantly began thinking about shoving everything into reverse; getting her airline reservation back, calling her sister and saying it had all been a joke. She suddenly doubted everything. She thought maybe she had not heard God correctly. Maybe she could not meet Betty's needs. After she finished with the "*maybes*" the "*what-ifs*" set in. "What if" Betty dies here and Rachel decides to sue me! *I COULD LOSE EVERYTHING!*

Within 5 minutes of hanging up with Rachel, Nancy's emotions were in free fall. "What have I done?" Bernie looked up at her as if to say *I didn't see anything!* She looked at her watch, 3:45 p.m. Claudia would be on her way home.

"Hi girl! Haven't heard from you in awhile. Hope you are calling to invite me to dinner!" Claudia was Nancy's best friend. She owned a consignment shop on the main island, which bore her name. 'Claudia's Closet.' Claudia commuted 6 days a week to the Big Island.

"Not unless you want a stupid maniac making your dinner!" Nancy sobbed.

"What on earth?" Claudia was shocked. In the 15 years she had known Nancy she could count on one hand the times she'd heard Nancy cry. "Calm down and tell me what's happened." Homeward bound, Claudia had pulled her car into a lane at the ferry. She wasn't going anywhere for at least 20 minutes.

It all came pouring out: Nancy's initial prayer about the house, her awareness of Betty needing help, the phone call from Rachel, the sleepless night...all of it, including God's comforting presence. Then Nancy told her about canceling her trip, her sisters' hurt feelings, and finished with all the negative thoughts she'd had since she spoke with Rachel and offered her home to Betty. "What have I done!" Nancy sobbed as Claudia quietly listened.

For a moment, Claudia didn't say anything. She was thinking. "Are you still there?" Nancy croaked. "I'm here." Claudia said softly. Silence again. Nancy considered hanging up the phone. Then in a low, calm voice Claudia said, "I was trying to decide whether or not to come to your 'pity party'." It wasn't what Nancy wanted to hear. She wanted to hear at least one "poor baby." But she didn't get it. Silence again. "Is that what I'm doing?" Nancy finally sounded a little calmer. "I think so my friend. It's fear Nancy, plain and simple. You are afraid to trust God. Do you trust Him Nancy?" Silence. "I don't trust *me*, Claudia. I wonder if in fact I did hear from God on this or was it something in my own ego - some latent rescuer thing in me. You know what a sucker I am for rescuing people." Claudia knew.

"Well if you ask me -- and you did," Claudia said, "you ought to pray a little more on this then wait and see how the meeting with Rachel goes. If she thinks it won't work or acts weird about it or something, then maybe you should back off. Call me after she leaves, OK?"

At 5 p.m. Rachel knocked lightly on Nancy's kitchen door. Since she'd hung up with Claudia, Nancy had washed her face and taken Bernie for a short walk to help calm herself. On her walk she had prayed, taking in deep breaths and slowly exhaling. Over and over again she said "I breathe You in, Holy One, and I breath myself out!" "I breathe You in, Holy One, and I breathe myself out!" By the time she returned home she felt better. She knew that on her own, she could not take care of a dying woman in her home, but with God's help - well...she'd see.

"Hi Rachel, please come in" Nancy swung the door open wide." Nancy looked directly into Rachel's eyes, trying to take in her mood or get some sense of how Rachel might be feeling about the proposition she had made to her on the phone. Rachel's appearance was about the same as it had been the day Nancy ran into her at the hospital. Shoulder length, stringy brown hair covering part of her face, overweight and wearing clothes that look like they had belonged to someone else first. Nancy noticed for the first time that Rachel did have one redeeming grace. She had huge brown eyes; so brown they were almost black. "I made a pot of coffee, would you like some?" "Yes" Rachel said simply.

As Nancy poured the coffee she noticed how Rachel sat perched on a bar stool at the kitchen island and looked around the room. In a small circular motion Rachel ran her fingers across the smooth wooden finish of the kitchen island. Nancy suddenly realized that Rachel had never been inside her home. The thought occurred to her that she might like to see the rest of the house. "Bring your cup, I'll give you the $5.00 tour." Nancy was aware that somewhere between opening the door and pouring the coffee, she had relaxed. All of the fear that had overwhelmed her earlier seemed to have simply disappeared. As she headed into the living room Nancy silently said *thank you Lord for the Peace that passes understanding.*

Nancy took Rachel though the downstairs rooms, stopping to comment on some of the furnishings and paintings. She showed Rachel into her own bedroom and bath. Then they went upstairs and through the three other bedrooms and baths. She finished her tour in the bedroom directly above her own. "This would be your mother's room. It has an adjoining bath and gets the morning sun, when we have sun that is," Nancy smiled at Rachel. The room had been fitted out with twin beds, which Nancy had covered in heavy cream comforters. Nancy had made the blue plaid curtains for the windows and matching dust ruffles for the beds. A tranquil landscape hung on the wall, which were painted a soft blue. A large mirror hung over the dresser sitting opposite the windows and pulled light across the room. A low bookcase filled with books formed a window seat under the double windows. Rachel noticed a light fragrance of cedar in the room. Family pictures were clustered on top of a chest of drawers.

Rachel turned her dark eyes on Nancy. "Why are you offering to do this? You don't even know my mother." Rachel was glaring at Nancy again. "She's not some little sweet saint of a person you know." Nancy prayed again silently. She saw something dark and angry in Rachel and responded to it negatively. *Lord you heard the question; please answer it -- for both of us.* Nancy knew she had to be completely honest.

Nancy sat down on the foot of the bed and looked up at Rachel. She motioned for Rachel to sit down in the big blue club chair that filled one corner of the room near the windows.

"Rachel, I don't know a thing about you or your mother except that God must love you both very much. You see, He spoke to me -- well I don't mean like you and I are speaking to each other -- but like God speaks to people sometimes. He let me know that I was supposed to offer your mother a place in this home and to help you. I believe that this house and everything in it, including me, belongs to Him. And I long ago gave Him permission to use it anyway He chooses." Nancy tried to read Rachel's face.

"I also don't want you to think I'm a nut or something, because I am honestly very nervous about doing this. I had plans to spend my birthday with my twin sister in Atlanta, which I have canceled, by the way. I also love the work I do at the hospital and caring for your mother might be very disruptive to my schedule there. And I'm worried because Betty is really sick and I might be stretched beyond my ability to care for her. She might fall, or rebel about being here. There are so many things I don't know, I honestly started to call you and back out of it." Nancy fell silent, waiting for Rachel to respond.

The whole time Nancy had been talking, Rachel stared at her. Her eyebrows were drawn together and her lips set in a thin little line. Rachel now looked down at the floor and after a moment, looked up at Nancy. Her expression was softer. She was no longer glaring. Nancy continued. "I've asked Mrs. Clifton if she can help me as a sitter when her kids are in school, you know, on the days when I'm scheduled to work." Nancy waited a moment and then continued. "I'll need your help to do this Rachel." Nancy wondered where her calm words were coming from. Rachel slowly moved her head up then down forming a nod that Nancy understood to mean yes…maybe. "I guess next step is to talk to mama," Rachel said. "She may not go for it --but I sure do."

Later that evening Nancy went back upstairs into what would become "Betty's room." *The blue room.* She felt tired from the strain she had put on herself. Worry always left her feeling tired as if she had been carrying something around all day that was too heavy. She sat down on the foot of the bed, dropped her shoulders down stretching her neck. The tension seemed to flow out of her. She began to imagine herself as a stranger in the room. She wondered what she would think of this room if she had never seen it before; if she had nothing to do with picking out the furnishings or how they were placed in the room. She remembered a fancy Bed and Breakfast that Frank had taken her once and how curious she had been about every detail of the room until she had gotten familiar and comfortable there. *It didn't take long,* she remembered, *but then, I wasn't entering the chamber in which I would probably die, either.* A shudder crept over Nancy. *She'll need something to do with her time, when she feels like it. I wonder what she is interested in. Maybe writing her memories, painting or something like that. I have some 'killer views for a landscape from the back yard. 'Killer views!' Really Nancy! I've got to stop using words like that while she's here.*

Nancy's eyes fell on the cluster of family pictures sitting on top of the chest of drawers. She was drawn to them and picked up the one of Frank Jr. made when he was about 10 years old. Staring back at her was a smiling boy, perfect white teeth showing, dark haircut into a crew cut. His cheeks were still a little chubby and there was a trace of a dimple on one cheek. His nose was like his dad's, large for his face and rounded at the end. He'd been a head taller than any of the other 4th graders at Elm Street Elementary when that picture was taken. He was a gregarious little boy with many friends. Nancy was always getting notes home from the teachers that he talked too much in class and goofed off during his lessons. She looked at the dark eyes staring back at her from the picture. A deep longing swept through her. *What happened to you? Where are you my precious boy?*

She went down the steps slowly, still thinking about Frank Jr. The steps seemed like a metaphor of his life—step by step he had descended lower and lower into drugs, alcohol and all that goes with addiction-- one step at a time. *Everyone has to hack their own way through this life,* she thought. *And somehow in the process of it all we are supposed to grow into responsible people.* Frank Jr. never seemed to take personal responsibility for his actions, or lack of them.

She carried all the family pictures back downstairs and put them in her room. She sat the picture of

Frank Jr. on the table beside her bed, gently stroking it as if *it* were her child. She'd invite Betty to put her own family pictures up in the blue room - maybe that would make it feel a little more like home to her.

"Hel-lo Clau-di-a" Nancy spun the syllables out in a "sing song" voice. "Feeling a little better, eh?" Claudia could tell from the change in the tempo of Nancy's voice that her friend's attitude had swung back to center. "Rachel and I talked. It went well. I feel calmer, maybe even a little excited that I am doing something I'm pretty sure God wants me to." "Atta-girl." Claudia's voice was pitched lower by an octave than most female voices and Nancy loved to hear her low intonations of "Atta-girl!"

"Rachel is going to talk to Betty tomorrow and see if she goes for it. Rachel said as soon as she had spoken to her mother, she'd call me and let me know what her mother says. I'll make my plans from there." Nancy didn't pause but continued... "you know Claudia, I didn't tell you this before because, well, I'm not sure I wanted you to know this about me but..." Claudia interrupted, "when have I ever held anything over your head?" "Never," said Nancy and meant it. "Well I didn't tell you before but I really considered calling the psychiatric hospital that Betty is in and asking the staff doctors about this whole idea of her coming to my house to die before even talking to Rachel. I was seriously looking for an out with God. If they said no then there was my out, you know?" Nancy ended with a question. It was rhetorical and Claudia knew it. "Hon, you are a thinking person, left brained, remember? Of course you thought of getting professional advice. Now that you've stepped out on faith, you still may want to get some medical advice. I know I would. Now to this business of you inviting Jim and me for dinner. That's my fee for "hysterical woman counseling." Nancy smiled. "How about Friday night, it's my birthday. We'll have a little party! I'll do my fish and sherry." Claudia's mouth started watering "What time shall we start beating down your door?"

Here Here!

What I am actually saying is that we need to be willing to let our intuition guide us, and then be willing to follow that guidance directly and fearlessly. Shakti Gawain

November 15th broke grey with a heavy misting rain. Rachel slowly drove her old car through the empty parking lot up to the *porte cochere* of the psychiatric hospital. Betty sat in a wheel chair that had been placed there a few moments earlier by an elderly black nurse, dressed entirely in white. They stood there motionless, fixed like statues waiting. No expression on either of their faces. Rachel wondered for a moment what would happen if she just drove right on past them. What if she left her mother sitting there, abruptly abandoned, and disappeared into the mist -- just like her mother had done to her. *Turn about is fair play*, she thought.

Rachel forced a smile as she got out of her car and came around to help Betty into the front seat. Betty's small bag was placed silently on the back seat. There were no flowers, no hoorahs! No Yeah! I'm going home. Betty looked like a tiny child sitting there as Rachel reminded her to buckle up. Her feet were arched down so that only the toes of her house shoes touched the car floor. She weighed about 85 pounds now and looked shriveled and grey. "Won't be long now," said Rachel and Betty wondered if she meant the ride to her new home or to her death.

They entered a lane at the ferry landing and it began to load almost immediately. There were only two other cars going to Rainman today. In the summer the line up of cars would take at least half an hour to load the ferry and it ran several times a day. But in the winter season, travel to the island was blissfully short. Betty had not spoken in the 15-minute ride from the hospital to the ferry. Neither had Rachel. Three days ago, Rachel had spelled out to Betty what her choices were and given her all the information she could about what she thought it would be like living with Nancy. Betty hadn't said much, just nodded her head a couple of times, acknowledging what Rachel was told her.

Betty had given up. At this point, full of pain killing drugs, full of sorrow and grief, she really did not care what happened to her, with one exception. She desperately wanted to go home, back to Rainman Island. If living with Nancy Hogan was the only way to accomplish that, then so be it.

Thirty minutes later Rachel drove her car off the ferry onto Peterson Point Road and quickly swung right onto Honey Bear Lane. She looked over at her mother and suddenly felt pity for her. "Would you like to go by your house before I take you over to Nancy's?" It was the first time Betty's face had shown any emotion on the entire trip. "Yes, please." She said it politely, like she was speaking to a stranger. "No problem" Rachel said and drove slowly down Honey Bear Lane. The early morning mist had turned into a thick blanket of fog, almost concealing Betty's little house at 64 Honey Bear Lane. Rachel's car rolled to a stop on the gravel driveway near the back door. For a moment Rachel panicked she remembered finding her mother's body lying on the kitchen floor. She remembered how small her mother looked and how light she had been when she helped Dr. Alice and Big John carry her to his car and then onto his boat.

"I came by and cleaned it up a little for you the other day," Rachel said as she looked at the woman sitting next to her. She tried to imagine what Betty must be feeling or thinking, but could not. Something deep stirred in Rachel and she decided not to mention the suicide note she found while cleaning up the kitchen. "Wasn't much that needed doing, " Rachel said softly. Betty nodded slowly but never took her eyes off the back door of her house. She sat there as if trying to will herself to go inside. Times without number she had imagined Kenneth standing at that back door with a smile on his face to welcome her home. His love had been the only unencumbered love she had ever known. It just had not lasted long enough. Not long enough at all.

"You want to go in?" Nancy said. "I've already taken some of your clothes and pictures and stuff over to Nancy's house. You don't have to go in if you don't feel like it." "I feel like it" Betty said as she opened the car door and slipped out into the fog. Betty felt like she was walking through a dream. She pushed on the door but it did not open. "Guess it sticks a little in damp weather" said Rachel coming up behind her. Betty stepped aside and Rachel put her shoulder to the door. The door swung open sucking long tendrils of wet fog into the dark, stale kitchen air. "I had the power turned off, since you won't be using it. I didn't see any point in paying for it. That means the pump is off too, no water to flush so don't use the potty while we're here" Rachel said nonchalantly. Betty glided her hand along the counter top near the door and took two shuffling steps into the small kitchen. She put her hand on the gas stove then turned and looked at Rachel. "Did you get the picture of Kenneth in my bedroom, the one that hung over the dresser?" It was the most Betty had spoken all day. "No, I got the small one that sat on the nightstand. Do you want the big one?" "Yes." Betty drew the 's' out making a hissing sound. "Anything else?" Rachel asked over her shoulder as she made her way across the living room into Betty's bedroom. Betty didn't answer. She walked slowly through the house, trying to memorize every detail, the smells, the position of furniture and pictures, the way the grey light slanted in through the windows. Finally she came into her bedroom. Rachel was standing there, holding the 8x10 picture of Kenneth Betty had taken right after they met. Betty looked blankly at the room. She felt suddenly drained and lifeless. "Let's go" she said and turned resolutely toward the door, toward the unknown.

Nancy's house was full of light and sweet buttery aromas when she heard the car pull up in the driveway. She smoothed down her apron, glanced into the mirror by the back door and swung the kitchen door open with a big smile of welcome. Nancy had practiced this in her mind a few times as she busied herself making Betty a birthday cake. She remembered that she and Betty had the birthday from her hospital record. "I knew you were coming, I knew it was your birthday - so as the song goes -- I baked a cake!" Nancy sang out as the two women struggled into the warm, fragrant kitchen.

Betty stood there weaving back and forth looking like she was going to faint. Nancy quickly guided her to the kitchen island and settled her into one of the comfortable bar seats. "I'm all ready for you" Nancy chirped. Betty looked at her blankly as if she was still trying to see through the fog she had just left. "Would you want something to eat or drink or do you just want to go up to your bed?" "To my bed" Betty said with the minimum amount of energy and emotion. Nancy glanced at Rachel who was still carrying the picture of Kenneth and her mother's small suitcase she'd had at the hospital. "Let's just get her upstairs then," said Nancy and they each took an arm.

They had to almost carry her up the steps. Nancy turned back the covers on the single bed nearest the window but Betty lay down on top of the cover without crawling under them. She closed her eyes and said she just needed to rest a minute. It was the most exercise she'd had in weeks.

Rachel told her mother that they had put a baby monitor beside her bed so that if she needed anything she was to speak in the direction of the monitor. Nancy told her where the bathroom was and that there was water beside her bed. Betty nodded in acknowledgment of their words. She did not open her eyes. Rachel quickly turned and walked back downstairs. Nancy noticed Rachel's abrupt exit. It was another reason why Nancy did not like her.

Nancy looked down at Betty lying in Frank Jr.'s old bed. She looked frail and gaunt. *She's probably near death.* Nancy had seen many people die in her years working around hospitals. She had watched her own husband die, gasping, writhing and struggling against it. She remembered how his face had finally relaxed. He looked like he was about to speak -- his mouth had gaped open a little. But it wasn't him anymore -- clearly he was gone.

Everybody dies. Nobody gets out of this thing alive. But why does death offend us so? Is it because we are made in God's image? Is it the God-fragment in us - the immortal part, the unassailable part that is outraged by the very thought of death. After all, we were originally made to live forever, in fellowship with God eternally. Somewhere that design must still linger in us, in our cells, our DNA, subjected now to God's punishment for our willful disobedience.

"Is Betty made in your image Father," Nancy spoke softly. Betty's eyes fluttered open as if she had been sleeping. She looked up at Nancy but did not speak. Nancy looked at her with deep compassion. "Welcome Betty, I hope you'll be comfortable here. I'll let you get some rest. Please use the monitor if you need anything. I'll be back in a while with your lunch." Betty lay there looking at Nancy. Nancy could not read her face and was once again reminded that she knew almost nothing about this stranger who now resided in her home. *I'll have to change that* she thought as she closed the door and walked down the steps.

Rachel was waiting in the kitchen. She had poured herself a cup of coffee. It made Nancy smile to think that Rachel was comfortable enough to help herself. There was a sudden squabble in the bird feeder outside the kitchen and both women looked out the large window over the sink in the direction of the loud squawking noises. "Territorial issues, I guess," said Nancy. Rachel took a sip from her mug and said, "here are her meds." She pushed 6 prescription bottles across the counter-top. "Most of them are twice a day. She's already had the morning ones today. I'll keep up with getting the refills to you." Rachel paused and looked down at her wet shoes. "It's mighty fine of you to do this for my mother," she said.

"Would you like to stay for lunch?" Nancy said impetuously. "I made chicken salad -- Oh, is your mother allergic to anything or does she have any diet restrictions?" "No and no" said Rachel. No diet restrictions and no allergies and no I'd rather not stay for lunch." Nancy looked at Rachel again. *Help me Lord to find a way to like her* she prayed silently to herself. Within minutes, Rachel was gone back out into the fog. Nancy looked at the beautiful strawberry birthday cake she had just iced. It was her favorite. She cut herself a piece, poured a cup of coffee and raised her mug into the air. "Here Here!" she said. "Here's to you Nancy and Laura on this your 57th birthday!" She made the same gesture toward the upstairs bedroom. "And here's to you Betty Bishop, may you have at least one more!" She went to the back door and let Bernie in. "You'll need to get used to someone being here besides us, boy," she said giving him a good scratch behind his ear. He followed her into her office wagging his tail. She settled into her desk chair and called her sister.

"HI - it's your twin sister. You can't stay mad at me forever! After all, it's my birthday - well it's yours too. I thought it would be within your power to grant me forgiveness as my one birthday wish!" Nancy rattled on for a couple of minutes leaving Laura a message that she hoped would raise a response. Her sister had been silent since the big announcement that she wasn't coming to Atlanta this year. She missed being with her sister, going out to dinner and doing all the big city stuff she didn't get to do on the island. She felt lonely and slighted, after all this was her special day. "You're probably out with that good looking, rich, talented man you had lined up for me! You are a shameless hussy! No wonder mother loved me best!" she said forcing a giggle and hung up.

"Bernie, I'd better brush up on death and dying if I'm going to turn my house into a hospice center." Nancy stood in front of the wall of cluttered bookshelves and searched for Kubler-Ross' book *on Death and Dying.* It had been required reading somewhere along the way in achieving her PhD. Sitting right next to it on the shelf was Harold S. Kushner's *How Good Do We Have to Be.* She took them both down and ran her hand over the jackets. "Thank you Lord" she whispered "for the gift of Your wisdom that You place in this world through people like Elisabeth Kubler-Ross and Rabbi Kushner. I pray that some of it will enter me or pass through me to Betty and Rachel."

Forgiven

Forgiveness is the fragrance that the violet sheds on the heel that has crushed it.   Mark Twain

It was almost 3 p.m. by the time Betty woke up. Nancy had been reading for a couple of hours when she heard the toilet flush in Betty's bathroom. She opened Betty's bedroom door and peeked in. "Ready for your lunch? It's so late you may want to skip it and go straight to dinner." Betty looked at her as if she wondered who she was. "I'm still a little groggy. Maybe a glass of milk or something like that." She shrugged her shoulders. "Coming right up" Nancy said.

She cut a piece of strawberry cake and put it on her best china dessert plate, then poured a glass of cold milk into a crystal glass. She dug around in the silver chest and pulled out a gleaming sterling silver fork and finished the creation with a small porcelain rose bud in a little china blue vase. *That should say welcome and happy birthday,* she thought, and headed back up the stairs.

Betty was sitting in the blue chair by the window when Nancy came back in. The rain had returned and filled the room with dark shadows. Nancy switched the lamp on beside Betty's chair and sat the tray down. "I remembered it was your birthday today - mine too. I baked you a cake." Betty's eyes widened in surprise. It was the first glimpse Nancy had gotten of any emotional response on Betty's face. "Thank you," Betty said softly. "It's been a long time since I thought about things like birthdays." "What do you like to think about Betty," Nancy asked sincerely. "I would like to get to know you better. We hardly know each other and here we are, thrown together by God." Betty's head jerked up when Nancy mentioned God. Her face hardened and something like anger pulled at the corners of her mouth.

After a moment she said, "I'm not sure God believes in *me.*" Betty spoke in a controlled voice as she pushed the cake around on her plate with the fork. "What do you mean?" Nancy asked, trying to draw her out. "My life isn't exactly what you'd call "blessed" is it?" "Why not?" Nancy said, ignoring the obvious. "Look lady, I don't know why you brought me here, but I sure do not feel up to having God rubbed in my face day and night." Betty was angry. She remembered some of her encounters with Fern. Her face was flushed and her left hand was clenched into a fist. Nancy knew she'd hit a nerve. Nancy sat on the foot of the bed for a moment and looked at Betty. She knew she had to choose her words carefully.

"Let me tell you why I brought you here, Betty," she said quietly. As they sat in the deepening shadows of the late afternoon, Nancy talked and Betty listened. Nancy told her the long version of the story of how God, in so many words, had told her to open her home to Betty. She ended with "Betty, I only mean to do you good. If at any time, you feel uncomfortable about how I am treating you, or if you feel you need a different living situation, I hope you will either tell Rachel or me. I am going to do my best to partner with Rachel on this. She felt desperate to try and get you back on the island."

"Rachel!" Betty snorted. "She doesn't give a rat's ass about me! I never see her unless it suits her timing and mood. I have no idea why she didn't just take me to my house and leave me to die." Betty looked down at her hands and picked at a fingernail.

She waited until she felt in control again. Nancy let the silence do its job. "Truth is, we just don't get along." She was a little calmer now. "Maybe that's why you're here instead of being back at your home," Nancy said. "Maybe you and I can work on that together." Betty looked up at Nancy. She had tears in her eyes. "It's time, Betty, to get things in order. I'm willing if you are." Betty's eyes went back to her folded hands. Betty slowly nodded in agreement.

It was a shaky start, but it was a start. As Nancy left the room to make dinner for Claudia and Jim her eyes fell on the small framed cross-stitch that she had made right after Frank Jr. disappeared. A stray beam of afternoon sun seemed to spotlight it in the otherwise dim room. *"Pardon one another so that later on you will not remember the injury."* Nancy tapped the glass with her finger and smiled. "Dinner at seven," she said over her shoulder. "I'm having a couple of friends over. Would you want to come down and eat with us or shall I bring you up a tray?" Betty didn't answer; she had closed her eyes again.

Rachel slumped in her chair eating a bowl of cereal and stared blankly at the images on the TV screen. She felt tired. *Why do I feel so tired and achy?* She mentally reviewed her day. *Just picked up mother and drove her to Nancy's house.* She didn't want to think about her mother any more that day, but the images of her mother trickled into her mind, unbidden. Rachel shook her head and straightened her shoulders trying to push the thoughts of her mother's face out of her mind. *Lead, guide, direct,* the prayer she had whispered earlier dropped into her mind. "OK Lord, help me!" She said it out loud to an empty room. It was a challenge. "If you can figure out this screwed up mess called 'my life', then more power to you!" She was sarcastic, angry. "I love her and I hate her. I guess I still blame myself for her disappearing act when I was a child but I know I didn't really have anything to do with it! I feel every feeling you can feel, grief, shame, guilt, anger, and love. God! Help me!" She cried it out to the unseen God. "I cannot go through her leaving me *again*," she sobbed.

Rachel realized she was on her hands and knees on the floor *wailing. How did she get there? How long had she been there?* The empty cereal bowl lay upside down on the floor across the room. Thirty years of intense feelings of anger and hurt and yearning were balled up inside her and demanding release. She cried like she had never cried before. Finally she lay down on the floor, curled up into a ball with her hands tucked between her knees, and her knees drawn up to her chest in a fetal position. She lay there exhausted, unable to move.

She had no idea how long she laid there or how or when the Prince of Peace had entered her presence. But He had. He had answered her prayer for help. She had put her burden down. She had laid it at her Savior's feet. She felt emotionally drained, but as clean and new as a newborn child.

In fact, that is exactly what she was.

What The ...

Ray rinsed out his coffee mug and sat it near the circa 1970 percolator. He took the wet dishcloth and wiped the counter around the coffee pot. There was nothing to clean up, just the force of habit. It had been his job to make coffee every morning. He loved bringing Linda a cup while she sat in bed and read. As he rinsed out the dishcloth and spread it out to dry over the faucet. He was thinking about the ducks that seem to be in permanent residence down by the creek behind his barn. *Maybe they got too old to fly south for the winter—like me,* he thought. Ray had been feeding them a couple of times a week for over two years. He saved his bread scraps and mixed them in an old metal pie plate with a little seed corn from the co-op. It had turned cold and he noticed a light dusting of snow covering his back steps when he went outside. *A rare winter blast* he told himself. He held firmly onto the handrail, his old knees needing the assurance as he descended into the frosty morning. His mind raced back to a boyhood memory and the thrill of discovering that snow had covered everything.

Ray flipped up the collar on his jacket and slowly walked across the yard. His feet made a crunching sound in the white powder. He glanced back and saw his footprints leading across the yard, the only tracks in this quiet, undisturbed world. Another boyhood memory surfaced. He and his best friend Gene had tried to make it across a patch of snow without leaving two tracks. He remembered Gene riding on his back for a few steps then dropped him on purpose in the snow and they both started laughing and making snow angels.

The familiar trail leading beside the barn was strangely unfamiliar on this snowy morning. Ray went slowly, not trusting his footing as the trail got steeper leading down to the creek. The words he had read earlier that morning came back to him: *"Breathe Me in with each breath. The way ahead of you is very steep. Slow down and cling tightly to My hand. I am teaching you a difficult lesson, learned only by hardship."*

He heard a loud crashing noise behind him. He snapped his head in the direction of the sound and his head met with something solid. He felt his body being hurled into the air as his feet left the ground. In a split second, everything went dark.

****

"Pam I'm going over there. I've tried all day to get in touch with Ray. Something's wrong." Micah spoke to Pam from his cell phone. He had docked his boat and his brother was on deck off-loading the traps they had used that day. It had been a pitiful day for crabbing. Trapping for prawn and crab was typically a sure bet this time of year. They had tried several depth settings and filled their bait canisters with cat food and fish oil. The men had started dropping traps about 8 a.m. and had made two slow circles back around, hauling in and refilling the bait canisters every 90 minutes or so. They had hauled in about 70 pounds of prawn but very few crabs. It was late afternoon and they were tired when they finally gave up and came in. "Must be the weather," Micah shouted at his brother over the noise of the twin engines. He shrugged his shoulders gesturing at his brother. "We'll try again tomorrow." Micah's brother Pete held up his hand and gave Micah a thumbs-up sign, as Micah cut the engines and began to tie up. Fifteen minutes later Micah was on Honey Bear Lane turning into Ray's dirt driveway.

He knocked on the door and heard Sally start barking furiously inside. He tried the door and it opened easily. *That man never locks his door! I'll have to scold him for that one of these days,* Micah thought. "Ray!" No answer. Sally came running out of the bedroom, still barking. *That's odd*, *Ray doesn't usually go anywhere without Sally, not even to the co-op.*

He looked around the small house. Everything was neat and tidy as usual. The bed was made, the clean dishes stacked in the drain. Micah bent down to comfort Sally. Her bark had changed to a frightened yipping sound. "Hey, good girl, calm down," he said, brushing the raised hair on her neck. He had seen Sally act this way once before during a thunderstorm. She was extremely anxious. "What's wrong, girl? Where's Ray?" Micah walked to the back door and opened it. Sally burst out between his legs almost knocking him down. She raced across the yard, disappearing behind the barn. Micah glanced at the lean-to where Ray parked his golf cart. It was sitting there with a little pile of snow behind one of the tires. Clearly it had not been moved in awhile. He looked over at the barn doors. They were closed. Micah could see the big pad lock on them from where he stood. He studied the scene for a moment and noticed the remains of a footprint in a small patch of snow. *Maybe he went off with somebody. But he would not have left Sally shut up like this,* he reasoned. "Here girl - Sally!" he raised his voice toward the dog, mostly out of fear. He listened intently. All he heard were the muffled sounds of Sally, still barking frantically down near the creek bank. Then it hit him. He lunged off the steps and into the yard. Adrenalin kicked into his tired body as he sprinted down the path toward Sally's barking.

Nothing could have prepared Micah for the scene that unfolded before him. When he saw Ray's body, he stopped so abruptly he slid down the bank in the cold mud. As he slowly stood up, trying to regain his balance, he did not notice the wet ooze of mud covering his hands and jeans. For an instant he just stood there – transfixed -- too stunned to move. His mind refusing to take in what he saw. Micah's hands dangled at his side. The cold mud slowly dripped into the top of his boot.

Ray lay in a pool of blood, sprawled out on his side. His right hand was bouncing up and down slowly in the rushing water of the creek, as if he was waving at somebody. His face was turned away from Micah but he could see sprigs of white hair poking up through the clots of blood and mud that covered his head. His legs were twisted back, grotesquely forming the appearance of someone trying to run lying down.

Something that looked like bloody butchered chicken parts were strewn all over the ground. The metal pie plate still containing the bread and corn sat upright near Ray's head. A stray bright blue feather had come to rest on Ray's ear. Micah wanted to reach down and touch the feather. It was the only thing he saw that looked real – that his mind could identify. In shock, he had no idea what to do. Sally had never stopped barking. She was alternately barking and licking Ray's face. Bark, lick, bark, lick. As if in slow motion, Micah knelt beside Ray. His CPR training slowly began to push its way forward. Time seemed to flatten out and slow down. *See-if-there-is-a-pulse*. He gently placed two fingers on Ray's neck, pressing in several spots -- trying to locate the jugular vein. He couldn't feel anything. Ray felt cold to Micah's touch but he noticed that his muscles had not stiffened into rigor mortis. It didn't make sense. Micah moved Ray's hand out of the water and reached into his pocket for his cell phone. He called Pam with one touch. "Oh my God, Pam, it's Ray. Get somebody over here with a stretcher quick. We're down by the creek behind the barn. He's hurt bad. He may be dead. There's blood everywhere. He's been laying here for I don't know how long." Pam did not engage Micah with questions. She was a trained triage nurse and she knew how to put first things first.

In less than 60 seconds Pam called Micah back. "Big John is on his way. He was at home, right down the road and should be there in about 5 minutes. He's got his boy with him to help lift Ray. I'm going to the clinic to wait for you. Dr. Alice is also on her way there. Be careful when you move him Micah - don't move his neck or back if you can help it. Try and see where the blood is coming from and apply pressure." Micah was still in shock and couldn't think of anything to say but "OK." "Pray for him, Micah" Pam's words pushed at him. "Pray, Micah. I'll pray with you." She knew her husband was in shock. "OK," he said.

Many times in her years of nursing Pam had recited a little section of Psalm 107. She prayed it now with emotion "Lord, help! We cry out to you in our trouble. Save us from our distress. Lord speak and heal - snatch this lovely man from the door of death." Micah took Ray's hand in his. He tried to find a pulse. More than anything in the world at that moment, he wanted Ray to turn and look at him and speak. Tears filled Micah's eyes as he stared into Ray's blood covered face. A light breeze stirred the feather on Ray's ear, but there was no other movement at all.

God Be With Us

When Micah looked up, Big John and Danny were running toward him with the stretcher. "Oh my God!" shouted Big John, when he got a look at Ray. Danny looked pale and started backing up. "Come 'ere son, and help me lift him onto the stretcher." "Pam said be careful of his neck and back, John." Micah gave the instruction without looking at either of them.

Big John had done things like this a few times and knew what he was doing. He laid the stretcher next to Ray and said, "son, you get his feet. Hold them tight! Don't let him slip. Micah on the count of three I want us all to lift him at the same time. You support his spine and middle, I'll get his head and neck." John slipped a crescent of foam around Ray's head to hold it in place. They lifted him smoothly onto the stretcher and within a few minutes Ray was in John's big van, which had been customized to hold the stretcher securely. They rolled out of Ray's back yard, down the overgrown driveway, past the grape vines and onto the main road toward the clinic. "Pile all the covers you can find on him, back there," John was driving fast and barking the orders. Danny and Micah were quick to respond.

Pam and Alice Mitchell were waiting with the clinic's double doors open wide. John backed the van in. They worked together as a team and moved Ray's lifeless body into the clinic then onto the exam table. "Help me get these wet clothes off of him," Alice handed Pam the scissors. "Strip him!" She was already searching for a heartbeat with her stethoscope. "It isn't much but I have a pulse! He's alive!" Alice shouted to everyone. "Pam - stat - get that crash cart in here!" Big John and Danny backed away and let Pam and Alice work on Ray. Micah striped what clothes he could without moving Ray's neck. His head was still bent sideways and he noticed that neither Alice nor Pam touched it. "He's lost a lot of blood," Alice was almost yelling. "Pam! get an IV started -- get a blood pressure cuff on him!" "Micah, take this phone out of my right jacket pocket and on "favorites" push emergency - When they answer get the ambulance from Comox on it's way." "John is your boat ready? If not go see to it. I'll have him as stable as I can in about 15 minutes." This was the second emergency run Dr. Alice had made in less than 30 days.

A few minutes later, Dr. Alice had finished a preliminary assessment and determined that Ray's neck was indeed broken, but she wasn't sure to what extent. Extensive Cat Scans and an MRI exam would be needed to fully assess his injuries. Also, the gashes on his head and face were deep and needed stitching, but that would have to wait. She had applied compression bandages to his head wounds and stabilized his neck with a brace for transporting him to Comox. He was suffering from exposure, dehydration and severe blood loss. His blood pressure was extremely low. His condition was critical and unstable. Pam had finally gotten two IV's going but it seemed to her to be a miracle. His veins were shutting down from dehydration and blood loss. "OK let's move him over!" Alice shouted from behind the curtained off exam area. Big John stepped in and pushed the curtain back. John and Alice lifted

Ray expertly onto the stretcher using the sheet from the examining table then secured the stretcher in the van. Ray's face and upper body were still covered in mud and blood, but Alice had wrapped him securely in insulated blankets to help hold in his body heat. Micah thought Ray looked like a bloody mummy with two IV's dripping. "I'm going over with you - taking the portable crash cart stuff," Alice said. "He may tank on the way." "Come on Ray, don't go out this way," Alice whispered in her friends ear. Micah said, "I'll be over as soon as I get cleaned up. I want to sit with him tonight."

Micah, Pam and Danny stood in the early darkness of the cold November evening and watched the taillights of Big John's van blink on and off as he drove the short distance to the dock. Micah thought that the blinking lights were like Ray's life right at that moment, blinking on and off. "Come on guys," Pam said softly. "Danny I'll take you home and Micah, I'll take you back over to Ray's so you can pick up your truck." "I'll need to bring Sally home with me, OK?" Micah said. "Of course," Pam whispered.

Micah leaned in and kissed Pam hard before he got out of the car in Ray's back yard. He needed her comfort, her warmth, and her calmness. He wished he could just go home, take a hot bath and climb in a warm bed with her, feel her warm body next to his, holding him. He drew in a deep breath as if to brace himself before going back into the hellish scene he had just left. Pam's fragrance drifted to him, comforted him. She always smelled good to him, a faint flowery smell that he loved. Micah looked down at the floor of the car. "If I had come by this morning like I thought about doing, this wouldn't have happened to Ray. Or at least I could have found him before he lay out there so long." A shudder went over Micah thinking of how bitterly cold it had been. Pam recognized that her husband was feeling guilty. Guilt feelings were almost always present when a loved one dies. As a registered nurse, she had seen it hundreds of times and she had learned that you couldn't talk someone out of feeling guilty. Oh, she had tried a few times to console people when they had lost someone by saying something like "there's no need for you to feel guilty, you could not have prevented it, you did everything possible to show them your love, etc." But along the way she had learned that the best thing she could do was not to try and talk them out of their feelings, but to meet them there with love. Pam looked at him and saw a man who genuinely deserved to be loved. She spoke to him quietly, lovingly. "I know you feel terrible about what has happened to Ray and I hurt with you. But you are a wonderful man, Micah. You've been a loving son to him, and I love you for it." Micah looked at his wife and smiled. Tears were rolling down his cheeks. "I'll be home in a few minutes to get a shower before I go over." Micah took one more look at her. She was smiling slightly and the exchange that passed between them was complex, an unspoken paragraph of compassion and commitment.

It was completely dark now and the silence of a winter night crashed in around him, chilling him to the bone. Ray's house was dark. Sally had retreated to the back door waiting there for her master's return. When she saw Micah she started barking again. "Come on girl" Micah said, and opened the truck door for Sally to jump in. "You're going to spend the night with Uncle Micah" he said.

Then wondered why we talk to dogs like they are children. They don't understand a thing we say, or do they? She acted reluctant so Micah picked her up and sat her gently on the front seat. She'd been through a lot today. He gave her a good scratch behind her ears and tried to reassure her. "I'll treat you good girl. You're Ray's baby." He grabbed a flashlight then closed the truck door and headed back down the path toward the creek. As he walked through the cold night, for the first time that evening he noticed how tired he felt. He was drained, cold, wet and hungry but he wanted to get one more look at where he had found Ray. *What in the hell happened? What were those chicken parts doing laying everywhere. What could have done this? Was it human? Was it animal?* His mind was whirling with questions.

He flooded the light onto the area where he'd found Ray's body. He saw the spot where he had fallen down the bank and he could still see part of the indention Ray's body had made in the mud. He thought about how Ray's hand had been bobbing in the water, as if waving to him or was he *beckoning*? He'd have to remember to tell Ray about that. The blood was harder to see in the darkness. *It must be disappearing into the mud -- the earth was sucking it in. From dust to dust,* Micah thought.

Big John, Danny and Micah's presence there had churned the soft creek bank into a slimy mud hole. Micah's feet went down several inches into the muck with every step he took. It was like walking in cold oatmeal. He scanned the area with his flash light and spotted something that looked like a bloody chicken wing. He picked it up and looked at it closely. He realized it wasn't a chicken wing at all.

It was a duck wing! *Aha!* Micah thought. *This is a feather from one of the ducks that Ray has been feeding down here for the last couple of years. But, so... ah...whatever came after Ray, had been dining on the ducks! Ray must have interrupted its dinner!*

He slowly looked around for any other clues but the area was a slimy mess. He saw where Danny and Big John had rolled in the stretcher. His flashlight picked up something bright blue. What a contrast the iridescent blue feather was to the black brown, bloody muck all around it. He picked it up gently, as if it were a priceless jewel, and put it in his jacket pocket. *I'll have to come back tomorrow when I can see better.* As he turned to go back up the trail to his truck he heard a cacophony of sounds nearby. He froze and switched off his light. He could hear better in the dark. He strained to hear what direction the sound was coming from. Something large was running, moving away from him, thank God! The crashing sound of branches and underbrush grew faint, as he stood motionless. *Could have been a deer.* A chill went over Micah. *I'd better get some men together with Rifles. I'll call Pat Roberts when I get to the house. He needs to know about this anyway.*

Dr. Alice didn't like to subject patients to the experience of being put through a trauma center. There was something dehumanizing about a trip through an emergency room at a major hospital. The focus shifts away from the person and onto machines and lab reports. Not only is there a loss of privacy but also dignity. She found it particularly distressing when the patient was her friend; a quiet, humorous man who she knew preferred to die in his own bed. And that brought up something else that was distressing to her. Ray was 75 years old recovering from pneumonia. His chances of s were slim. She knew what she was getting him into. It was the beginning of a long ordeal for him - something that would be extremely hard for him to endure.

And what did he have to look forward to at the end of all his suffering? Once entrapped in the *medical system* it was hard to escape. The patient didn't seem to have the right to make choices, even in the simplest things, like when he was thirsty, or needed to pee. He would be forced to wait on the availability and will of someone else. She wondered if she had made the right call by subjecting him to what lay ahead. *Should I have let him die peacefully in my arms in the clinic, surrounded by people who love him? Is it his time?*

As Big John's boat skimmed across a mirror calm sea, Dr. Alice thought about all the noise, lights, pumps, drugs, surgery, and voices that lay ahead for Ray. That would be hard to take for a well person, much more difficult when you are old and vulnerable and barely clinging to life. She looked down at Ray again and placed a loving hand on his chest. She checked his heart rhythm and pulse, glanced up at the drips to make sure they were still going. She took his cold hands in hers, bending over she whispered into his unconsciousness, "hang on Ray, we're going to try and make you feel better soon." She saw the lights from the ambulance waiting for them on the dock ahead. "Here we go, may God be with us." *Was He?*

The Dinner Party

Because of God's tender mercy, the light from Heaven is about to break upon us, to give light to those who sit in darkness and in the shadow of death, and to guide us to the path of peace.
                                                            The Gospel of Luke

Nancy sautéed the diced onions in butter then dredged the tilapia in minced garlic. As she placed the fish to cook in the bubbling caramelized onions she shouted "four minutes to dinner." Claudia was in the dining room showing Jim how to set a "proper" table with Nancy's collection of imported china and silver. She had shown Jim the bit about the knives, forks and spoons and where they go several different times in their 27 years of marriage, but so far, he was proving to be a most reluctant student. "Be sure and put the chargers out for the plates and bring three of them in here. I want to warm them before I plate the food."

"All right Miss Bossy Birthday Girl" Claudia said as she walked into the kitchen carrying her glass of wine. Jim came in right behind her carrying the plates. "Smells fishy in here," Jim said "but I bet the food is better than my other choice down at the Sleeping Pig." "Well I should think so!" Nancy said as she flipped the fish over and went into the pantry for the sherry. "This recipe is one of my favorites. My sister came up with it a few years ago. Well, she said she came up with it. But I think she got it from a chef in some fancy Atlanta restaurant. This is way out of her league." Nancy drenched the fish, capers, caramelized onions and garlic with dry sherry. The fragrant steam spilled out into the kitchen. She plated the mashed potatoes in the center of the warmed plates. Then placed a steaming fish fillet on top of the potatoes and built the stack on up with a mound of sautéed green beans mixed with cherry tomatoes. She garnished the savory pyramid with lemon slices and chives. "Dadaaaah!" She said smiling. As they carried their plates into the dining room, where freshly baked bread and wine awaited them, the phone rang. "Shall I get that?" Claudia asked. "It can wait," Nancy said.

The conversation at dinner was lively. Jim was a charming man who knew how to enliven any dinner party. He was an artist, a potter and often starred in the local theater productions. There was a thriving community of skilled artisans on the island and together with Camille Carmichael and several other artists, Jim was on the board of directors for the Rainman Island Art Association. Life on the island suited him. And Claudia suited him. They obviously enjoyed each other, sneaking a little kiss here and a little pat there. "Do you all remember when I started the Rainman Island Art Ala Carte Newsletter?" Jim said. "How could we forget?" Nancy said. "You sent your two ace reporters out to snoop around our neighbor's yards collecting stuff for the Yard Report column!" Claudia chimed in. "Do you remember when old man Riggins came running out with his shotgun and ran us off his place?" Claudia squealed with laughter. She was getting a buzz from the wine.

Betty made her way silently down the steps, unnoticed. She heard the voices from the dining room and moved toward them. She suddenly found herself standing in the archway that separated the entry foyer from the dining room. Nancy jumped when she saw her, startled. She had almost forgotten Betty was even in the house. Betty was bundled in a pink bathroom that made her look like a tiny, fat, and anemic elfin. "I called but no one heard me," she said quietly. "Can I get you something Betty?" Nancy asked. "I was going to bring your dinner up to you in a little while. I didn't know if you felt like company on your first day here." Nancy felt lame. Betty wasn't sure what to do. She didn't know Claudia or Jim, or Nancy for that matter, and she had no experience with dinner parties.

"I must have fallen asleep again," said Betty, "but I did wake up a little hungry. I really haven't had anything to eat today." "Sit down right here" Nancy said and pulled out a chair. "Yes, please join us," Jim beamed a smile at her that was hard to refuse. Betty sat down quietly and looked at Nancy's back as she quickly made her way into the kitchen. Nancy returned quickly with the fish concoction and placed it in front of Betty. Betty's stared at it. "What is it?" said Betty with a slight frown on her face. Nancy told her it was really just fish and potatoes and pretty bland, if she wanted to try it. "If you don't like it, I'll open a can of soup or something." She poured Betty some water. "Would you like a glass of wine?" Nancy asked. Betty shook her head and said "I had to give that up years ago. I'm a recovering alcoholic you know." "No, I didn't know," Nancy said. "But thank you for telling me."

Jim picked the conversation back up with Nancy as a way of forcing his wife and her best friend to quite gawking at Betty. Jim had a second sense about people, an insight that bordered on mystical. He had the gift of intuition and used it often in his approach to art and acting. And he used it now as he tried to absorb the essence of Betty Bishop. Betty took a bite of her food and chewed slowly. She looked up and met Nancy's eyes. "The doctor said you have no dietary restrictions so I guess we need to figure out what you like to eat, cause I sure do love to cook," Nancy said smiling. "You can make this for me any time you want to," Betty said shyly. It was a resoundingly positive statement and nobody at the table missed it. For the first time Nancy felt like she might have done right by bringing Betty to her home. Claudia shot Nancy a look that said, "I told you so" then smiled at Betty.

Nancy was surprised when Betty ate most of her dinner. When she offered strawberry cake and coffee in the den, Betty declined and said she was feeling tired again. She thanked Nancy for dinner and slowly retreated up the stairs. The phone rang again. The answering machine cut on this time. It was Rachel. All three of them sat there and heard her say "Just wanted to see how mother was doing and…pause…ah…pause…Miss Nancy I'd like to speak to you when you get a chance. Something happened to me tonight and I … ah…just…ah…wanted to tell someone about it. Call me back, please. When you get a chance, that is." Claudia grinned still a little giddy from the wine. "Well I want to know what happened to her! Maybe she took a bath, looked in the mirror at her cleaned up self and thought she had mysteriously turned into someone else!" "You are so mean!" Nancy said laughing.

"Hi Rachel, your mom is doing fine. She just came down and had dinner with us. Ate pretty good. I was pleased," Nancy started. "That's good, Miss

Hogan," said Rachel. "What's up?" Nancy asked. "You mentioned that something happened to you. What is it?" Nancy realized that every time she spoke to Rachel she used her 'business voice.' There was a hint of arrogance in Nancy's tone whenever she spoke to or about Rachel. It was so automatic that Nancy had never realized it before tonight. But for some reason, in this particular conversation, she heard herself loud and clear and knew what she was doing. Rachel brought something out in Nancy's personality that Nancy did not like about herself -- a judgmental, critical parent. Nancy had tried hard to rid herself of the damage done to her by critical and judgmental parents and grandparents and husband. But there it was, surfacing in her. *My mother, myself,* she thought as she listened for Rachel to speak.

Rachel had not noticed Nancy's tone. As far a Rachel was concerned Nancy's response to her was normal and routine. Rachel's self esteem bottomed out long ago when her mother abandoned her at the tender age of eight. Emotional vulnerability replaced what should have been healthy self-esteem. But the worst of it was her complete inability to bond with others. Rachel felt that people had always held her at a distance or rejected her entirely. Most of which was true.

Nancy eyed Claudia who had moved over in front of the mirror and was mimicking someone looking startled – mouth wide open, eyes bulging. Nancy didn't want to start laughing again so she turned her back on her friend and closed her eyes to concentrate.

"I don't know exactly what happened to me tonight.

I think I met Jesus, I mean...I don't know...but...I feel different...I'm ..." Rachel's voice trailed off.

Nancy felt disoriented, as if she had been floating upside down and now was suddenly jerked back into reality. Instantly she desperately wanted to say the right thing, but what was it! "That's wonderful, Nancy." She forced the words out and for the second time in one hour, she felt lame. Nancy's voice was gentle now. "Tell me what happened."

As Rachel talked, Nancy walked slowly out of the den down the hall into her bedroom and quietly closed the door behind her. She was sitting on her bed when Rachel finally hung up twenty minutes later. Tears were streaming down Nancy's face. *What a birthday Lord! You have blessed me in so many ways, Father -- but I cannot remember ever receiving the gift of being the first one to know that You just brought another of Your children into Your kingdom. I ask you to forgive me for rejecting her and for my feelings of superiority. Teach me Father to love as you love. I'm sure glad that You are God and I am not.*

Nancy heard a light knock on her bedroom door and suddenly Claudia was standing in the open door. Claudia could see that Nancy had been crying. "What's going on?" Claudia asked softly.

Nancy looked up at her with the tears still filling her eyes. "Somehow Jesus has taken Rachel, just as she is, sandblasted her clean and into the Kingdom of God!"

"What!" Claudia was almost shouting. "Tell me the whole story!"

Arm in arm, the old friends slowly walked down the hallway and back into the den, beaming. When Jim saw their faces he knew something important and good had happened. He didn't need to ask them. They both started talking at the same time.

It was almost 11 p.m. when Jim and Claudia started toward the back door. "What a wonderful evening we've had" said Jim. Claudia nodded in agreement and hugged her friend. As she backed out of the embrace Claudia said "Oh! I almost forgot to tell you something interesting happened the other day at the shop. I saw a man that looked exactly like Frank Jr., except he was a little older and a little weird. I guess Frank has a look-a-like running around. When I saw him he was looking through that row of men's jackets I put up front by the window." Nancy looked stunned. "Did you speak to him?" Nancy asked. "Well I really didn't get a chance. As soon as he spotted me coming over, he almost ran out of the store."

Betty Bishop

Rainman Island is a place that nurtures creativity, cherishes nature and harbors an innovative community. Many organizations and countless volunteer hours have gone into making this year's Rainman Island Art and Seafood Festival the best one ever!

Camille pushed back from her computer and read the paragraph through glasses perched on the tip of her nose. She grunted and pushed her glasses back into place. Sam, one of the Island's talented teenagers had offered to create a website to advertise the festival this year and Camille was rushing to get some script to him. She had already made several cuts at format and content. She wanted to have something ready for the council meeting this afternoon. All sixteen members of the Festival Society needed to proof read the text and approve it before she gave it to Sam to publish over the Internet.

This year's Festival will foster appreciation of and interest in the arts through the presentation of artistic and cultural events (see calendar below). The admission of $15 per person includes all activities. Food and beverages sold separately.

I wonder if we should charge more than $15 per person. She made a note to ask the committee about admission. She tried Nancy Hogan's number again. This time Nancy caught it on the second ring. "This is Camille Carmichael" she started. Nancy wished she had not answered the phone, she was running late. "I don't think I have spoken to you before which seems impossible living on such a small island," Camille said. Nancy vaguely recognized the name but couldn't place her. Nancy wondered where the conversation was going. If she didn't hurry she'd miss the 10 o'clock ferry to the main island. "What did you need, Mrs. Carmichael?" Nancy used her "business voice" again. "Is this a bad time to call?" Camille asked. "Why yes, I was just leaving," Nancy said. "I need to catch the 10 o'clock ferry." "Oh! I'll call back later, then. What's a good time?"

Never thought Nancy. *Probably wants money, food cooked and delivered by me or another one of those volunteer things.* "I'll be home tomorrow, all day. Perhaps you would call me back then," Nancy said, dismissing Camille.

When Sarah Clifton arrived there was only enough time for Nancy to quickly show her around, tell her about Betty's meds and show her how the baby monitor worked. She almost ran up the stairs to introduce her to Betty. Nancy lightly tapped on Betty's door but did not wait to enter. They found Betty sitting in the big blue chair by the windows with her eyes closed and her hands folded in her lap. She was wearing the big fluffy pink housecoat again. Nancy had brought Betty's breakfast tray up to her earlier. It sat untouched on the foot of her bed. "Betty this is Mrs. Sarah Clifton. She's going to stay with you on the days I'm over at the hospital. She has my number and Rachel's if she needs them. Can you think of anything you want me to do before I leave?" Nancy asked sincerely. Betty smiled at them both and whispered "no thank you." As Nancy was leaving, she told Sarah that Betty seemed very low to her today. "Maybe if you get a chance you could go up and talk to her a little. Try to draw her out of herself."

Sarah Clifton is 30 something, heavy set and friendly. When engaged in conversation Sarah will give you her opinion, whether you ask for it or not. She has two little girls in the island elementary school. That's how she came to know Rachel, rather she knew *of* Rachel. Rachel doesn't keep close company with anyone.

"Will do, Mrs. H" Sarah said. "You are going to miss the ferry if you keep standing around here telling me what to do. Remember I have to leave at 2:30 and pick the girls up from school. I can bring them back here and stay till you get home if you want me to, or leave Betty on her own until you come. It's up to you. Either way it'll be $20.00 a day."

This was all so new for Nancy. She hadn't had anyone in her home when she was away in years; since Frank died and Frank Jr. disappeared. This felt like an army of strangers had moved into her private world. "I guess she'll be OK on her own after 2:30. Why don't you ask her what she prefers? Either way is OK with me. Just give her some lunch and make sure she's in no distress when you leave. Rachel is the one to call if anything happens. She's closer to you than I'll be, and it is *her* mother."

Nancy prayed as she backed her car out of the drive: *help me Father to be as gracious with my home and my things, as you have been so gracious to me with everything.* Betty watched from the upstairs bedroom window as Nancy's car backed out of the drive.

Another pair of timid eyes also watched Nancy go, unobserved.

Sarah wasted no time bounding back up the stairs and trying to engage Betty in conversation. "Can I clear away your dishes Betty? Say, you haven't eaten anything, didn't even drink your coffee. How do you feel today? Want me to read to you or anything?" Betty didn't know which question to answer first. For a moment she wondered if Sarah was on drugs she was talking so fast. Betty remembered she used to turn into a motor mouth herself when she got high.

Betty leaned forward. "You know Rachel, don't you?" "Yes Mam," Sarah said. "She helps the teachers over where my Lizzy Beth and Hannah go to school."

"Tell me what you think of Rachel" Betty said quietly, fixing her eyes directly on Sarah's. Sarah had not expected that question, but true to form, she blurted out the first thing that came into her mind. "I think she's kinda weird. She doesn't talk much; never smiles and I've never seen her when that hair of hers wasn't half down in her face. Makes her look sort of like -- retarded -- if you ask me." Betty continued to stare at Sarah, but her mouth had slipped open without her even realizing it. *This young woman was certainly outspoken, I wonder what she thinks of me?* Betty thought but decided not to ask.

A few minutes later, Betty heard the TV come on

downstairs and assumed Sarah was occupied. She felt a little stronger today, and attributed it to the good food and more rest that she had had in weeks. After two long hospital stays, preceded by several months of chemo, her mind, body and spirit were depleted. She silently opened the door of her bedroom and walked down the hall toward the other bedrooms. She stopped and noticed the art on the hall walls, big lively floral paintings. One had a cat in it. All 5 doors in the hallway were closed. She opened the first one and found a linen closet. The next one was a bedroom and the warm colors and luxurious fabrics immediately engaged her. The bedside tables were covered with inlaid mirrors giving the whole room the feel of a luxurious Hollywood movie set, she thought. There was a bathroom that connected this bedroom with another one. Betty thought a connecting bathroom was a good idea. She'd never seen a "Jack and Jill" bathroom before.

Betty suddenly felt like a little girl in Disney World for the first time. She walked through the connecting bathroom into the next bedroom. It was stark white; walls, carpet, furniture, fabrics, everything was done up in shades of white. There were white silk orchids clustered on one of the dressers. They looked so real Betty bent over and sniffed them. "Am I in heaven?" she said out loud. A smile crossed her face and she drew in the pink robe a little closer around her tiny frame. Across the hall, she went into the bedroom that adjoined hers. Blue toile fabric covered the walls and cherry canopy bed. The room looked like something Betty had once seen in a magazine at the doctor's office. She wasn't sure about this room. She didn't feel like she could even sit down in it without messing something up.

Come to think of it, of all the rooms upstairs, Betty liked the one she was in the best. *I guess Nancy does know a little something about me.*

Before returning to her room, Betty glanced out the window at the end of the hall. She noticed a man walking slowly down the road away from the house. Something was odd about the way he walked, she thought. Instead of walking on the shoulder of the road like most locals did, he stayed in the ditch. And it had been raining a lot lately. *He was bound to be walking in water*. She watched him until he slowly moved out of sight, around the bend in the road. She suddenly felt so weak she thought she was going to fall. She held herself up on the wall and moved slowly back into her room and lowered herself into the big blue chair. Within a moment she had drifted off to sleep again.

"I think she's been asleep most of the time I've been here" Sarah said when Nancy called at noon. "Did you take her lunch up yet?" "Not yet, I'm about to. I warmed up that homemade soup you showed me and got the crackers out. This soup sure looks good Mrs. H." "Well call me or Rachel if the train goes off the track," Nancy said lightly and hung up.

Sarah knocked and entered Betty's room as she had seen Nancy do. "Got your lunch Miss Betty." Sarah could tell that Betty had been coughing. There was a little pile of blood stained tissues piled up in her lap. When Sarah came in, Betty grabbed the tissues up quickly and put them in the small trashcan beside the big blue chair. "You know we have that oxygen over there if you get to where you think you need it," Sarah said. Betty nodded. "Feel like some homemade soup? Mrs. H. sure is a good cook."

"She sure is" Betty agreed and Sarah tucked the napkin into Betty's pink bathrobe and sat the tray down in her lap." "Thanks, Betty said quietly. "I've never been one to eat breakfast much. Hope I didn't hurt Nancy's feelings this morning." "Aw, I doubt it. Everybody has to get used to new people, you know?" Betty liked Sarah. There was something wide open about her. You knew where you stood with her. Very unlike Rachel. Betty had no idea where she stood with her own daughter or how to fix the gulf that lay between them. Rachel was sweet to Betty one day and caustic the next. She'd come by the house to see her, then get up and leave abruptly after only being there 5 minutes.

Betty tested the warm soup with pursed lips then swallowed a little. It was home made chicken noodle, one of Betty's favorites. Sarah watched Betty's shoulders relax as she started to enjoy the soup. "You know what I said about Rachel earlier. I have a big mouth, Miss Betty and I know that's your daughter and all and well, maybe I shouldn't have said she was weird and looked like she was retarded." "Maybe she is retarded," Betty grinned at Sarah. Sarah howled with laughter. "I'm gonna like this job just fine," Sarah said. "Tell me about your girls," Betty prompted, and for the next 30 minutes, Betty ate soup and listened…and Sarah talked.

Good News Bad News

Micah's body ached all over as he sat in the waiting room of the ER at Comox General Hospital. It was very late or very early, depending on how you looked at it. Micah was bone weary from his long day of fishing and then the shock of finding Ray. The adrenalin rush it had taken to get Ray's lifeless body to the clinic, then his frantic rush to get to the hospital himself had all taken their toll. But he was wide-awake, too keyed up to relax. He'd been walking around and around the ER waiting room for hours. He was now very acquainted with the little hallway outside the ER. He'd sat in there on the cold, tiled floor and prayed his heart out for Ray as the hours ticked by. He'd begged God for Ray's life, for his healing. Then finally, mentally and physically exhausted he reached the plateau of surrender. Like the Christ in Gethsemane, finally, Micah came to that place of acceptance. He had given the entire outcome of this tragedy over to God and felt God's peace surround him.

He glanced up at the big black and white clock on the wall again. It was only fifteen minutes later than the last time he'd looked. 5:15 A.M. It startled Micah when the double doors leading back to the treatment center swung open and Dr. Alice walked out looking for him. "Can I buy you a cup of coffee, you look like you could use one," she said. Micah got up without speaking and they walked over to a closed door with a card reader on it. Dr. Alice slid her ID badge through the card reader and the door swung open. The Doctor's lounge is down this way. There's always a fresh cup of coffee in there, well...sometimes it's fresh."

"I been praying all night, Dr. Alice. Is he going to make it?" She looked at him with tenderness, then down at the floor. "I'm just the doctor, Micah. It's in God's hands now. Medically speaking, he's alive, that's about it. I don't know if he can pull out of this or not. To complicate everything else he's dealing with, the pneumonia has kicked back in. We've maxed out on his drips - he's getting blood, fluids, and antibiotics - a whole bunch of stuff. His blood pressure keeps bottoming out. There is some good news. You want to hear it?"

She looked at him and half smiled as she poured them each a mug of freshly brewed coffee. They sat down facing each other in the deserted lounge. Micah thought, "here it is 5:30 in the morning. I know Alice has not slept at all for at least 24 hours but she looks exactly like she always does, red hair pulled back in a pony tail, face shiny and fresh and a big toothy smile. I wonder how she does it?" "I sure do want to hear some *good news*!" Micah said as he blew the steam from his coffee. "Although he does have two fractures of the cervical vertebrae, there is no evidence of neurological injury" her smile widened. "That is very good news, Micah, especially keeping in mind his old bones and the adventure of getting him here - all the handling, etc. You and Big John did an excellent job with your part."

"You mean that if he can make it over the hump of exposure and infection, he won't be paralyzed, he'll be OK?" Micah raised his eyebrows so high they touched a lock of dark hair that had flopped down in his face. "That's what we are hoping for, Micah. It is certainly a possibility. It's really up to his body now. We're doing everything we can think to do. There have been two other doctors back there with me tonight. One is an infection specialist and Dr. Lowe just left. He's the neurosurgeon on call tonight. Together we reviewed the MRI's of Ray's neck with the radiologist. If we knew of anything else to do, we'd be doing it." Dr. Alice shrugged her shoulders and met Micah's eyes. "But Micah, it's a long uphill battle for him and I don't want you to get your hopes up too high. It really is in God's hands now." A slight smile crossed Micah's face. "Ray would say there is no better place to be than in God's hands. Has he come around yet?" Micah asked.

"No, we're keeping him under, taking everything off his plate, so to speak. We had to put him on a ventilator. I hope it's temporary. I hated to do it because now he can't talk. Even if he does come around he can't tell us what happened to him. He's in trouble with his lungs and breathing. There was no other choice."

Dr. Alice's eyes scanned Micah's face. "You should go home and get some rest. We'll probably keep him out for a while -- maybe days. I'll let you know even the slightest change. I'm charted as the admitting physician, so I'll be notified immediately of any change."

Dr. Alice changed the subject. "How did you get here from your boat?" Micah smiled and said, "Aw, I keep an old motor cycle over at the ferry. I have to come over here so often that I needed a quick ride.

I always leave Pam the car, in case she needs it with the kids and all. Why?" "I'm going home too," said Dr. Alice, "and I wanted to catch a ride to the ferry." "Fine by me, if you don't mind a little wind in your hair," Micah said and then looked down at the floor, suddenly feeling embarrassed.

"I was born to ride!" Dr. Alice said as she pushed a small fist up into the air.

It was 7:30 a.m. by the time Micah made it home. He could smell bacon cooking when he came in the front door. His kids were finishing breakfast and Pam smiled a big warm "welcome home smile" at Micah. "How's Ray, dear?" Sally trotted into the kitchen at the sound of Micah's familiar voice. "He's still in critical condition but Dr. Alice says he has a chance. I am so hungry I could eat a horse," he said as he reached down and teasingly snatched the last piece of half eaten bacon from Abigail's plate. "Go get a long hot shower and I'll have your breakfast ready when you finish. I've got to run the kids to school, but I'll be back in about 10 minutes or so. I want to hear everything." Pam started to usher the kids toward the car. *It was good to be home* Micah thought, as he walked slowly toward their bedroom. He hesitated halfway down the hall and ran his finger over a picture of his family that had been taken about a year earlier. *Thankful, that's what I am, Father, thankful.*

When Pam came home about 15 minutes later, the house was quiet. The shower was not running. She peeked into the bedroom and found Micah lying across their bed sound asleep with his clothes on. She lovingly drew the blanket over him and slipped his shoes off and closed the door.

Bear Hunt

"Hey Pat, this is Micah Stillmore," he said into the phone. "I need to tell you about what happened to Ray Phillips." Micah listened as Pat told him to hold on for a minute while he turned down a radio that was screeching in the background. "Ok Micah, sorry about that," Pat came back on the line. "I found him last night down behind his barn. His neck was broken and he had deep gashes in his head. He'd apparently been laying there most of the day. Dr. Alice got him over to Comox last night. He's real low. He may not make it." Micah stopped so that Pat could ask him some questions. He wanted Pat to get this right. Pat was a retired cop from Vancouver. He was likable enough but Micah didn't think much of his detective abilities. He had been the island's Constable for over 3 years.

Pat asked him a few questions about the time of day Ray was found, commented about the cold weather and snow then asked if there was any sign of a struggle. Micah told Pat about the half eaten ducks everywhere and offered to meet him at Ray's house when he got ready to go over. "Oh and I heard something when I went back over there last night to get Ray's dog. Sounded like a large animal, or *something*…well…large. Sounded like it ran away from me."

"Two or four?" Pat said. "Two or four what?" Micah said feeling a little frustrated that he had to deal with

Pat. "Feet. Sorry. Was the thing you heard running away -- running on two feet or four?"

"Hard to say, Pat. I was cold, tired, wet and more than a little rattled. But Pat -- I'd take a *big* rifle with me if I were you. Whatever it was, it was big."

"Yeah, I can meet you over there about three this afternoon and show you around," Micah said as he ended the call.

At 3 p.m. Micah sat in his truck waiting for Pat in Ray's backyard. The day was overcast and had warmed a little. From where he sat he could see patches of fog moving slowly along the creek bank. *This is a pretty place,* he thought, *I hope that Ray gets to enjoy it a little longer*. He really did not want to go back down to the creek but wondered what it looked like in daylight. He was still groggy from loss of sleep even though Pam had let him sleep about 4 hours. Every few minutes the image of Ray's face and his grotesquely bent legs and neck dropped into Micah's thoughts.

Pat tapped on the window and startled Micah out of his thoughts. He slipped out of his truck and led the way down to the creek bank. Pat had a camera and started taking pictures as Micah described everything he could remember. Pat made a few notes and looked around. He saw a couple of the blue feathers still stuck in the mud and the *now* empty metal pie plate. "What's this over here?" Pat had walked about 6 or 8 feet upstream from where Ray had been laying. He pulled back some low hanging branches so he could see better. Micah and Pat looked down at a large paw print. "Look at those claw marks, and the four toes," Pat said. They both bent down to have a closer look. Pat took out a small ruler from his shirt pocket and measured the depth of the print and noted it in his book. He measured the width of the print then started looking around for more. But the ground changed up the bank near the paw print to moss covered rocks. "Hard to tell which direction he was traveling with only one print," Pat said, "but he's a big one. Guess you can go any damn direction you want to when you're that big. Wonder what he's doing roaming around this time of year. Don't bears hibernate in the winter?" Micah looked at Pat and shrugged his shoulders. "Guess that's why we need a detective on the job around here." Micah knew he sounded sarcastic without really meaning to.

As they walked back to their trucks, Pat said "I think I'm going to write this one up as a suspected attack by a dangerous animal, until I can talk to Ray, that is. Have you heard anything about his condition today?"

"He's the same," Micah said. "Critical, unconscious, struggling to live, as Dr. Alice put it. I phoned her right before I came over to meet you."

"Have you looked around the place, made sure no one broke in or anything like that?" Pat asked Micah.

"I did look around a little. Barn's still locked -- golf cart still here. He never locks his front door but everything inside looked like it was in its usual place." "I'll have a look around myself," Pat said. "Then I plan to head over to the co-op and put up some dangerous animal alert posters."

Pat looked down at his muddy boots, then up at

Micah, who towered over him. "I need to get some men together and find this bear. Could you help us later on?"

"I've got to pull traps in the morning and I'm going back over to see about Ray this afternoon. But me and my brother Pete can both help tomorrow afternoon." Micah looked up at the darkening sky. "It's supposed to rain hard this afternoon and into tomorrow. It won't be any fun looking for a bear in this weather."

"Guess we'll have to learn to think like a bear. Where would you go if you were a bear around here?" Pat looked up at Micah and at almost the same moment, they both said "the Hell Hole."

Micah floored the gas as he followed Pat's truck down Honey Bear Lane. Gravel spun from Pat's wheels and splattered across Micah's windshield. Pat had thrown on the blue LED deck light he had recently installed on the top of his truck. They both made the left turn onto Peterson Point Road without looking in either direction. A squirrel, munching on an acorn, looked up in time to see the big black wheel rolling directly at him. Stunned, he froze. Pat noticed the bump and glanced into his rear view mirror but could only see Micah driving fast behind him. They both parked along the road directly in front of the path that led down to Hell Hole. Pat reached into his truck and pulled his 660 Remington rifle off the gun rack behind the drivers seat. He checked to make sure it was loaded. He hoped it would be enough to stop a bear, especially to stop a mad, charging bear. "Have you got a good light for the cave?" he asked Micah as he picked up his headlamp and put it over his head and switched it on. "I've got this one" Micah said and held up a high-powered flashlight. High powered flashlights were necessary equipment for the several jobs Micah was frequently called on to do around the island. He always kept one charged up and ready to go in his truck.

"Wait a minute, I've got to radio Bill over at the co-op and tell him what we're up to. He's my backup and it's smart to let someone else know what's up." Micah's impression of Pat was improving by leaps and bounds. As Pat spoke to Bill, he not only gave him a brief outline of what they had seen at Ray's place, but what they suspected and where they were. He also asked Bill to start circulating the dangerous animal alert. "You'll find a few of those fliers in that black filing cabinet in my office" Pat said into the phone. "Yeah, about 15-20 minutes I'd guess. Hey, I've got Micah Stillmore with me. Yeah. I've got the key. Talk to you in a few" he said then snapped his phone off. He dropped the cell phone into his jacket pocket as they walked toward the barred entrance to Hell Hole. "Scout around a little and see if you can see any noticeable paw prints while I find the key to the gate. It's been raining so much lately the prints may be hard to see." As Micah looked around, Pat pulled out a big wad of keys and fumbled around for the one labeled Hell Hole.

As he started down the steep bank toward the barred entrance to the cave he noticed that the lock had been broken and the gate was standing open about 2 inches. He looked down at the ground. "Somebody's been using this entrance - look at the ground there. This gate has been swung open and shut a few times lately. The grass and moss are pushed back. A bear wouldn't do that!" They looked at each other nervously. Pat wondered if he should get some additional backup before going in. His mind was whirling with possibilities.

Some crazed person could have attacked Ray as easily as a crazed animal could have attacked him. It was the first time he had considered that angle.

Pat pushed the gate open far enough for them to enter the cave. It was the first time Pat had been in the cave in a couple of years and he'd never gone very far. Micah had never been inside at all. He didn't like caves. Especially caves named Hell's Hole. Things slithered in caves. Both men stood perfectly still. Pat laid his finger over his pursed lips in a shushing motion, and then tapped his ear to indicate he wanted Micah to listen with him. Outside a large bird flew past the cave opening, momentarily blocking the dim light coming from outside. They both heard an eagle squawking on a high branch outside the cave entrance. In between the eagle squawks they strained to hear any sound that might be coming from the blackness before them. Pat took small steps forward moving the light on his head in every direction.

Light bounced off the wet walls as they slowly made their way down the man made corridor. The cave floor sloped gently. Small alcoves line the corridor on both sides and were filled with grotesque stalagmites and stalactites. The ceiling in the corridor was 7 or 8 feet high. *So this was the entrance to the old timers poker and drinking room,* Micah thought as he tried to calm himself.

The corridor ran about 50 feet then opened into a

much larger room with a 40 or 50 foot ceiling. Micah held up his flashlight so that the entire area was illuminated. The light flooded out to reveal a room about 60 x 60 with irregular walls and at least 4 other corridors leading off in other directions like the spokes on a poorly made wheel. Pat slowly rotated his body so that his headlamp washed across the walls about 6 feet off the floor of the cave. As their eyes adjusted to the half-light they saw a small ledge about 4 feet off the floor at the rear of the room. Laying on it was what appeared to be a sleeping bag, a red fuel can, and some stacked cans. "I think I've solved a couple of crimes today," Pat whispered. "This looks like the stuff that was reported stolen from the co-op a few days ago." They walked slowly toward the sleeping bag and were startled when it moved. Micah felt the impulse to run and Pat must have sensed it because Pat reached out and caught Micah's arm, turned and made eye contact with him. "Steady," whispered Pat and laid his finger over his mouth again, indicating silence, then raised his rifle and pointed it directly at the moving lump in the sleeping bag.

"Come on out of there" he said in a surprising calm voice. Micah's eyes were fixed on the large lump. All sorts of stupid thoughts were flying through his mind at lightning speed. "If it was a bear, could he understand English? And what was a bear doing sleeping in a sleeping bag in the middle of the afternoon?" Both men waited. "I said come on out of there" Pat raised his voice and kept it as level as he could under the circumstance.

The sleeping bag moved again then dropped away, revealing a man with rumpled, dark, shoulder length hair and a dark beard growing out of a filthy face.

There was a look of utter bewilderment on his face. Pat and Micah stood transfixed as the man slowly moved his legs out of the bag and stood up on the ledge. He put one of his arms up over his eyes to try and see beyond the light that Pat was shining directly into his face. "Step on down here, son" Pat said calmly, like he did this every day. Micah thought, "yeah, he's definitely got my vote next year." The cave dweller did not resist and without speaking, slowly started his descent down from his perch. He dropped himself the last couple of feet onto the floor and swayed to catch his balance. Micah quickly started formulating ideas about who he was and what he was doing here. It was obvious from the litter around his "bunk" that he'd been staying in the cave for a while. Pat reached around to his back and pulled a pair of cuffs off his belt loop. He slung the gun back over his shoulder and took several steps toward the man. "Hold your hands out, son." The man did as he was told. "I'm going to take you into my office for some questions. You shouldn't be in here. Where'd you get those groceries up there?" The man didn't answer Pat. He looked confused and still half asleep. When asked about the groceries, the man slowly swung his head and looked back in the direction of the ledge. "What's your name, boy?" Pat asked. "Frank. My name is Frank Hogan."

You Never Know

On the commute home Nancy remembered the call she'd received earlier from Camille Carmichael. *Might as well get it over with and call her back - see what I've volunteered for this time*. She retrieved her cell phone and pressed the number from her 'recent calls' list. Camille answered on the first ring. "Hi this is Nancy Hogan. I have a little more time to chat now. You called me this morning?" Her voice ended high, with a question. "Ah yes, Mrs. Hogan," Camille said. "Please, call me Nancy," she interrupted. "Mrs. Hogan was my mother-in-law's name." *Where did that come from?* Nancy chided herself. "Just a moment, please" Camille said and Nancy could hear her rummaging through some papers. "Yes, Mrs…ah…Nancy, I wanted to speak to you about the commission piece that has been ordered - get a date so I can get you and your sister on my calendar." This woman wasn't asking her to volunteer. Nancy was confused. She changed gears and said "I'm not sure what you're talking about, Mrs. Carmichael. Do you have the right person? "I think so," said Camille. "And please Nancy, call me Camille. No one calls me Mrs. Carmichael." Finally the name clicked with Nancy. *Rosewood.* "You are Nancy Hogan and live at 354 Honey Bear Lane, right?" Camille snapped. "That's me alright but I have no idea what you're talking about. What is a commission piece?" Nancy's confusion wasn't clearing up. "Oh, I apologize. Let me read you the letter," said Camille, "just a moment."

Camille adjusted the ever-present glasses and held the letter up next to the lamp. "Dear Mrs. Carmichael. I have long enjoyed your work. My sister, Nancy Hogan, who is apparently your neighbor there on Rainman Island, introduced me to your art. She sent me some greeting cards you had printed from some of your watercolors. They have delighted my friends and me. The detail of your shadow work and the vivid colors you can pull from watercolors is remarkable. Which brings me to ask would you consider doing a commission piece of my twin sister and me? Are you still there Mrs...ah...Nancy?" Camille asked looking over at the clock on her desk. "I don't know anything about this," said Nancy, honestly surprised. "Wonder how she's planning for us to get together for this...commission piece?" "Oh," said Camille, "she says somewhere in here, let me see...here it is...she says she'll be here Christmas week through the end of the year."

There was complete silence on the line. Camille thought the call had been dropped. "H-e-l-l-o," Camille said. "Oh, yeah, I'm here," said Nancy. "I am just totally surprised. I didn't know she was coming." "Sounds like you two better talk before we set a date then," Camille offered. "Maybe this was supposed to be a surprise for you or something. Sure hope I didn't steal her thunder."

"I'll certainly call her tonight and get the details on this. I'll have to call you back - maybe tomorrow. Is that OK?" "Sure," said Camille. "Actually those two weeks are some of the slowest for me in the entire year so anytime in there would work OK. I'll talk to you tomorrow," said Camille and hung up.

Why had Laura not told her she was planning on a visit? She had not been to the island in over 10 years, maybe longer. I always go to Atlanta. She was so consumed with her thoughts about Laura's visit that she automatically drove her car off the ramp from Big John's Ferry service onto Peterson Point Rd., then made the right onto Honey Bear Lane, without thinking. As she drove past "Rosewood" she slowed down a little and tried to see into the lighted windows. *Finally, I'll get to go inside that house. This should be interesting.*

Nancy's big yellow house seemed to loom up out of the fog that floated in patches around the house reflecting her headlamps as she slowly pulled into the driveway. It was only 6 p.m. but in late November it was often completely dark by 5 p.m., especially on rainy days. *It's almost Christmas and Laura is coming and I have Betty here, and Rachel and Sarah! How is all this going to work?* As she made her way to the back door she heard Bernie barking his greeting from inside the kitchen. It seemed strange to Nancy to come home, expecting someone to be there. *Good strange.*

As she entered the kitchen, she could definitely tell that someone besides her had been there. Little tell-tell signs were everywhere, though nothing was really wrong with the sponge being left in the kitchen sink, or the coffee pot still plugged in. "Hello!" she spoke softly into the baby monitor. "Hello" Betty said back. "You home?" said Betty -- she couldn't think of anything else to say. "Was everything OK today, with Sarah and all?" Nancy asked into the monitor. "Sure was. I like her," Betty said. Nancy thought Betty sounded almost cheerful. "I'll be up as soon as I change. Can I bring you anything?" said Nancy. "No, I'm fine," said Betty.

Betty put the small picture of Kenneth she had been holding down in her lap. "Oh, and I have to call my sister before it gets too late on the East Coast. I'll be up in a few," said Nancy. "All right" said Betty.

Laura answered the phone and said, "I know you're calling me to tell me you've won the Canadian lottery. They do have a lottery up there don't they?" Nancy couldn't help but giggle. "Well, I think I have. I'm not sure how I landed a visit from you, which is as good as winning the lottery. You hardly ever come up here. What's up?"

"Well, since you couldn't come to visit me for our birthday, and since you are apparently starting up some sort of hostel for the dying, and since you have started getting messages from God! Well! I thought I'd better come check you out. I may have need of your facilities and abilities in my future -- you never know," Laura said.

"Well, whatever your reasons are, it will be grand having you for Christmas. Anybody coming with you?" Nancy said.

"Well, if you mean that short, blonde, ugly man I wanted you to meet-- he has been exported back to Iraq or something, so I don't think he can make it."

"You alone will be all the Christmas present I could dream of," Nancy said. "And so you contacted Camille Carmichael to commission a portrait of us? Where is it going to hang? There will be a custody battle!" Nancy said laughing. She was very happy her sister was coming to visit. She had not realized how much she missed her.

"Changing the subject a little, did you get the birthday present I sent?" Nancy asked. "Sure did," said Laura. "It was an amazing night - all those guys, roaming around my bedroom till the wee hours of the morning. They said they were coming back - didn't need to be paid. I guess they had a good time, too. I know I did!" They both laughed until they were sobbing. Laura was the queen of exaggeration.

Laura gave Nancy her travel plans and times she'd need to pick her up at the harbor in Nanaimo. Before going up to see about Betty, Nancy shuffled through the mail she'd thrown on the counter. As usual, there was one from Laura. This one had stickers of flying insects all over it. *I'll read it later*. She noticed something stuck in her mail that was not an envelope. It was a yellow slip of paper with some handwriting on it. She picked it up and saw that it was a note from Rachel. "Came by today after school. I guess Mom was asleep. No one came to the door. I'll call tonight. Rachel"

She carried the note with her as she climbed the steps. Betty's door was closed. Nancy tapped on it and walked in. Betty wasn't there. She glanced toward the bathroom door. The door was open and the lights were off. Nancy stepped out into the hall and noticed Betty standing in the dark, looking out the single window at the end of the hall.

"What'cha doing?" Nancy asked. Betty turned slowly to face her and said, "I'm watching a peeping Tom. Damn fool boy next door has been spying on you ever since you got home."

"What!" Nancy was shocked. She quickly closed the distance between them and peered out the window. Betty glanced over at Nancy and said, "he went into his house, and I watched him. I guess his daddy will be home in a few minutes. It's about time for the Ferry to shut down for the night." The idea of a creepy adolescent standing around outside her windows staring in at her sent a wave of nausea through Nancy. She looked at Betty with her mouth gaping open in shock. "What should I do?" Nancy whispered when she wanted to scream. "You probably need to start by talking to John. Then I think you ought to try and scare the hell out of Danny!" Betty said flatly.

"How?" Nancy hissed still whispering and reeling from the feeling of being invaded. "You could call Pat Roberts and ask him to arrest Danny! He needs to be jerked back into reality."

Nancy almost fell into the chair in her office. She had been sitting there talking to Laura, now she felt…exposed, like someone watching her take a shower. She reached up and closed the blinds over the bank of windows above her desk and dialed Big John's number. "I'm going to have to make this brief," she said when he answered cheerily "Hi neighbor." "Betty saw Danny staring in my windows tonight, John. I feel violated and just awful. I don't know what you think we should do about it but I want to call Pat Roberts and get him involved. I want to scare the hell out of Danny for doing this."

Betty had come down the steps and was standing in the middle of the room. "John! Did you hear me?"

the line sounded dead. "Yes, I hear you," Big John said. "You sure it was him?" "Yes, Betty saw him looking in my windows then watched him go into your house." Betty nodded at Nancy confirming what she was saying. "Damn it to hell!" John said angrily. "I'll be home in about 5 minutes Nancy, we'll be over and talk this out." "I don't want to talk it out. I want to call Pat!" Nancy countered angrily. "Well do what you have to do," John said, still angry.

Nancy, like almost everyone else on the island, had Pat Robert's number in her phone. Pat answered on the 2nd ring "Constable Roberts." "Nancy Hogan, Pat." "Oh!," said Pat. "I was about to call you", Pat said. "I don't know how you found out so quick, but I've got your boy Frank down here. Can you come down to my office?"

A Glimpse Of Heaven

Micah sat watching the machine pump air into Ray's lungs through the trach tube. He tried to make sense of the technical data that flashed on the screens around the room. He noticed the pulse oximetry on his arm that monitored his 02 levels. Yesterday it had been hovering around 90. Today it had slipped into the 80's. What did that mean? Was Ray getting better? Dr. Alice had come by to check on him. *Was it Tuesday already?* Micah thought that time seemed to move differently in hospitals -- slower.

Dr. Alice had told him that it was important to remember that like the laws of physics, a patient is the sum of all his parts. "The infection in Ray's lungs is not our biggest concern now. He has gone septic and has MRSA," she said. "His age and general condition aren't helping."

"What does *gone septic* mean?" Micah asked. "The infection from his lungs has apparently spread into his blood stream, Micah. And his kidneys are trying to shut down," Dr. Alice responded. "We've kept him more or less unconscious with medications for 7 days now and today we plan to slowly bring him out of it. See where we are, so to speak. Also, we've decided to remove the ventilator. That's a risky bit of business, Micah. But the longer he's on it, the more dependent he becomes. It may have to go right back in. We'll have to wait and see." Dr. Alice had turned to face Micah. She fixed her eyes on his and said "we are maxed out, Micah, on what we know to do for him, medically. It's in God's hands." Dr. Alice had finished speaking with a slight shrug of her shoulders and a weak smile. She promised Micah she'd be back around 2 p.m. "He should be waking up a little by then." She told him that Dr. Andrews would be coming in shortly to remove the ventilator. "But Micah," she said, turning toward the door, "Ray is very likely to be confused and disoriented when he wakes up. He may even be violent. He's been through a lot."

More than anything Micah wanted to ask Ray what happened to him. At the very least he wanted to tell Ray how much he loved him. "I know you want to talk to him, Micah, but I don't know if he will even be able to speak." Micah heard the words and smiled weakly. "I'll be back around 2 this afternoon."

Micah had brought Ray's Bible to him and sat reading some of the notes Ray had written in the margins. There were lots and lots of notes. Occasionally Micah would read one out loud to Ray. Pam told him that the hearing is the last thing to go -- and even when you are in a coma you can still hear. He wanted Ray to know he was there, and that he cared. From time to time he covered Ray's hand with his own and patted it gently.

****

Dr. Andrews had come and gone. The ventilator was out. Surprising everyone, Ray was breathing on his own. Two hours slipped by. Micah really had not noticed the time as he read Ray's Bible. A movement caught his eye and he shot to his feet.

Ray was moving his hand! It was the same hand that Micah had last seen bobbing up and down in the rushing water. Micah's eye's traveled quickly from Ray's hand up his arm and he was shocked to see Ray's bright blue eyes locked on his.

"Hey Buddy! Where ya' been?" Micah whispered the words as his face rose in a huge smile. For a moment, Ray looked wildly around the room, down at all the tubes running into him. He looked at the window and the light from the overcast day streaming in. He looked frantically at all the monitors and bags and tubes around the room. Then he looked at Micah with eyes full of questions. He slowly raised his hand and felt the picc line that had been inserted into his chest. Micah knew that Ray was trying to understand where he was and what had happened to him. He saw Ray's fingers begin to tighten on the tube in his chest, as if he meant to pull it out and he quickly grabbed Ray's hands and held them.

"Ray, you can't remove that. You need it right now. All this stuff they have on you is keeping you alive, making you better. You've had a really rough time."

Ray watched Micah as he spoke. His expressive eyes showed hurt and pain and bewilderment.

"Ray, if you want to, if you try, you might be able to speak." Micah spoke tenderly as if he were speaking to a young child. "Do you feel like giving it a try?"

The door behind Micah opened then closed quietly. Micah did not turn around. Dr. Alice laid her hand on Micah's shoulder as she came to stand next to him.

"Hello handsome" Dr. Alice looked down at Ray and smiled.

"How long has he been awake?" she asked Micah without taking her eyes off Ray.

"About 2 or 3 minutes, not long." Dr. Alice glanced around the room at all the monitors. Micah glanced at her and wished for a moment that he could interpret the data as easily as she seemed to understand it.

"I was trying to get him to speak" Micah said.

"Want to give it a try Ray?" Dr. Alice said cheerfully. "You'll probably have the worst sore throat of your life--we've been working on your lungs."

Ray's eyes widened. The halo brace attached to his skull with screws rendered his head and neck completely immobile. Ray looked at them steadily. The wildness in his eyes began to change as he started to understand where he was. The two people he loved and trusted most in the world were hovering over him. He tried to relax.

"Want to try and speak now?" Ray batted his eyes once. "OK, I want you to try and say HI, OK?"

Ray waited a minute and was able to say something that sounded like wind rushing through the word Hi. Micah noticed that he winced in pain.

"Excellent!" Dr. Alice said, genuinely delighted. "Not many patients can do that on the first try!"

"You have something to tell us, don't you Ray?"

Micah said. Ray batted his eyes slowly. Micah knew it meant yes.

"Bat your eyes once for yes and twice for no, OK?" Micah said.

"Ray I'm going to get a speech therapist in here in a little while so she can help you practice. But you're going to have to take it real easy, you understand?" He batted his eyes *twice*.

Micah looked at Alice. "I think he just said no." They looked at Ray. "You don't want to take it easy, Ray?" Dr. Alice said, smiling. He waited a moment and then clearly said "NO."

"Went to heaven" Ray slowly pushed the words out then waited for his lungs to fill with air again. "Want to tell."

Stunned, Micah and Alice looked at each other. "Get your notebook Micah and write this down, this is going to be good," Dr. Alice said as she beamed a smile at Ray. Ray put his hand on his throat and said "hurts." Dr. Alice flew out of the room and was back at his side within moments with pain meds.

"This should help," she said. It did. Ray closed his eyes and dozed.

On and off for the next six hours Ray dozed, then spoke, then dozed again. He could only manage a few words at a time. Then he had to rest. It was exhausting work for him to speak. Several times Dr. Alice told him to stop. He stared back at her and slowly blinked his eyes twice. Every word he pushed out was an effort. The speech therapist had come and gone. Several doctors and nurses came and went. But Ray continued.

Ray carefully picked his way through his encounter in Heaven. He seemed determined that Micah and Alice know where he had been and what he had seen. Micah wrote down every word. Occasionally Micah asked Ray for some clarification of what he meant. He tried to always ask yes and no questions to conserve Ray's energy and voice. He and Ray had quickly worked out yes and no signals either with his eyes or a squeeze of his hand when his eyes were too tired.

And then Ray simply stopped. Quietly and serenely his life began to ebb away. Dr. Alice never left the room. As the dim light of afternoon gave way to darkness, Ray slipped back into a coma, this time, without the aid of drugs. "It won't be long now," Dr. Alice said, smiling at Ray. She leaned over and whispered into his ear "thank you Ray, for that last gift from your life. We will treasure it always." After 20 minutes or so of repeatedly checking for a heartbeat, Dr. Alice reached over and switched off all supporting systems. Ray was gone.

Together Micah and Dr. Alice sat in the growing darkness of the room. They did not speak; they did not turn the lights on. They did not ask each other questions. They both, in their own way, were trying to comprehend the priceless gift that Ray had left them. Finally, Dr. Alice spoke.

"Ray and I worked out his funeral arrangements over a month ago, back when he was in the clinic with pneumonia. He wanted to be cremated." Micah slowly nodded as he listened to Dr. Alice. She continued, "he said he didn't want a funeral, just a party of some sort and let all his friends have a drink together and a laugh. He wanted it to be light and fun." Micah nodded again.

"When should we do it?" Micah asked slowly.

"His birthday is Christmas eve. He was a Christmas baby, did you know that?" Alice's voice was almost a whisper.

"I guess I had forgotten it. You know I have small kids and they dominate Christmas."

"Well, I say we have a Christmas Eve birthday party on the island, maybe at the Community Center, in honor of Ray's life. Have it on his birthday."

"That sounds just about perfect," Micah said as he looked up at Ray's body, still lying there, as if he had just dozed off again.

"Can you make the arrangements for the cremation?" Micah said. "He doesn't need that body anymore."

Micah looked at the notebook in his hand. "He's with Linda and their daughter Becky now. And his beloved Jesus. Don't you know there is a celebration going on in Heaven about now!

I wish I could just have a peek," Micah said.

"You just did," said Alice.

"It"

Every saint has a past and every sinner has a future.
                                                    Oscar Wilde

"Where's she gone?" Rachel asked Betty, stiffly. Rachel had come by Nancy's house anxious to talk what had happened to her. For the last few days Rachel had felt like she was walking on pink clouds. These were brand new feelings for Rachel.

"Didn't Nancy tell you what happened to me the other night?" "No," said Betty. "She only said you had something to tell me that was important." "Oh," said Rachel looking down at the swirling, muted shades of blue in the carpet. For a second Rachel thought about how it would feel to descend into the depths of the soft watery colors in the rug; to submerge herself until all sound and thinking was muffled out.

She forced her eyes away and looked directly at Betty. "Well, mother," she wasn't sure where or how to begin. "I was sitting at home last Tuesday night. Alone as usual. I had just finished grading some papers and felt too tired to get into my weaving. The radio was on my favorite country western station. I had turned it down low. I wasn't really listening to it anyway. I made myself a bowl of cereal for my supper...and...well," Rachel stumbled for a place to start. She knew that whatever she chose to say could not possibly capture the experience -- the feelings, the release, and the days of contentment that followed.

"Well, you know ... same old--same old." She was stalling. "Nothing different going on from any other night," Rachel spoke slowly as if she were backing up, like a child getting ready to run forward at top speed then leap. Rachel smiled weakly at her mother then took the leap. "All of a sudden I felt that someone was in the room with me, I mean I sensed a Presence, but I wasn't afraid or anything, in fact it felt kind of good. I looked around the room to see if anything was different. The feeling was so real and powerful. I don't know how to describe what happened next. I...I started crying. I mean really crying, like the saddest thing in the world had just happened to me. I started to remember stuff I hadn't thought about in years." Rachel looked at her mother, trying to figure out if she should go on or not. She *felt* a voice inside her that seemed to say *now or never, Rachel.* "I sort of recognized the *Presence*, or maybe I should say I just sort of understood Who *it* was...and I trusted *it*...I knew *it* was something good."

She lunged ahead. "I remembered when you left me, mother, and how bad it hurt, how afraid I was." Betty winced and Rachel saw it. Betty felt vulnerable. Naked. "I remembered how me and Robert cried for you...that first day we didn't know what to do. We kept thinking you would come back. That night we lay in the bed holding each other and crying. We did that for most of the next day, until Robert finally figured out how to call Daddy and he came and got us. We stayed with a neighbor until he got there."

Betty's mouth clenched shut. A muscle in her cheek twitched. She dropped her head, looking down toward the floor. The room went silent. Rachel waited wondering whether or not to go on. Then Betty looked up again and straightened her shoulders. The gesture seemed to say "come on, let me have it--I can take it."

Rachel was sitting on the foot of Betty's bed. For a moment Betty thought Rachel still looked like a little girl with messy hair, baggy clothes and huge brown eyes. Betty knew Rachel needed to finally come to terms with what she had done to them, to her. Betty had known it for a long time. But she never had the courage to start...how could she begin to explain. It was so long ago now. She was another person then -- a person who abandoned her children for drugs. They had never talked about *it.* The big *it,* the why and the how of *it* - Betty had abandoned Rachel and Robert. Just walked out of their lives. Leaving them to fend for themselves. It was an unspeakably cruel blow. Devastating. And now, after all the years of ignoring it, trying to somehow outlive the past, to run ahead of it somehow, it had surfaced again. Through the years they both hoped *it* would just disappear, be swept away by time. It was not.

   Betty thought to herself *well I'm dying now, time is running out. I've probably avoided **it** long enough.* She had only been brave enough once, while Kenneth was alive and supportive of her to try and talk about *it* with Rachel. But at the last moment, she had chickened out and simply told Rachel that she hoped they could let the past be past. But *the* *past is not dead. It's not even past.* Rachel's childhood trust had been destroyed, crushed again and again as she cried out for a mother's love that never came. Never. The 8-year-old Rachel could not reason *it* out; she did not have the maturity, knowledge or skills to do so. And she never received the help she so desperately needed to cope with the trauma of abandonment. Emotionally she became stunted. And remained in many ways an 8-year-old girl, blaming herself for the wound that had been inflicted on her.

Both Rachel and Betty sat quietly, not sure what to do or say. Finally Rachel pushed forward. She brushed the wayward lock of hair from her face and folded her hands in her lap, waiting for the words to come so that she could continue. This was hard and she chose her words carefully. With all her heart she wanted her next words to tear down the wall that had been built up between them for a lifetime.

"Mother, I forgive you."

Betty jerked her head up. Her eyes widened in surprise and then filled with tears. She was completely unprepared to hear these words from Rachel. A sheepish little smile came on Rachel's face. She looked at Betty as if trying to push the words across the room and into her mother's mind and heart with that smile.

Betty sat quietly for what seemed like a long time in the big blue chair looking down at the floor. She needed time for the words to form in her. Rachel waited. Finally she said, "Rachel, I have needed to hear those words for a very long time. I did not know how to ask you for them. I have been unable to forgive myself...how could I possibly ask you to forgive me...when I couldn't even forgive myself." A slight smile traveled across Rachel's face. Rachel knew she had said exactly the right words to open the door that had been shut for so long.

Betty slowly continued, "A person that is not an addict can never understand how drugs and alcohol could possibly become more important than a woman's children, or husband or even her own health and safety. But -- it happens, Rachel -- it happened to me."

The room fell silent again. Rachel looked at Betty and said "mother, there's something else. I've never told anyone this before, not even Robert. There are times, long periods of time that I wondered if I imagined it. But I didn't. All this came back to me the other night when I was crying so hard.

Uncle Jack, daddy's brother molested me when I was 9." Rachel's eyes locked onto Betty's.

"He came to our house one afternoon in the summer. Dad was working. Jack had been drinking. I remember he smelled funny. Robert was not home either. I was alone." The impact of her words struck a guilty place in Betty, scattering acid. The pain was physical. Betty repeated Rachel's words in her mind: *I was alone,* then added her own -- *it is your fault that I was alone.*

"Uncle Jack...forced himself on me." Rachel studied Betty's face for a moment, searching for some sign of condemnation. But what she saw was compassion. Rachel continued. "I was so ashamed I locked myself in my room for days. I thought this was my fault, too. Something I deserved. I was so confused. I had no one to talk to about it. I told dad I was sick. He wasn't the kind of man that paid much attention to Robert or me. I don't know what happened to Uncle Jack. He never came back to our house. Maybe he thought I'd told dad or something. I simply never saw him again. But I always worried that I would."

Betty looked down at the floor again, collecting her thoughts. Time seemed to have stopped for both of them. They were walking through the pain of the past while standing safely in the present. Somehow they both realized it could not hurt them anymore. *It was past.*

A sense of peace was so thick in the room it was palpable. Betty looked at Rachel. "I know how you must have felt, my precious girl. I was raped, too. It's been a long time ago. I always thought it was my fault or that I deserved it somehow." Silence fell in the room again. Rachel had no idea her mother had also been raped.

Betty suddenly felt as if someone else had entered the room. She looked at Rachel who did not seem to have noticed. "Do you feel that, Rachel?" "Feel what?" Rachel asked, fixing her eyes back on Betty. "That Presence you were talking about. It's here." Rachel smiled at her mother. The room seemed to be filled with peace. Tears welled up in Betty's eyes. "All my life, Rachel, I always wanted to believe that no matter how much I messed up my life, that God would not give up on me. And somehow now I understand that He did not give up. He loves me and always has -- even when I couldn't love myself. God knows what I have done and he doesn't hate me. You know what I have done and you have forgiven me." Betty hesitated. "When you found me in the kitchen with the gas on... I wanted to end my life...not because of the cancer, but because I could no longer live with the guilt of what I did to you and Robert -- and with my own life. Now I feel that ... well... I feel like I don't have to be perfect. I can't change the past but I can change the future – or what I have left of it."

"If you can forgive me Rachel, I think God will, too."

Focus on Me

It was almost midnight when Nancy pulled into her driveway. As she switched the engine off she heard Bernie barking in the kitchen, announcing her arrival as usual. For some reason the Christmas song *Hark the Herald Angels Sing* popped into her mind. She tried to focus her thoughts. *What day was it? What date was it? Was it December already?* She couldn't think. She felt she had to connect with something of the present, something that would pull her back from the surreal encounter with her long lost son.

He sat silently on the seat next to her. *He smelled like stale mushrooms, like dirt.* He had not spoken in at least two hours. She looked at him. He was looking down at his lap. "Are you hungry?" she asked gently. She had no idea what else to say. He moved his head slowly up and down. "Let's go inside. I'll make you some eggs."

She reached the back door before he did and stepped in to greet the barking dog. She clipped the leash on Bernie, not knowing how he would react to the stranger -- *that was her son.* She left the door open a little so that all Frank needed to do was give it a push. She walked over to the baby monitor and said "Betty it's me, did I wake you?" Betty said, "I was just dozing a little. Bernie let me know you were home. What's going on?" Nancy realized that she had not taken the time to tell Betty anything before rushing out the door. "I know it's late Betty, but if you feel up to it you might want to come down to the kitchen. I have some pretty shocking news."

As she said this, Frank pushed the door open and for a second, their eyes met, then he dropped his head again, still silent. Bernie pulled at the leash Nancy was still holding. He lunged at Frank barking furiously. The hair on the dog's neck was raised. Nancy bent down and stroked him. "It's OK Bernie" she soothed. Frank stepped closer, crouched down near Bernie and held out his hand for Bernie to sniff. The strange smell of him, the dirty shoulder-length graying hair, and the wild bushy whiskers that covered his face, his filthy clothes -- it was all so bizarre to Nancy. The only thing that looked familiar at all was his eyes. They had not changed since the last time she had seen him over ten years ago.

Betty made a little sound behind them. Nancy turned toward her while Bernie continued to sniff vigorously at Frank's shoes. "Betty, this is my son, Frank." Betty looked at Frank, then back at Nancy, then back at Frank. She did not speak. Frank stood up slowly and looked at Betty blankly. Betty did not even know that Nancy had a son and certainly not one that looked like this! She smiled weakly at Nancy, trying to comprehend what was going on. Betty pulled her pink bathrobe tight around herself and sat down at the kitchen island. The room was quiet. Bernie continued to sniff at Frank's shoes. Frank bent back down again and rubbed the dog's head and ears. "Hello Frank," Betty finally said, almost in a whisper. He looked up at her. *Something out of her weakness and vulnerability seemed to meet his*, and for the first time in several hours, Frank spoke. In a barely audible voice he said, "hello."

Nancy remembered the old saying *"if you have no idea what to do, do something familiar."* She pulled out her skillet, went to the refrigerator for eggs and said over her shoulder "I'm making scrabbled eggs, Betty, you want some?" "Sure," she said, "but just a little." Betty motioned for Frank to sit on the stool next to her and Nancy's heart rejoiced that she was not alone in this awkward moment. As the flames leaped around the bottom of the skillet, she reached up into the cabinet to take down a bowl and said to her Lord *"Thank You for all You have done and will do. You are my ever present help in times of trouble."*

****

Claudia's phone rang. It was 5:30 a.m. It had rained steadily all night. For a moment Nancy thought about all the swollen streams and waterfalls that appeared this time of year on the island. The image of a rainbow came to Nancy's mind. Another of God's promises right there in the sky for all to see.

On the third ring Claudia answered and said, "what's wrong - too early for a chat --something must be wrong. Is it Betty?"

"Slow down, Claudia. You really need to consider switching to decaf!"

"What's wrong?" Nancy's friend repeated.

"Are you sitting down?"

"Yes."

"Frank Jr. is home."

Nancy waited until her comment could sink in. She continued to wait until Claudia could ramble through "what, then how, then a few excited Oh My God's!"

"I really don't have any answers yet, Claudia. But he's upstairs right now, in the white room. I assume asleep. The constable found him yesterday apparently living in Hell Hole. He was covered in dirt and whiskers - but... Claudia... when you ask him something he just stares at his feet or hands, the wall, whatever. It's like he's not even here...just his body."

"You gonna have Dr. Alice check him out, right?" asked Claudia.

"Of course. I'll call her as soon as it's daylight. But Claudia I need some clothes for Frank. I asked him to shower before he went into the white room, but I didn't have any man's clothes for him and the ones he was wearing are now in the garbage. He's about Jim's size I think. Bring me some stuff, just a few things of Jim's before you go into work. And then maybe bring some stuff from the shop this afternoon on your way home."

"OK" said Claudia. "I'll be over there in a few minutes. Make a pot. We'll need to have a strategy meeting," Claudia said then hung up. Nancy loved Claudia. She was always caring without being judgmental. Nancy hugged the phone to herself after Claudia hung up. Then she prayed *Oh how good you are to me, Father, to give me such a friend. You knew long ago that I would need her in my life for such a time as this.*

Nancy let Bernie out then stepped out onto the deck herself. The rain had stopped. A cool mist hit her face. *A new day, one like no other, born of water, as all living things are.* She breathed in the early morning fog letting it refresh her and listened. The grey light of dawn mixed with the fog and created a barrier that she could not see through. *How appropriate. I'm in a fog, literally and figuratively.*

Water dripped from every branch. She heard the trickle of water in the downspout behind her and the tinkle of the wind chimes that hung all around in the fruit trees to discourage the birds. She lifted her mind and heart again to God. *Dearest Father, how am I to go, what am I to do? I have never been so stunned. I am happy and sad all at the same time. My prodigal son has come home Father, but ... there is only turmoil in my spirit. I don't even know this man, my own son.* She tried to sort out how she was feeling at that moment. Odd and unrelated thoughts tumbled through her mind. Images of all sorts of outcomes and tortures that she might have to endure as a result of Frank Jr.'s return into her life. She felt anxious. Fragmented thoughts darted in and out of her consciousness. *What if he's violent, mentally sick, still addicted?*

She remembered the disappointment and stress of trying to help him through so many years of his life -- the fights, the confrontations, the hopeless feelings of being disappointed over and over again. Looking back it all seemed so complicated. But there had always been that ray of hope. She had always imagined, hoped for, a homecoming – but one quite different than this. *Hope does that. Hope wraps*

*ight Christmas paper and allows our
to create the perfect son or daughter,
relationship.* And now... all the feelings of
a̶e̶ nd dread were back. She could not keep
them in the closet of her mind anymore. Frank was
real again, not a memory, not a grinning child in an
old photo, but a man.

An *exhumed* man!

She forced her thoughts back to God. *You got this one, right Father?* She smiled faintly as she looked up into the swirling fog. Bernie raced back up onto the deck, paws and nose wet from crashing through the garden in hot pursuit of a squirrel. The words dropped into Nancy's mind. She knew the Lord was speaking to her. All of her attention was drawn to *the Voice* in her mind. *Keep your focus on Me, My child. Bring every thought captive to Me. I will light your way.*

Thirty minutes later Claudia walked into Nancy's kitchen carrying a large garbage bag. Nancy assumed it was full of men's clothes. Claudia was jumpy -- like she had entered a funeral home and wasn't sure where the corpse was. She was overly quiet and respectful and kept looking toward the steps leading to the upstairs bedrooms - *the white room*. Nancy studied Claudia for a moment. She knew her so well, but she had never seen her exactly like this.

"I brought some of Jim's shaving stuff, too. I didn't figure you had anything." Claudia gave Nancy the impression that she might run out of the kitchen if Frank suddenly appeared, ghost like in the doorway. Claudia looked wide eyed at her friend, "Well, how are you doing?" Nancy shrugged.

"How can I help you?" Claudia said, trying to calm herself.

Nancy shrugged again. "The Lord just told me He has this one," Nancy said and meant it. "Soooooo, what happens next *is not up to me*. I don't own the outcome. God does. He made Frank, I just helped out a little. He has a plan, Claudia. I just don't know what it is yet."

Claudia slowly nodded. "You are my dearest friend on earth, Nancy. I just love it that we have the same Father. I'm your true twin you know."

A Good Day

Sometimes God just shows off.

Nancy lugged the heavy bag of clothes up the stairs. Silently she went through the empty bedroom opposite the room Frank was in. She tip toed into the adjoining bath with the lights still out and slowly opened the door to the white bedroom. She peeked in. The blinds were closed and the room lay in semi-darkness. She saw a large lump under the white down comforter and heard the slow rhythm of Frank's breathing. She studied the familiar room for a moment -- everything pure white -- everything new. *Was Frank's return to be a new beginning - a blank white canvas?* She felt an old dread nudge at her. *Was it even possible to start over, to be a new creation as the Bible promised? A new creation?* The questions lingered in her mind. *Do people ever really change?* She thought about Rachel and the phone call she'd received on her birthday. *Had God made Rachel new?*

She quietly closed the door to the white room. Carefully, she opened Claudia's bag and spread out some of the things on the bathroom counter, hoping Frank would understand they were for him. Then she opened the bathroom door again, just slightly, hoping Frank would not wake up disoriented. He could at least see where the bathroom was.

Claudia had thought of everything, *she even put in a*

toothbrush, God love 'er. As Nancy was coming back down stairs the phone rang. She glanced at the clock. It was 7:15 a.m. Someone was up early.

"Hi, Dr. Alice."

"Yes! Can you believe it?"

"I would really appreciate it."

"Can I just call you when he wakes up?"

"Yes, that would help too."

"Alright, thank you."

She laughed, "Yes, just think of 354 Honey Bear Lane as the *new clinic - annex*!"

Before she made it into the kitchen the phone rang again. Nancy sat down at her desk this time and pushed the talk button on the phone. She glanced out the bank of windows in front of her and noticed the fog was slowly lifting. Once again she thought how much she loved the view from her office window. This call was from her Pastor, Dr. Susan Weaver.

"News certainly travels fast on this island," she said smiling. Nancy heard Susan chuckle. Nancy admired Susan. She found her weekly sermons insightful and motivating.

"Claudia called me before I even got out of bed this morning!" Susan said. "She was so excited I thought someone was having a baby the way she was squealing."

"Yeah, she's pretty thrilled that my prodigal son has come home, although not entirely on his on," said Nancy. "I'm still trying to figure out how I feel about it," she said honestly.

"Well, I am pleased for you," Susan said in her "pastorally" voice. "But I'm also calling about that other situation Claudia mentioned."

"What other situation?" Nancy frowned.

"That Parker boy, Danny -- you told Pat that he'd been sneaking around your place, peeping in the windows."

"Gaah! I had almost forgotten about that with Frank and all."

"Thought you might need some reinforcements -- you've got a lot going on. Betty Bishop is staying with you too, isn't she?"

Nancy heard a noise behind her. She turned and saw Betty and Frank standing together. Betty reached over and slid her hand into Franks. He glanced at her briefly then looked down at Bernie. Betty looked so tiny standing next to Frank. He was over six feet tall. Betty barely came up to his shoulder. Nancy also noticed that Frank was wearing the clean tee shirt and jeans she had laid out. Betty, of course, was in her fluffy pink bathrobe.

"Ah... Susan...can I call you back...I seem to have a couple of hungry looking customers wanting breakfast..." Nancy smiled up at her houseguests. She hung up the phone after promising Susan she'd let her know if she needed reinforcements.

"I was telling Frank you are a good cook," Betty was trying to bridge the awkward silence. Frank looked at Nancy. She tried to read the look in his eyes, in his face. Was it confusion? Pain? -- some unspoken agony? She wanted to ask him how he got so *lost*. Something deep inside Nancy told her *to go slow, be gentle, no sudden moves – hope but do not expect anything from Frank, for now.*

"My friend, Dr. Alice, wanted me to make her some pancakes this morning, Frank. Would you like some, too?" Frank nodded and a slight smile shadowed across his face.

"I better call her right quick and tell her to get over here or she'll miss out," Nancy said as she called Dr. Alice's number. As Betty led Frank into the kitchen Nancy wondered how Betty was able to connect so quickly with him. He seemed to trust her. Nancy looked at their backs as they walked into the warmly lit kitchen. *They looked like wounded comrades returning from some distant war.*

Nancy simply said, "Now is good," and then hung up the phone.

****

The breakfast dishes were washed and put away. Nancy and Alice stepped out onto the deck and watched Bernie race across the back yard. "Well, what do you think?"

"Let me start with the good news," said Alice. "Betty looks wonderful -- impossible to know anything really until she's had a few tests, but she looks like she might be going into remission. I listened to her lungs and they sound relatively clear. Her face has filled out a little so I'd guess she's gaining weight. That is a good sign. She told me you prescribed 3-4 fruit smoothies a day."

Nancy grinned. "Did she tell you I talked with the nutritionist at the hospital and then I hit the health food store? I have her on foods and vitamins that are supposed to build up her immune system."

"Seems to be working," said Alice. "You know there is no cure for stage 4 lung cancer, but when she came to you, she had just finished up a round of chemo. It could have kicked in. The food and vitamins could have kicked in, too."

"Did she mention that we started praying together yesterday?" Nancy asked.

"No, but ... so... maybe God kicked in, too?" Dr. Alice Mitchell was a scientist. She was not given to spiritualizing a medical situation. "Could be He's using everything we're doing, especially the prayer," she granted.

Nancy looked at her again and said, " I do know that she told me she felt like she was being pulled out of a black hole. She said that when she was going through the *medical machine*, she felt like she was just another number, another '*grey head*' that didn't matter to anyone anymore. I think that may be why she tried to end her life. She had lost hope. Then she saw me trying to help her. She told me she decided, the second day she was here, she was going to stop wallowing in despair and fight back.

She didn't feel alone anymore. Dr. Alice, that just thrills me." Nancy noticed Bernie sniffing along at something in the grass. It was quiet between them for a moment.

Then Nancy looked back at her and said "well...what about Frank?"

"I'm not sure what's going on with him. Was he always quiet and withdrawn like that?"

"Honestly, Alice, I don't know him. I haven't seen him in over 5 years...and you know... before that only rarely for a number of years." Nancy paused and looked out past Dr. Alice, toward the deep blue outline of the distant mountains, remembering. "I knew him best way back when he was high school age. He was talkative then, even demanding sometimes. I always thought those wild mood swings were just teenage hormones. And you know about the drug use." Bernie started barking at a squirrel and Alice turned toward the sound.

As if speaking to herself, she said, "There seems to be some sort of memory loss going on. It's not my field but I know there are lots of causes and effects. Could have been some trauma to the brain, but I didn't notice any wounds or scars. Could be the drug use. Or it could be schizophrenia - just not sure.

"SCHIZOPHRENIA!" Nancy looked stricken.

"There are good meds for that now, Nancy. Don't over react. And I could be completely wrong."

There was a long pause as if Alice was going down some mental checklist in her mind. "Other than that, my quick once over didn't turn up anything. He looks healthy enough and his reflexes are normal. Maybe some of that food and vitamin therapy you've been using on Betty would bring him around, too. He does appear a little undernourished."

"Did he tell you anything about where he's been for the last 5 years?" asked his mother.

"No. I did notice that he keeps looking at Betty like she's some sort of lifeline for him. What do you make of that?"

"I was going to ask you the same thing," said Nancy.

"Could be because Betty is a recovering addict just like Frank, she seems more familiar to him than you do. Just a guess."

"Do you think he is *recovering?*" Nancy's face and voice was full of hope.

"All just a guess, Nancy, but I see no evidence of needles in the arms, pupils dilate when they should, eyes are clear, the interior of the nose is in good shape, heart rate and reflexes good. I could only do cursory testing. I'd need to do a full workup on him, get some labs, to determine anything further about recent drug use."

"So, what should I do now?" asked Nancy.

Dr. Alice stuck her hands deep into the pockets of the white lab coat she was wearing, and then straightened herself up to her full height. "I guess you've got to just wait and see for the next week or so. He needs time to adjust. I talked to Pat Roberts on my way over here to see if he'd come up with anything -- you know any criminal record -- if the police were looking for him -- that kind of thing."

Nancy had not even thought of it. "What did he say?"

"He said he hadn't had time to look into it but would let *you* know, not me, if he found anything incriminating."

"Was he rude to you?" Nancy asked, frowning.

"Not really. He and I just don't run in the same herd, you might say. We had a little run in a couple of years ago. I pulled rank on him with the authorities over on the main island. I think his pride got hurt or something. There's a lot of Barney Phife in that man, you know." They both laughed.

It was late afternoon when Nancy noticed Frank throwing a stick for Bernie to chase in the back yard. Bernie and Frank had become friends. *Unconditional love,* thought Nancy. *That's what dogs are created to teach us.* Frank was wearing one of the jackets that Claudia had packed. She noticed Frank kept to himself most of the day. Nancy played along. She had decided to let him come to her, when he was ready. She had no reason to force him to tell her anything about his sudden disappearance, his absence. For the moment, Nancy felt comfortable with her decision. After all, she was as much a stranger to him as he was to her. Time was needed to grow something between them again, and what would grow was not known to her. She had left it in her Father's hands. Claudia had called at least three times during the day wanting to know what was going on.

It's time to turn my attention to Danny," Nancy thought. She knocked on Betty's door and went in. She was surprised to see Betty reading the Bible. There was so much she did not know about the people living in her house.

"Can I interrupt you?"

"Sure," Betty said, moving the ribbon bookmark to hold her place in Genesis. "Is it Frank or Danny or me or maybe Rachel you want to talk about?" Betty grinned at Nancy. Betty was definitely feeling better.

"You know Betty, you have only been here for a little under a month and I can't even think of what it would be like if you weren't here!" They both smiled. "I've talked to Pat Roberts and Big John about Danny. They both liked your idea of scaring the hell out of Danny. Pat informed me that I could prosecute Danny, for trespassing or something. And so I can legitimately use that. Just not sure how to go about it -- I guess Big John has talked to him – told him that he was seen."

Betty studied her hands for a minute. "What if we set a trap for him? I mean really...set a couple of little traps...you know, those kind you put out to catch beavers and small pesky animals. Put them out under your office windows and bedroom windows. When he is caught, and I'm pretty sure it won't take long, Bernie will let us know." Betty looked at Nancy and knew by Nancy's expression that the idea was appealing to her. "The traps can't really hurt him but they do need to be secured to the house someway so he can't pull them lose, or carry them off. Then we'll call Pat and Big John over and confront him, threaten to take him off to jail, maybe even let him spend a night in that little lock up Pat has over at the co-op."

"I like it!" Nancy sounded exuberant. "But just in case…do you have any other ideas?" "Well there's always the shooting over his head with a shot gun strategy, or maybe putting a little trip wire under the windows that sets off a siren and lights or something," Betty said. Nancy wondered where this was coming from. Betty was rattling this off like she'd been planning it for days!

"Mom!" The sound of Frank's voice calling out to her crashed through something fragile inside her. Tears instantly welled up. Nancy jerked her head toward the hall door as Frank stepped in. Betty and Nancy both looked at Frank, not knowing what to expect. "Someone's in the kitchen. Wants to see one of you."

"Which one?" they said in unison. Frank shrugged his shoulders.

"I'll go see," Nancy said. She was surprised that Frank followed her down the steps. His movements and voice were still so strange to her. When they entered the kitchen, Rachel was standing there. She looked different somehow. Her stringy brown hair had been pulled back away from her face in a ponytail and her large brown eyes looked softer. She was actually smiling.

"I just came by to see how things are going." Betty heard Rachel's voice and came down.

"Things are going fine, Rachel. I was about to serve up some dinner for us in a little while. Would you want to stay?" Rachel looked down at the floor. The aroma of something Italian had been swirling around her since she walked into the kitchen.

She looked directly at Frank. "Who is he?" *The glaring was back.*

"This is my son, Rachel. He's been...away...and just came home," Nancy said self-consciously glancing at Bernie.

"Oh..." a long pause. All eyes were on Rachel. "I guess I could stay, if you have enough."

"It's lasagna night, Rachel," said Nancy. "There's enough for a small army."

Rachel caught Betty's eye. She was smiling. For a second Rachel wondered if she had ever seen her mother smiling before. "Rachel, how about setting the table?" Rachel glared at Nancy. Nancy just ignored it and pointed to where things were.

Frank leaned against the bar awkwardly. Bernie walked over and sniffed at Rachel's feet. Frank stooped down to give him a scratch. Bernie's help did not go unnoticed by Nancy. She had often thought of how a dog's behavior was superior in many ways to humans'. *Dogs neither judge nor criticize.* As Nancy tossed the salad she looked again at the stranger petting Bernie. Moments before he had called her *Mom* and something deep inside her had stirred. *She wasn't sure how to be a mother to him. He was a grown man now, a stranger. And she apparently hadn't done too good a job at mothering him the first time around. What was her role to be in his life now? Friend? Mentor? Financial patron? Was she being given a second chance?*

****

Betty looked at Frank across the dinner table. "Rachel could cut your hair." She paused to assess how the words impacted him. "If you want her to -- she's a licensed beautician, you know."

All eyes went to Rachel. She looked down at her plate. Nancy struggled to suppress a giggle and quickly drew her napkin over her mouth and nose in case she lost the battle. *Surely Rachel had never even seen the inside of a beauty shop. How could she be a licensed beautician?*

"You could sure use a cut and a shave, son," Betty continued.

"All right" said Frank, to everyone's surprise.

"It's been awhile since I cut hair," Rachel protested. "Are you sure?" She looked at Frank with her large dark eyes opened wide in apprehension.

"I'm sure," Frank said almost in a whisper.

"Well, Betty, let's get the dishes cleared so Rachel can perform some magic on Sasquatch. I can't wait to see who's under those whiskers!" She handed Rachel scissors from her sewing basket. "Everything else you will probably need is upstairs in Frank's bathroom. He'll show you the way."

Rachel silently followed Frank out of the kitchen toward the stairs. Nancy held Betty's eyes in an expression of surprise at this interesting development. Then Betty changed the subject.

"I want to ask you something about God," said Betty as she carried her dishes to the sink.

Nancy stood at the sink and rinsed red sauce from plates before placing them in the dishwasher. She glanced at Betty without speaking.

"I'm a little late getting started, but I've been reading the Bible in my room. I was thinking maybe I ought to start cramming for my final exam...for getting into Heaven." Betty smiled at her own joke. "I might be taking my entrance test just any day now." Her face wrinkled up into a grin.

 She settled herself at the kitchen island. Her mood shifted and she looked down at the smooth, polished wood. Then quietly she said, "What I'm trying to understand is how forgiveness works. Since I was a little girl, I always thought God would...reject you, yeah...reject you, and not forgive you if you did *one* bad thing? I mean...if you weren't...perfect, or something. I mean, look at poor ole' Adam and Eve...one bad thing...and BAM! they were OUT!"

"What's your question," Nancy said, drying her hands and joining Betty at the kitchen island.

Betty's voice changed to almost a whisper. She continued to push at the wood grain with her fingertip as if she were trying to move it around. "I've sure made a lot of mistakes in my life, wrong choices...over and over again. I don't know why God didn't kick me out of His world a long time ago. Who knows, maybe He's about to with the cancer and all." Betty paused trying to find the next words.

"I lost a son too, Nancy. But I abandoned him and Rachel when they were real young - just walked off and left them." Her eyes filled with tears. I guess it's sort of the opposite way that you lost Frank...but I have grieved that loss for most of my life. The worst part is that I caused it. ME!" Betty went silent for a moment. "God's grace, that's what it is...God's grace is helping me and Rachel to begin to sort things out, you know, find a place of peace between us from all the old *stuff.* But I don't even know how to start with Robert. I have not seen him or spoken to him in many years. But I want to, Nancy, I want to! How can I even start?"

Both Betty's confession and question startled Nancy. "I may have to get a theologian over here to help us get through that part about Adam and Eve," she said with a little smile. Nancy hesitated for a moment, trying to figure out what to say. "If you're interested I could ask my pastor Susan Weaver to come by and talk to you. She's wonderful. I know she'd like to meet you and may have the deep answers you're looking for."

Betty didn't say anything. She focused on her coffee cup. Nancy understood from Betty's expression that she wanted to talk with her, not a stranger. "But -- let me take a swing at an answer, or at least try. Sounds like when you were a child you had God figured out as someone who punishes for each wrong move." Betty met Nancy's eyes and nodded slightly.

"You know us self absorbed humans have a bad

habit of automatically judging God by ourselves, by human standards, I mean. We seem hard-wired to magnify the behavior of human authorities in our lives, our parents for example, to a divine level. In other words we create a God that we could never trust! God is not like us, Betty. I bet your parents were strict and judgmental, like mine."

"I guess they were," said Betty. "My mother was very judgmental and my Dad, well he was just not around much."

"Well the stories of God's judgments are certainly in the Bible," Nancy said. "But God is also love. At the end of the story of Adam and Eve, you know when their eyes are opened to moral choices because they ate of the Tree of Knowledge of Good and Evil? That's when they discover that they are naked! And do you know what God did?"

"Kicked 'em out of the garden?"

"Yes, but! He made them CLOTHES! Imagine that! He still loved them and took care of them. His love was constant. Yeah, I think He was disappointed in them, maybe even angry. But God loved them despite their poor choices and selfishness."

Nancy reached down and picked up Betty's hands and held them. "And the other part of what you asked is about forgiveness. And all we can really do, when we've done someone wrong is to sincerely ask them to forgive us. If Robert is willing, if the timing is right for him, then like Rachel, you can start to form a new relationship with him." Nancy hesitated. "Have you thought about writing him a letter?"

Betty was startled. She had never thought of something so simple. She was sincerely grateful for the idea. "A letter is a great idea. If he isn't ready to forgive me, he can just tear up the letter. But if he is ready, then maybe God will help me know what to do next."

"Well," said Nancy, "He sure seemed to guide you and Rachel along."

"NO! He jerked Rachel and me by the neck!" Betty said and they both laughed.

Rachel cleared her throat as she stepped back into the kitchen. Right behind her was Frank. The change in him was amazing. Nancy and Betty stared in stunned silence. Rachel had cut his graying hair very short revealing that the hair near his temples was almost white. Nancy thought it made him look even more like his father, whose hair had grayed exactly the same way. Rachel had shaved him clean and Nancy stared at the face she had not seen in many years. There were dark circles under his eyes and Nancy noticed a small scar under his left eye she'd never seen before. But there was no doubt that the handsome man standing before them was her son. No doubt at all. Nancy could not hold back the tears. Rachel stood off to the side, beaming.

It had been a good day.

Ho! Ho! Ho!

Nancy listened to Christmas music on the car radio as she drove to the ferry. She glanced at the outside temperature. -4 Celsius. She could hear the wind whipping around her car. *Might be a bumpy crossing.* Laura would be arriving tomorrow and she had a list of items she needed from the big island. Laura had never visited her sister in the winter. *She'll have a few choice words about the weather, no doubt.* Several days had slipped by since she last made this trek -- days full of the unexpected. She had a long talk with Big John about Danny. There was something about Big John's gentle ways and generous spirit that made him both a good father and a push over for his son. She did not know what he had said to Danny, but Betty had reported that she had seen no sign of him lately.

Nancy glanced down at her list and added "trip wire and alarm - Circuit City." John had assured her his son's unauthorized visits to her windows were over. But she was not so sure. She pulled her car onto the ferry and inched it up toward the rear bumper of Alice Mitchell's jeep in front of her. She gave Big John a small wave and cut the engine. *Must be Tuesday*, she thought. *Alice is going over to the free clinic.* She noticed that Alice was on the phone. Nancy had brought along a letter from her sister. It had arrived in last night's mail. She hadn't had a chance to read it yet. Her sister's letters still came almost daily, this one had Halloween ghosts all over it. She'd 'doctored it up' so that each ghost had a little bubble over its head. The ghosts were busy booing and hissing at each other - or the mailman - or her - who knew! *Uh oh, I wonder what that means.*

December 8

Dear Sisterwoman,

The Ghost Hunters house tour was the second best gift you have ever given me (the patio slabs still rank as 1). But the guys from "Southern Paranormal Investigators" rank way up there! The tour, both inside and out went splendidly. Once they set up the equipment and went "light's out," they had activity and responses almost immediately. Also, they had researched my house and property's history and found that it was built in the 1860s. I had thought it was 1870s. Anyway, they stayed late and I fell asleep. When I woke around 4:00 a.m. to go to the toilet, the cameras were gone. So were the 5 guys. Now they have to go over the footage and EVP's to find out how much they "caught!" Early in the evening they said something about a young Cherokee Indian girl and a Civil War soldier! Prior to the visit, I had invited the spirits to come to the party. No details yet - it takes awhile to go over all the videos, etc. It sure was fun! I'm so glad you thought to do this for me. What a wonderful birthday present. Lost power this a.m. for an hour - ate breakfast by candlelight, just like the old days. Felt great. Thank you so much.

Love to you my twin,
Laura and those on the "other side"

Down in the lower side of the note was a fat bunny rabbit sticker. Laura had drawn in a bubble above its head and written in the word "BOO" in capital letters. Nancy smiled. She was glad she'd taken the time to arrange the visit of the "paranormal investigators." She thought Laura would get a kick out of it and maybe be a little consoled since she had missed her annual birthday visit. Nancy remembered the many times she had visited Laura. Thursday nights the TV was locked onto the SiFi channel for the next episode of "Ghost Hunters." Laura thought the idea of dead people's spirits living in her house was delicious. Nancy thought it was all *hooey*.

We don't see things as THEY are...we see things as WE are. And, she added, *we are opposites. How on earth could twin sisters be so different?* Big John blowing the ferry whistle signaling their arrival on the main island interrupted her mediation. She looked up to see Dr. Alice wave at her through her rear view mirror then drive off the ferry.

Rachel had started coming by Nancy's house almost every afternoon after school. She said it was to check on her mother but Nancy and Betty both thought Frank was the real draw.

"Infatuation or something," Nancy told Claudia as they chatted over lunch in the hospital cafeteria.

Claudia responded, "Who knew Rachel was a beautician! - I mean...hair down in her face, no makeup, dumpy clothes...I couldn't have been more shocked if you told me she was a brain surgeon! I know! I know! Maybe she has -- you know... dual personalities or something."

Nancy just shook her head at her impetuous friend. "You certainly can't predict life, can you?" "And Betty!" exclaimed Nancy. "She seems like my long lost sister, or sage old aunt or something. Claudia, I am shocked at some of the things she comes up with... extra- ordinary... I mean deep questions, full of wisdom and insight. But then the next day she'll come up with some cock-eyed thing like she never learned how to drive a car, or make bread, or something. This is just a wild ride, I'm telling you!"

Claudia looked at her friend; her expression had turned serious. "I don't know how to make bread either, Nancy." They chuckled. "When is Frank's appointment with the shrink?" Claudia switched gears.

"Next week," said Nancy. "He's seeing Dr. Davis. I've given the doctor all the info I can on Frank, but I know so very little about his adult life. Dr. Davis said there is no blood test or MRI or anything that will help provide a diagnosis for mental illness, including schizophrenia. He said his approach would be to ask Frank a bunch of questions."

"Is the doctor going to fill you in on what he finds out? I mean Frank is an adult and all. He could tell the doctor to keep it all confidential. He hasn't been very forthcoming with any details, has he?"

"No. And I don't even know how he'll get along with Dr. Davis. He might clam up, just like he does with me," said Nancy. "Like every thing else right now I'm in the *wait-and-see* mode."

Nancy's shopping took most of the afternoon. She stocked up on everything, including wine and what she called 'fancy fixin's.' She also stopped by the post office and was delighted to find, in her P.O. box, the tickets she had ordered. Late in the afternoon, she stopped by *Claudia's Closet*. "I'm going to be so busy with my sister's visit and all the rest of my *house guests* during Christmas. I didn't want to forget to give you your Christmas gift - give you something to look forward to, I hope." Nancy handed Claudia a bright red envelope.

Claudia grinned and bounced her eyebrows up and down doing her imitation of Groucho Marx as she slid her finger under the flap and popped open the envelope.

"Two tickets to *Wicked*! You darling girl! WOW!" Thank you so much. I've been dying to see this musical for a long time--as you know...and now I get to!" Nancy held up her hands and said, "Now I called Jim and asked about dates before I purchased them. He said the date would work for both of you so blame him if I screwed up!" Claudia looked down at the tickets again. "New Year's Day!" she whooped. "Perfect!" "I have something for you, too. I'll drop it by after Laura settles in. I'd like to see her again. OK?"

"Of course" said Nancy.

It was completely dark by the time Nancy got home. Rachel's motor scooter was parked in the driveway, *again*. For a second her mind went back to the night in October when Rachel had almost run over her with that stupid motor scooter. *Was that a little warning from God that Rachel and Betty's lives were about to collide with hers? One more set of those little dots that I can't connect yet, Father,* she prayed silently.

Bernie was so preoccupied with Frank when she walked into the kitchen, he didn't bark his usual greeting. He just ran over and licked at her hand when he noticed her. "How about a little help with groceries and stuff" she said to Frank and Rachel, sitting together at the kitchen counter. They rose as one and went out to retrieve the packages, which completely filled the trunk and backseat of her car.

A few minutes later the entire kitchen was strewn from one end to the other with boxes and packages when the phone rang.

"It's me," said Laura. "Just want to make sure there's room in the Inn - so to speak...you know this time of year and all. You never know who might show up at *your* house! Could be Joseph and a pregnant Mary! Have you noticed any large stars over your place lately?" Nancy laughed and let Laura finish her monologue. "I must love you a lot traveling on one car, two planes, three buses, four ferries and a partridge in a pear tree to get to you! Why don't you live somewhere civilized?"

"Your room is ready," said Nancy softly. "I've put in padded walls just in case you need to scream or bang your head or something."

"Good idea" said Laura. "Well, good night my dear...if you want to call it that. I have to get up in two hours and catch that god forsaken flight, in order to make those god forsaken ferry connections work." Laura clicked the phone off abruptly to make her point.

Nancy looked at Frank. He had been watching her closely while she had been talking to her sister. When she turned to look at him, his eyes fell to the floor. "Frank, do you remember your Aunt Laura? She'll be here tomorrow for a visit."

"Yes, I remember her. She looks just like you, but acts different," Frank said.

It was the most Frank had spoken to her since he came home. And it was his first reference to a memory. She made a mental note to remember and tell Dr. Davis. Nancy decided to push ahead a little. "What do you remember most about her," she said as she stacked cream soups on the shelf.

"I remember she gave me $25 when I graduated from high school. I remember that she always sent me gifts on Christmas and my birthday," Frank said, then fell silent.

Funny what people remember Nancy thought. "Well I got her a gift today--for Christmas. I wonder if you and Rachel would like to wrap a few gifts for me tonight?"

Rachel smiled. She was grateful to have something to do besides just hang around and hope to get invited for dinner. Rachel loved being in this house. It felt safe. This home was full of life and love, good smells and a warmth Rachel had never known in her life. She sensed that God lived *in* Nancy. She now felt that He lived in her, too.

Betty joined them as they dined on the rotisserie chicken Nancy had purchased at the grocer and a hot fruit compote Rachel prepared following Nancy's detailed instructions. After dinner, Nancy put a pile of fancy and unusual food items in the living room floor and asked everyone to pitch in and see how many they could wrap in 30 minutes. Nancy promised a prize to the person who wrapped the most in the given time. Rachel was laughing trying to figure out how to wrap a giant bottle of maraschino cherries when Frank scooted over close to her and showed her how to roll the jar in the wrapping paper then twist the ends of the paper like a piece of taffy. Nancy lay back in a comfortable chair and kicked her shoes off. She was enjoying the moment when she heard the phone ring again. Reluctantly she pushed her tired body up and walked into her office barefooted. She could still hear everyone going at it in the living room with the radio blasting away some country western version of *Rudolf the Red Nose Reindeer* when she said "Hello."

"This is Pat Roberts, Mrs. Hogan. Hope I'm not interrupting your dinner."

"Finished. What's up?" she braced herself. This could not be a casual call. A shudder went through her.

"I had a call back from the Vancouver police regarding Frank Jr. today. I've been doing some inquiries you know." Nancy listened. Her heart was in her throat. "He does have a couple of warrants out on him, Mrs. Hogan."

Christmas Eve Eve

On December 22 the Duke Point terminal was crowded with Christmas travelers. Nancy had never seen so many seaplanes in the water. She thought they looked rather like a giant flock of sea gulls bobbing up and down in the water. She imagined they were all waiting to whisk some important person away to some secluded destination that could only be reached by air or boat. For a moment she wished she were one of them.

As she waited, she flipped open the book Claudia had given her the previous Christmas. She had just gotten around to reading Morton T. Kelsey's *The Other Side of Silence.* Mid-page she read, *"The flowering of the human soul, however, is more a matter of the proper psychological and spiritual environment than of particular gifts or disposition or heroism. How seldom we wonder at the growth of the great redwood from a tiny seed dropped at random on the littered floor of the forest. From one seed is grown enough wood to frame several hundred houses. The human soul has seed potential like this if it has the right environment. Remember that only in a few mountain valleys were the conditions right for the Sequoiadendron giganteum, the mighty redwood, to grow.*

...For both the seed and the soul, these things all take time. In both cases there is need for patience. Most of us know enough not to poke at the seed to

see if it is sprouting, or to try to hurry it along with too much water or fertilizer or cultivation. The same respect must be shown for the soul as its growth starts to take place. Growth can seldom be forced in nature. Whether it is producing a tree or a human personality, nature unfolds its growth slowly, silently."

Nancy closed her eyes and laid her head back on the wall behind her seat. *I seem to be living in the middle of one of your gardens, Father. Wouldn't be the first time you disguised yourself as a gardener.* She smiled as she thought about Mary Magdalene in the garden, consumed with grief and fear and all sorts of emotions. In that state of mind she had mistaken the risen Jesus as a gardener. It was one of Nancy's favorite Bible stories. *How often in her own life had she been so consumed with fear or grief that she also missed identifying God's presence? Pain plows through the soil of the soul - uproots some things so that others can grow.* Nancy let the words of Morton Kelsey sink into her. She imagined the faces of Frank, Betty and Rachel in the middle of giant sunflower blooms, bobbing and shifting in the wind, trying to find the "Son."

"Well! There you *finally* are!" The face looking down at Nancy was like looking in a mirror except..."oh my god! What have you done to your hair! Laura's gray hair was chopped off and gelled up into short spikes. She wore dangling gold earrings and an orange sweatshirt. The ever-present 22k gold Spiga necklace hung around her neck. Nancy thought she looked spectacular. Nancy leaped into her outstretched arms. As they walked through the terminal, Nancy noticed the eyes turning toward them, the smiles, and the occasional nod. Nancy fought off the old compulsion to think they weren't noticing her, but her beautiful, accomplished artistic sister. Nancy had chosen her outfit carefully; Christmas green silk shirt under a pearl grey cashmere jacket and slacks. After a few moments, Nancy realized that people weren't just looking at Laura; they were looking at both of them. Together, the identical twins of a *mature* age, were striking! Nancy tucked her arm around Laura's waist and pulled her a little closer as they headed for baggage claim.

Nancy navigated the familiar route through the City of Nanaimo and up onto the highway that was one of the main arteries of Vancouver Island. They'd be on this route for at least 2 hours, Nancy calculated. "Next stop Big John Parker's ferry," she said. "Do you remember him?" Laura had laid her head back on the seat and closed her eyes. "Of course I do, he's your next door neighbor, isn't he?" With her eyes still closed, Laura said, "So catch me up on the latest episode of 'A*s The Worm Turns.*' It was a pejorative reference to the people whose lives had recently intersected Nancy's.

"Well," Nancy started "the most interesting piece of news came in just last night." Nancy paused for effect.

Laura opened one eye and studied her sister's profile. "It would be hard to top some of the news you've been distributing lately. I mean ranking something as the-most-interesting, well, what in the hell is it?"

"Apparently I have a grandchild." The news struck Laura's ears like an unexpected clap of thunder. She jerked up wide-eyed and stared at her sister.

Nancy glanced away from the road and looked at her twin. Laura's face epitomized the word "dumbstruck."

"Frank has a CHILD?" Laura blurted it out.

"Apparently so. A child whose mother lives somewhere around Vancouver." Nancy paused again for the words to sink in. Laura sat silently. Nancy continued. "Pat Roberts called last night and said there were two warrants outstanding against Frank. He'd been searching around since we know so very little about where he's been for the last 5 years."

"Well, that was smart, I guess," said Laura still trying to absorb the news. "Did you ask Frank, I mean…about a child?"

"Not yet. Wait till you're around him a little, Laura, you'll see what I'm up against. He seems mentally fragile to me. I don't want to do or say anything that might be considered by him as threatening--you know…push him into a corner with questions. He might run away again. He has an appointment with Dr. Davis, the psychiatrist at the hospital, in a couple of days, and I'll let him ask Frank where he has been--or whatever he decides."

Laura's mouth was still hanging open with a surprised look on her face. Laura had married and divorced three times. She and husband #2 had produced a daughter, Kelly. Kelly was now grown and living in Milwaukee, near her father. Laura had two young granddaughters from Kelly but she only got to see them a couple of times a year.

Laura closed her eyes and laid her head back on the seat again. After several minutes of silence and without moving Laura said, "so, what does having a grandchild have to do with warrants for his arrest?"

Nancy cut her eyes over at her sister. When they were young, the twins had always been able to understand each other, often without words. They knew at a glance how the other one was feeling. They anticipated each other accurately most of the time. But right at this moment Nancy had no idea what Laura was thinking.

"One warrant was for failure to pay child support, Pat said, and the other one was a bench warrant."

"You mean he stole a park bench?" Laura jerked up in surprise again.

"No silly!" Nancy was suddenly not enjoying the conversation. She didn't like the tone of her sister's comments. A bench warrant is issued when someone doesn't show up in court when they are supposed to, that's all. It's not like he's done anything really bad, Laura. He's not like a murderer or a thief or something. At least...I don't think he is."

"Well, that's a comfort!" Laura snorted.

"For really bad stuff they issue arrest warrants for felony charges, and stuff... I guess..." Nancy's voice trailed off. Once again she realized there was still so much she did not know about her son.

Laura could see that Nancy was getting upset. Laura

paused then said, "Nancy, I love you and I'm here to help you in any way I can. You obviously don't need me drilling you for information when we both know you don't have any." Nancy's shoulders visibly relaxed.

"I brought some art supplies with me," Laura changed the subject. "I thought I'd try and paint some landscapes. You have some great views on Rainman Island, so the brochure says," she looked at Nancy and smiled. "I've never been here in the winter," she said glancing out the car window at the overcast day and misting rain. "Does the sun even come out here in the winter?"

****

"Hello Aunt Laura," Frank said as he walked toward the car. "Can I help get your luggage in the house?" His tone was flat and his face lacked expression. Laura looked at him but he did not make eye contact. She thought about his serious little face as a child. *He didn't smile much even then.* She had nicknamed him *poker face* because he always looked so solemn. She thought now how much older he looked than the last time she had seen him. He was in his 20s then, a handsome young man with a perfectly oval face surrounded by soft brown hair. She knew then that he had an on again, off again problem with drugs, even as far back as middle school. But here he stood, waiting for her to answer.

"Uh, yes... please...," she sounded unsure as if she were talking to a stranger.

"Thank you Frank," Nancy said as she got out of the car. "I think she packed enough to move in - do I need to help you?" Frank moved past them and started getting her bags out of the trunk without responding. Nancy and Laura exchanged glances that communicated something like *since we don't know what to say, we're not going to say anything.*

Laura looked up at the big yellow cape cod looming in front of her. "My God! Your house has grown! I don't remember it being this big!"

"Yeah," Nancy said. "God waters it every day. It indeed has grown," she was thinking of the people now inside. *His garden.*

Laura thought she meant the daily rain.

"Come on Laura, I want you to meet Betty." Bernie heralded their arrival with joyful barking from his tethered spot in the back yard.

Betty was standing in the middle of the kitchen again wearing her fluffy pink bathrobe. She had tied it neatly in the front and smoothed her short, curly, grey hair down with a damp comb, though strands of it once again were reaching toward the ceiling.

The first thing Laura noticed about Betty was how small she was -- how thin. Her face and neck were deeply lined with wrinkles. Her eyelids sagged into soft folds of skin making her eyes appear to be slits in a wrinkled mask. The puffy dark circles under her eyes gave testament to recent suffering. Laura knew that Betty was her exact age, though she looked years older. And then Betty smiled. The warmth her smile told Laura that this woman sincerely welcomed her. Laura knew a little of Betty's history - the parts that Nancy had shared with her. But the person standing before her was not the woman Laura had been expecting. Laura moved toward her like someone on a conveyor belt and took her outstretched hands in hers. They stood there that way for a moment, just looking at each other and smiling. Laura didn't know this woman at all, but she knew they would be friends. *Yes*, thought Laura, *this is going to be a fine visit.*

Frank stood at the bottom of the stairs surrounded by Laura's suitcases and packages. "What room do these go in?" Frank sounded impatient. Nancy looked over at Laura.

"You want to share a bath with Frank or with Betty," she said grinning. "Well you are not putting me in that god-awful, blue toile room! I hate that room! I want my old room back - top of stairs, first door on the left as I recall -- you know -- the Hollywood suite!"

"Well, then you'll share a bath with Frank," Nancy said. She looked past her twin sister directly at Frank. She studied his face for a moment to see if she could detect any change in his expression, any nuance that would indicate embarrassment or displeasure with the idea. Nancy didn't want to do anything that would make him consider leaving again. Just the thought of it caused her to shudder.

"Frank, you'd better speak up if you don't like the idea. No one knows better than me what a mess she can be," Nancy said with a little laugh.

"Am not!" Laura interjected, getting a small laugh out of Betty.

"No problem." There have been plenty of times in the past few years that I didn't even have a bathroom," Frank said then disappeared up the steps with the first load of luggage. Betty, Laura and Nancy glanced at each other. They all knew what Frank meant. He had been homeless.

It was just after 7 p.m. when Nancy finished clearing away the remains of the light supper she had served -- cold chicken and steaming homemade cream of broccoli soup. Laura announced her exhaustion having been up for almost 24 hours, and went off to bed almost immediately after dinner. During the small talk at dinner Nancy laid out a few plans she had made for Laura's visit, including the trip to Camille Carmichael's for the *commission piece* Laura had ordered. She had also remarked that Frank had a doctor's appointment on the main island the next day, and that they could attach a shopping trip, too, if anybody wanted anything.

"After all", said Nancy, "it's Christmas Eve, Eve." "Eve, Eve?" Betty questioned and then smiled - "ah...I get it," she said, then quickly asked to go along. She said she wanted to see her doctor and tell him how good she was feeling. Her remark brought big smiles from all around the table, even one from Frank.

"Oh, and on Christmas Eve," said Nancy, "I'm going down to the community center. They are having the wake for Ray Phillips, a lovely man I've known since I first moved to the island. He died recently following an apparent bear attack."

"Good God!" shouted Laura. "You have wild bears on this island?"

"Apparently we have at least one!" Nancy said. Nancy caught the change in Frank's face. For a moment she thought he either looked extremely guilty or hurt. "Do you remember Ray, Frank?" Frank nodded yes and left the table.

It started to rain again.

Reparation

Our greatness lies not so much in being able to remake the world as being able to remake ourselves. Gandhi

Dr. Davis's office was on the 3rd floor of the doctor's building adjacent to Comox General Hospital. As the little group walked in, Christmas music blared out at them in the lobby.

"What the hell does a roasted chestnut have to do with anything?" Laura mumbled. She glanced around the room. It seemed to her that every possible nook and cranny had been decorated with white lights and greenery. A giant Christmas tree stood in the corner. It had been festooned with tiny white lights and small round glass balls that held pictures of children's faces.

Betty said her doctor was on the 5th floor and suggested that everyone meet back in the lobby when they were finished. Earlier that morning, when Betty had made her way downstairs wearing something other than a pink bathrobe, Nancy realized she'd never seen Betty in street clothes. Apparently Rachel had brought her a nylon warm-up suit, which now swished as she walked away from them to the elevator. Nancy took one more look at Betty's back and for a moment was torn between going with Frank or going with Betty.

Dr. Davis was actually waiting for them when they

arrived. Nancy introduced Laura and Frank to him and said she was surprised that his waiting room wasn't full.

"I guess people are too busy this time of year to..." he trailed off. He looked directly at Frank. "Come on in Son, let's have a chat. I've looked forward to meeting you."

Laura and Nancy sat down in the empty waiting room. Laura reached over and took Nancy's hand. "I honestly hope the doctor says he'll be OK, and that we can start asking him some questions. I'm dying to know where he's been and if he has a child, or maybe more than one." It was the first time Nancy had thought that there might be more than one child. She slowly nodded.

An hour passed. The twins had been deep in conversation when Dr. Davis finally stepped into the waiting room and asked Nancy if she could come into his office. "My receptionist is off for Christmas," he said smiling. "I have to do everything!" Nancy didn't say anything. She suddenly felt an old fear rising up in her. *No more guessing, now. This could be bad news.* As she followed Dr. Davis down a short hallway and into his office, she prayed *Father, may I feel your hand on me. Your touch tells me You are in this with me.*"

She settled into the chair next to Frank and imagined Jesus standing behind her with His hand on her shoulder. With this image in mind, she felt that nothing could be said that He did not personally allow.

"Frank and I have had a good talk" Dr. Davis said,

relaxing into his leather chair and straightening his long legs. "We plan to see more of each other in the next few weeks." He paused a moment and looked at Frank. "Frank and I thought I should fill you in a little on what we talked about today." Nancy nodded her head slowly and kept her eye contact on Dr. Davis.

"My first impression is that we might be dealing with some level of brain damage. He might have received a trauma to his brain as a result of a motorcycle wreck he had a few years ago. Frank told me a little about it - said he was drinking and driving a friends motorcycle without a helmet, went off the road in a curve and hit the guardrail. At least he thinks that's what happened." "That's what my buddy told me," Frank interrupted. "Frank's reflexes are slow," Dr. Davis continued, "Which could mean a lot of things...and his facial muscles seem to be involved. I'd like to run some lab tests on him, get an MRI--I haven't ruled out Parkinson--any history of that in the family?"

"No!" Nancy said, glancing quickly toward Frank.

"Did he have any type of injury to his head as a child, Mrs. Hogan?"

She thought for a moment. She wasn't expecting the question. "The usual stuff, I think. I don't remember anything severe enough for him to see a doctor."

Dr. Davis focused on Frank. "And the long term use of alcohol and drugs could have contributed to something we refer to as ARBI or alcohol related brain injury which can have a permanent impact on cognitive and motor functions in the brain." Dr. Davis reached up and stroked his chin as if trying to think of what to say next. "He tells me he is not delusional, in other words, does not hear voices, so for the moment I'd rule out schizophrenia."

Nancy shifted in her chair. She sensed that Dr. Davis was beginning to reach, to speculate.

"I'd like to know", Nancy said slowly, almost in a whisper, "if Frank would be willing to talk with me and tell me why he disappeared so abruptly after his father died, where he's been for 5 years and does he have a family somewhere - children - are the police looking for him? I've been afraid to ask him anything Dr. Davis for fear I'd lose him again. I'm terrified of losing him again." Nancy's voice broke with emotion and tears filled her eyes. It had just all tumbled out.

"Frank" Dr. Davis said, "Do you feel up to answering some of your mother's questions?"

"I'll try," he said slowly. Frank glanced at his mother then back down at the floor. "Mom, I don't remember stuff too good." There was a long pause as if he were searching through a stack of laundry trying to find two socks that matched.

"I've been thinking about this...how to help you understand who I am...where I've been. I didn't know how to start. So I didn't. But...I remember when I was a kid. I wanted to please you and dad, especially dad. I remember I thought he wanted me to be like this great baseball player. When I went out for little league, you remember?" He paused and looked at Nancy. She nodded. "He'd sit up there in the stands and shout stuff at me when I got up to bat, or scream at me when I'd miss the ball. It was the year I was in Miss English's third grade. Lots of stuff like that went on with Dad, all the time. I don't think you noticed it," he looked at Nancy. "I just don't remember you being around very much," Frank said. "And with him, I just never felt like I measured up. I mean, somehow I knew I was a born failure. I think that sort of started me on the wrong path. I remember by the time I was a young teenager, Dad would just throw money at me to get rid of me and you know--I wanted to be rid of him, too--and he was willing to finance it!" Frank snorted a little laugh.

"A kid offered me some marijuana in the 5th grade and when I smoked it I felt better than I had ever felt in my whole life." Frank stopped, took a deep breath then haltingly started up again. Nancy intuitively knew not to interrupt him. "I also felt worse than I had ever felt because I knew it was wrong--what I was doing -- it was wrong. But I already knew I was a failure, even when I was 11 years old -- my dad told me I was -- and I believed him. After awhile, I guess I just didn't care. I figured I couldn't make my old man like me whatever I did."

The room was quiet for a while. Then Frank continued. "I guess when he died, I was so into drugs and alcohol, I thought I had to be near a supply and Rainman Island wasn't it—it's too isolated and everybody knows your business." A slight smile crossed Nancy's face. It was the truth.

"That's one of the reasons I wanted to come back...the isolation. I haven't used in almost 6 months, now." He straightened his shoulders when he said it. "There was a woman I met, she looked pretty good, said she wanted to help me get sober and stuff. She had a kid. I kind of liked the kid; he was about 4 years old. She said she wanted to get married, so we did. She told everybody the kid was ours, but he wasn't. I didn't mind. I liked the kid. I thought she was just trying to--you know--make us into a family, or something. But it wasn't long before she took off with another guy. She left the kid with me. His name is Tommy. Tommy Johnson. I thought I could help him a little and you know..." Frank looked directly at Nancy. "He's the one that helped me get sober. He's about 5 now. His mom showed back up a few months ago, made my life hell. Finally I just took off, hitched rides, worked a few day jobs here and there to eat and buy the ferry tickets over here. When I got back to Rainman Island, I couldn't figure out what to do. I was broke. There are no jobs on the island this time of year. I didn't even have the money to leave the island. I thought about hiring out one of the fishing boats but I get so damn seasick.

I came around to your house a few times—watching to see who came and went. I didn't know if you even still lived on the island. I got up the nerve and knocked on the door once. When Betty came to the door, wearing her pink bathrobe, I figured you didn't live there anymore--figured you'd moved back to maybe be with Aunt Laura or something. I took off without speaking to Betty. It was cold and raining one night and I remembered Hell Hole. I used to sneak in there and get high. Got me out of the rain at least."

Nancy looked at her son, tears now streaming down

her cheeks. She forced her voice past the lump in her throat. "When you were young, Frank, I didn't know much about being a parent. I can't count the times that I blamed myself for not being the kind of mother you needed. Looking back, and I've had a lot of time to look back, I think I just gave up trying and absorbed myself in school. I guess education became my addiction." She stopped talking for a moment because she had never thought about herself in those terms. *She had addictions, too but they just weren't the self destructive ones that Frank had--or were they?* She looked at Frank again. He was just sitting there...waiting. *How many times had he waited for her? How many hours of his life had he—waited—for her?*

"Frank, if you will forgive me, I promise you I will do my best to discover who you really are or want to be and help you with as much wisdom and grace as God will grant me."

Frank looked at his mother and said "I guess we can learn how to do this together -- but as *friends.* I think we should give up on the mother - son thing." Nancy nodded slowly trying to understand how that could be. They sat in silence for a moment, neither of them knowing what else to say.

The Christmas music that had been piped into the waiting room pushed in and filled the silence. *Let there be peace on earth, and let it begin with me.*

A sudden loud thump followed by a groan grabbed their attention. They all stood up at the same time and went in the direction of the waiting room. Laura was sprawled out in the floor and laughing - a small blue bump rising on her forehead.

"What in the world!" Nancy said.

"I must have fallen asleep in this quiet warm spot and fallen out of the chair! I'm a little messed up with the time change." Dr. Davis helped Laura back into a chair and looked closely at her injury.

"Let me get some ice on that" he said and disappeared into the employee's lounge area. They were all laughing when he came back into the room with ice in a zip lock bag.

"What is so funny" he said smiling. "Just think of the fun stories we can make up about this one!" Laura said. She was already looking forward to the surprised look on Betty's face.

Farewell

Betty was indeed surprised to learn that Dr. Davis had not liked Laura's suggestions about treatment for Frank and had knocked her out in a rage! None of them could quit laughing long enough to tell it straight. Betty said they should all practice a straight face so they could tell it to Rachel without laughing. The bump was gleefully explained over lunch. After the laughter again died down, the focus shifted to Betty.

"Remission," Betty repeated to them. She told them that she wanted to roll that word around in her mouth like a morsel of sweet Christmas candy, savoring every nuance of flavor. "I have made my peace with death," she said. "It will come some day, but...just not today. I've finally at peace with myself and I'm starting to make peace with Rachel. And thanks to you Nancy, I have started a letter to Robert. I pray that God will grant me peace with him."

Frank looked at his mother. "It is possible Betty," Nancy said. "Life is so full of twists and turns and wrong way streets. You just never know what's up ahead."

"I read a book about that not long ago," said Laura. *Me too*, thought Nancy. *My book is called the Bible and the author is God!* "Tell us about it" Nancy said, stifling the judgmental thoughts of her sister. She knew Laura loved an audience.

After lunch Betty told them she had a couple more things she needed to do before going back to the island. She said she'd meet them at the ferry for the 4 p.m. crossing and that she could take a taxi around to the places she wanted to go. She acted so secretive that they assumed some special secret Christmas shopping was on Betty's agenda. And that was exactly what Betty hoped they would think.

****

By 6 p.m. Christmas Eve, the community center was full. Dr. Alice and Pam had set out an enormous assortment of Christmas cookies and punch (adult and children's versions). People just kept pushing in. Someone opened the windows to get some cool air circulating and laughter spilled out into the full parking lot. A few pictures from Ray and Linda's life sat around the room.

Micah took a seat on a tall stool set up for him in front of the mike. He slowly strummed the first few bars of the familiar Jim Croce song on his acoustical guitar:

> *Well, I know it's kinda late,*
> *I know I shouldn't wake you,*
> *but what I've got to say can't wait,*
> *I know you'll understand.*
> *Every time I tried to tell you the words just came out wrong.*
> *So I want to say I loved you, in a song.*

Micah had changed the words a little, his eyes and

heart filled with tears.

He stopped playing and looked into the crowd that had fallen into a quiet and reflective mood. "Ray loved Jim Croce's songs. How many of you knew that?" A few raised their hands. "He wanted us to get together like this -- a few friends -- a few drinks -- a few laughs and a few songs.

Dr. Alice and I decided to make it Christmas Eve. Today was his birthday." A ripple of whispers and a few muffled laughs went through the room.

"Yeah, he shared it with Jesus!" Micah laughed at his own joke and was instantly joined by others. "I'd say Ray came to a place in his life where he shared just about everything with Jesus, good and bad. I'll bet Jesus was the first person he looked up when he got to heaven a few days ago." Micah's voice filled with emotion and he hesitated, again.

Dr. Alice came to Micah's rescue and moved in a littler closer to the mike. She told everyone "If you don't have a drink of some kind in your hand, I'll give you a minute to get one then we're going to hear some 'Ray stories'...and toast him--or roast him, whatever you decide."

Micah strummed a few more chords of the song while people scurried to the several punch bowls set out around the room.

Yeah, I know it's strange,
but every time I was near him,
I'd just run out of things to say,
I know he'll understand.
Every time I tried to tell him, the words just came out wrong,

So I'll have to say I loved Ray, in a song.

When people again starting turning toward Micah and Dr. Alice with their drinks, she said, "Who'd go first with a memory of Ray?"

Dr. Susan Weaver held her glass up above her head and said, "I'd like to be first." All eyes turned toward her and folks near her turned so that a little open space was formed around her. "Ray was a charming man. I knew him for about 5 years and I never caught him without a smile for me. He loved to tease me about wearing pants in the pulpit - he said he was sure it was a sin and then he'd just burst out laughing. There was a lot of mischief in that man!" Dr. Alice raised her glass and said "Here! Here!" in agreement and everyone sipped something.

"I want to be next," said Jack Murphy, the manager of the island co-op. "I knew Ray so well, known him most of my life. It would be hard to pick out one story to tell you cause I just have so many. But I think he'd want us to have a good laugh tonight cause he's done broke loose from this old world and I just know he is having a ball up there in heaven! One of my favorite Ray stories was around that wine he and Linda used to make and sell at the co-op." Heads nodded around the room. "Some of you know this story, but not everyone. Well a tourist bought a bottle of it one year while he was here on vacation and came back the next year wanting some more of it, course I sold out of it real quick each year. Ray happened to be standing there when this tourist said Ray's wine was so good it tasted like an angel was pissing on his tongue! Ray started laughing so hard he had to fake a coughing spasm and leave the store. We always called his wine Angel Piss after that!" People were wiping the tears away when the laughter finally stopped.

Micah smiled at Pam as he wiped the tears away. He realized that he felt lighter, like something heavy inside had been released.

Cindy Blackstead was next. She said "you all know how handy Ray was - how he loved to make things or fix things for us in his shop. I took a bunch of chairs over to him once--I got them at an auction. I thought Ray could fix them up--so I could use them at the restaurant. He took one look at those rickety old chairs and told me that 'those who sit in darkness' are the only ones that would sit down in one of these chairs! I think he was quoting the Bible or something.

He told me the best thing I could do with those chairs was to burn 'em. But you know what? He fixed every one of them! Took him weeks. Ray was special. I think he was the most patient man I ever knew--kind and lighthearted. You all sit in those chairs every time you come into the Pig."

Story after story, toast after toast went on for the better part of an hour.

Then Micah came back on the mike and started strumming the familiar chords of Amazing Grace. One by one the voices melded together into a familiar chorus of praise. Folks started to leave after that. Some in small groups, some as singles, but each feeling that this was one of the best Christmas Eves they could remember -- the celebration of the One coming to earth and another going home.

The rain had stopped. Nancy, Betty, Rachel, Frank and Laura all got out of Nancy's car and stood in the driveway of the big, yellow, cape cod house. Laura looked up and saw the Northern lights and gasped. She nudged Frank then the others saw them too. "Nothing like this ever happens in Roswell, Ga." Laura said. They stood there in silence for a while then Nancy said quietly, "it's like we are watching the hem of heaven as She dances."

Full House

There is born to you a Savior. Luke

Christmas Day arrived on schedule. Nancy rose early while everyone was still sleeping and slipped into the living room. She switched on the Christmas tree lights and sat comfortably and watched as the lights danced and blinked against the darkness. Her thoughts drifted to Christ as The Light of the World. She held out her hands and tried to grab a ray of pulsating light - *it cannot be done* she thought. *I can't hold light -- I can only reflect His light.*

She thought of her full house. The people that meant the most to her were all under one roof – well, except for Claudia and she'd be over soon. Even Rachel had spent the night. She was sleeping in the dreaded "blue toile" room. *Yes, she had a full house this Christmas morning. All rooms were taken. Thanks be to God!*

Her mind drifted to that well known passage 'there was no room for them in the inn.' *Is there room for You in me--dear Lord--in the hearts of those sleeping in this 'inn'?* Nancy thought.

She heard a small sound behind her as Laura came and sat on the floor beside her and tucked her arms around Nancy's legs in a warm embrace. She laid her head against Nancy's knees and together they sat quietly watching the lights of the tree. Each of them lost in their own, *very different* thoughts and memories. Nothing was said. Nothing needed to be said.

Betty arrived in the living room shortly after sunrise, followed by Frank a few minutes later. They greeted each silently, almost reverently, so as not to intrude on the peace-filled silence of the room filled by the softly flickering light.

Rachel did not make her appearance until mid-morning looking a bit disoriented. Nancy saw how sweetly, almost bashfully, Rachel looked at Frank. Betty saw it, too.

Homemade cinnamon rolls, cheesy breakfast casserole and fresh fruit salad seemed to magically appear on the dining room table laid out with Nancy's best china and silver. "Who made all this?" Rachel asked as her eyes danced across the cornucopia of delights. "Christmas Elves!" was the predictable answer the twins said simultaneously. Halfway through the meal Nancy jumped up to answer the phone. Everyone heard her say, "Yes, anytime - we're just hanging out." When she returned she told everyone it was Claudia. She and Jim were coming over.

After brunch, Nancy invited everyone back into the living room to play a game she had made up. After everyone was seated, she brought in a laundry basket full of the gifts Frank and Rachel had wrapped a few days earlier. She instructed them to bid on each gift as it was pulled from the basket. "But! the bid price," she said, "is limited to something you will do for the others in the room, such as rake their yard, carry out their garbage for a week, and tell them a story--stuff like that. And we will each take turns at being the auctioneer."

The bidding was outrageous. Rachel screamed out "Mother!" and everyone went sprawling in the floor laughing when Betty bid that she could make Rachel drive around the island at midnight on New Year's Eve, on her motor scooter screaming, "The British are coming!" That bid won Betty the jumbo jar of maraschino cherries.

One by one the gifts were auctioned off to the highest bidder until only one gift was left in the basket. Everyone glanced around the room. No one could remember wrapping it. They didn't have a clue what was in it. They all looked at Nancy who only raised her eyebrows and shook her head.

"Top bidder gets it--might be something "s-p-e-c-i-a-l," Nancy teased.

"I bid three art lessons," said Laura.

"No one can out bid that, Aunt Laura," said Frank, and the mysterious package was passed to her. Laura stood up and laid the package on Betty's lap.

"You take this one," she said. "I still have to figure out how to get that can of refrigerated crab meat through customs!"

All eyes were on Betty as she ripped open the loosely wrapped package and held up the contents. A river of chocolate brown and beige paisley velvet rippled to the floor.

"What is it?" asked Betty. Laura smiled and said, "It's your new bathrobe, Betty. See, I had it monogrammed for you."

Betty looked at the small cursive BB on the cuff. "I ordered it from the Smithsonian for you. It's called the 'Robe of Impunity.'

"What does that mean?" Rachel asked with her dark eyes squinting.

"Impunity means freedom from punishment or harm. So, it means that nothing can harm your mother while she is wearing the robe," said Laura.

Betty laid the soft fabric across her lap. "I think there was a bit of a conspiracy going on here," Betty said as tears filled her eyes. "I mean a monogrammed robe, with my name on it didn't just show up from..."Claudia's Closet."

"Might have!" laughed Claudia as she and Jim walked into the room.

****

Christmas dinner was a progressive affair; Hors d'oeuvres at Rachel's house, main course at Claudia's house followed by dessert back at Nancy's house. Over the years, Claudia and Nancy had often organized progressive dinner parties with their supper club friends, but this was the first time Rachel had ever been included. They were both surprised when Rachel had volunteered for Hors d'oeuvres. Apparently she had overheard Claudia and Nancy discussing plans one night, right before Laura arrived. Nancy had thought Frank and Rachel were watching TV, but she quickly found out that Rachel was interested in just about everything that went on at the "Hogan Hotel" these days, especially since Frank Jr. had checked in.

Claudia later told Nancy she could not even imagine what Rachel's house looked like inside. She'd driven by it and thought it looked like the home of someone on the witness protection program!

"You are so mean!" Nancy told her. "How could someone as sweet as me, like you so much!" "I'm-just-saying...Claudia had teased, exaggerating every syllable.

They had all been surprised to find a large weaving loom dominating Rachel's living room floor. Rachel patiently explained all the working parts of the loom as her guests huddled around. She pointed out how each part was used, depending on what she was making.

"When did you take up weaving?" Nancy asked, sincerely interested.

"While I was still in high school. I worked at a summer camp one year. My job was to help a professional weaver teach the young campers how to weave. I got *hooked*, so to speak." Everybody laughed.

Large baskets of brightly colored yarn sat around the room on the bare wooden floor. Nancy asked Betty if she had anything that Rachel made on the loom. Betty looked a little embarrassed and said "no."

"I put a few things in the Seafood Festival each

year," Rachel said. "Mostly hall runners, sometimes a blanket or two."

"Do you have anything you have finished that we could see?" asked Nancy, still wide-eyed with interest.

Rachel took the little group into her bedroom and switched on the light. Covering her bed was a throw Rachel had woven depicting scenes from Rainman Island. They all recognized the art center, the co-op, and the island's stone schoolhouse. She had woven in eagles and herons and flowers.

Nancy caught her breath. She could not believe that someone that looked and acted like Rachel was capable of making something so beautiful. Claudia stepped over to the tapestry hanging above Rachel's bed to take a closer look. In the foreground Rachel had woven black, leafless trees that stood in stark contrast to the frosty blue air surrounding them. A light snow lay on the ground. Along the distant horizon were hazy blue mountains. "That's one of the views from up on Mt. George," Rachel told them with a touch of pride in her voice.

Claudia met Nancy's wide-eyed stare. She gave voice to what they were both thinking. "Rachel, I had no idea—no idea," she slowly repeated herself touching the edge of the wall hanging, "that you could make such beautiful things. You are a very skilled weaver."

"You are a *fiber* artist!" interrupted Laura, with a distinctly professional tone.

Betty ran her hand over a woven blanket folded at

the foot of Rachel's bed. Betty had never been in this room before. The blanket felt soft and warm to her touch. Rachel stepped over to the bed, picked up the blanket and handed it to her mother. "I'd like you to have this, mother" she said.

Betty's eyes flew open in surprise. No one spoke. Everyone there understood the significance of the gift, especially Betty. Finally Betty managed to simply say "Thank you, Rachel," and hugged the soft folds close to her chest.

The Commission Piece

The average individual should be able to cook a meal, change a diaper or plan an invasion.
Specialization is for insects.

Late Monday afternoon Laura and Nancy glanced at each other as Laura tapped lightly on the back door of 14 Honey Bear Lane...a.k.a *Rosewood.*

"Why did she want us to come so late in the day?" Nancy asked Laura.

"She said our faces would not be as puffy or something," said Laura.

Nancy had always wanted to go inside this house ever since the day she had delivered Camille's mail accidentally left at her home.

"What does *Rosewood* refer to I wonder" Nancy asked, as they stood on the screened porch and listened to the thump of Camille's cane coming toward the back door.

Laura shrugged. "Let's ask her. It's probably not a secret."

The door swung open and Camille beamed one of her 1000-watt smiles at them. "So! The twins have arrived! Welcome!" she said in a booming voice.

Camille backed out of their way so that they could enter the kitchen. When Nancy stepped in her head jerked involuntarily at what she saw. She was stunned. It was NOT what she expected. Camille saw the glazed look come over Nancy's face and said, "I'll show you around before we start if you would be interested. It's sort of *hodge-podge-lodge*.

"Yes! I'd love a look around," said Nancy in a sudden resurgence of her Southern accent. Neither of them asked Camille why she used a cane.

Stepping in, Nancy felt engulfed, swallowed up, by the soft shadows. Time seemed suspended, though the large antique wall clock betrayed the passage of time with its steady ticking. There was a shabby sort of grandeur everywhere she looked that seemed glamorized and accentuated by the shadows. *If a few cobwebs were added, it could easily be a movie set for some ghostly encounter*, thought Nancy. A sense of the mysterious, the absurd was palpable.

This house reflects the life of the one who lives here, Laura thought. *One who has discovered that there is a Divine order, a place and a purpose and a time for everything. The only difference between the bizarre and the beautiful in this place is in the eye of the beholder.*

"All of life is art and art, is life," Laura said to Camille. Camille simply nodded.

Original art and elaborately framed photos hung 'gallery style' from the high ceilings to the floor in every room. The windows were heavily draped, as if to block out the invasion of time. As they passed through the archway that separated the kitchen from the dining room, Nancy noticed a life size wooden arm jutting out from the wall at a 90-degree angle. It was well above their heads, but visually, it was unavoidable. The hand of this wooden arm held a baton, something like a drum major might hold as he leads a noisy parade. Underneath the arm was a brass plaque bearing the words: "Jesus Christ."

With Camille leading the way, they moved slowly into a small sitting room opposite the library. The twins noticed a wall in the library completely filled with diplomas and citations. "Are all of these yours?" asked Laura.

"Yes," said Camille, "I'm afraid I'm a kudos junkie."

"Well," said Laura, drawing a little closer and inspecting the ones nearest to her, "they scream authority, accomplishment and substance." Laura turned to her sister and said, "We are in good hands, Nancy."

Nancy smiled weakly, still trying to analyze the wooden arm and brass plaque in the dining room. Nancy scanned the "kudos wall." She had often thought that only insecure people displayed all of their diplomas, etc. She herself had discretely placed her most prestigious diplomas so that they could only be seen as a person was leaving her home office.

A little dazzled by the sheer magnitude of them all, Nancy's eyes wandered from left to right, upward. In the dim upper corner of the wall, near the ten-foot high ceiling, Nancy observed an ornate gilded frame holding the picture of a woman's bust and with what appeared to be a blue ribbon attached to the frame. It looked so out of place Nancy questioned Camille. "What's that one up there? Something one of your grandchildren did?"

"No," said Camille. "That's where it all began for me. A blue ribbon at the county fair when I was six years old. I've been addicted to blue ribbons ever since."

They padded across a thick oriental carpet then headed toward Camille's studio. As they passed through the small sitting room, Nancy noticed a wall of bookshelves. They appeared overly burdened with thick volumes on art and psychology.

She is completely right brained, thought Nancy, *just like Laura.*

"Any ghost around here?" Nancy thought she was making a joke. Camille stopped so abruptly that Nancy thought she had tripped on something.

"Did one speak to you?" Camille said in earnest, her grey blue eyes blazing at Nancy.

"Ahhh…no…" said Nancy, startled at Camille's sincerity.

Laura saved the moment by bending slightly toward Camille and whispering "she doesn't believe in ghosts, I don't know what's wrong with her."

Camille's mood changed suddenly again as the two artistic women exchanged some sort of non-verbal communication--a connection that left Nancy with the distinct feeling of being an outsider. It wasn't the first time Laura and her artist friends had dismissed Nancy as a--Nancy struggled to think what must be going through their minds. *A non-entity.* She shrugged it off. Nancy knew who she was.

Camille pushed open the double French doors leading into her studio. It was a large room full of natural light. Three sides of the room were glass, from floor to ceiling.

"Welcome to my sanctuary" Camille said to Laura's delighted gaze.

Every nook and cranny of the room was crammed full of mismatched cabinets. There were several work tables sitting at odd angles around the room covered with smudges of paint and plaster. Laura saw at least three large easels. The room smelled of oil paint and turpentine mingled with cigarette smoke. Row after row of colorful mat boards had been stuffed into slots specifically designed to accommodate their various sizes under one of the worktables. A profusion of open trays holding all sorts of curious looking tools lay everywhere. Nancy noticed several old coffee cans stuffed full of every conceivable size and type of artist brush.

The room gave the immediate impression of organized mayhem. A stool had been pulled up close to one of the easels standing in the corner. On it was mounted a small, half finished watercolor. Both Nancy and Laura went over to inspect it. "Just a little something I'm doing for myself," Camille said. "I'm calling this series 'The Corners of My Life.' Arthritis has crippled my body. I am so limited now in my range of motion that there are many days I feel like a prisoner in my own body. And, as is true for most prison cells, my range of vision is limited. But the other morning, with the sun streaming in, I saw how lovely the light played around the corners of my garden box, and in my sitting room, and in my studio. Corners are mysterious," she said, "you don't always know what's around them..." Camille trailed off as if she were continuing the conversation with herself. The room fell silent for a moment.

Camille moved differently in this room – almost gracefully. She went over to a small table covered with boxes of plaster gauze, the kind doctors use to set broken bones. The table also held a small bucket, a large roll of gauze and a jar of Vaseline. A square of black plastic had been thrown over the back of a tall stool beside the table. "Are you ready to get started? I can do one today and one tomorrow. Who wants to go first? I figured that the one that isn't sitting will be my assistant and hand me stuff, when I ask for it."

Nancy had no idea what Camille was talking about. She knew enough to know this was not the way you start an oil painting. Laura saw the surprised look on Nancy's face. It was exactly what she had hoped for. At least she had been able to keep one part of the surprise from Nancy.

"Nancy, Camille is renowned for her work in *life casting.* She's not going to paint our portrait, she's going to cast our faces, first in plaster, then from the plaster cast, I've ask her to take it to bronze!" Laura said grinning broadly. Both Camille and Laura thought that was plenty of explanation, but Nancy was still confused.

"I tell you what," said Camille, "Laura you go first, Nancy will help, that way she'll see how we do this." Nancy took a step back without realizing it. Camille studied her for a moment then said, "Come with me, Nancy." With cane in hand Camille walked past them back into the adjacent sitting room then into the library. They both followed obediently.

In one corner of the library, Camille stepped aside and pointed to the bronze bust of a very old woman. Nancy's eyes flew open. "That is beautiful!" she said. "That is "life casting," Camille said. *Life casting* simply means that you don't have to be dead for me to get an exact copy, or cast, of your face. Before someone invented dental alginate, a person had to be dead to get a cast of their face. That's because the only way they could get such accurate detail was to pour *hot plaster* over the face - that's what they did to Abraham Lincoln..."

Laura picked up the task of enlightening her sister. Camille will first apply a layer of dental alginate over my face and neck. She doesn't put any alginate into my nose holes so I don't have to worry about breathing. But I have to sit dead still for a few minutes. I've heard it feels really good, sort of like getting a facial. On top of the alginate, she applies a layer of wet plaster gauze. The plaster gauze sets up firm in about 5 minutes. The alginate doesn't even take that long. So after a few minutes the whole thing pops off your face. When the alginate sets up, it looks and feels like the white of a boiled egg."

"That's the negative mold," Camille continued. "Then I pour a milk coat of plaster into the negative mold. I follow the thin milk coat of plaster with a heavier plaster mix, filling up the negative mold. When the plaster sets up, I peel away the plaster gauze and alginate and viola! I have a positive mold, an exact replica of your face and neck, or whatever body part you want me to do," she grinned as if enjoying some private joke.

"That's when the real work starts for me," Camille continued. "I have to clean it up. I use dental tools mostly. I open the eyes; give it some hair and eyelashes. The alginate sticks to hair, so I use Vaseline to lubricate all facial hair before I apply the alginate. When I'm satisfied that I have the exact image I'm looking for I'll send them out to get bronzed."

"Oh" said Nancy. Her eyes were the size of saucers.

Laura stepped in to examine the old woman's bust. "Who is this?" she asked. "She's the oldest looking woman I've ever seen."

"A few years ago I was asked to cast the tribal leaders of the Seminole Indians of South Florida. This is Susie Billie. She was the tribe's Shaman. Six of the tribal leaders were women. Progressive huh?" Camille gently touched the statue. "She was 96 when I cast her. No white person had ever touched her before I worked on her that day. The tribe commissioned me to do the work and it was later displayed at the Smithsonian." Deeply impressed, Nancy took a closer look. Every wrinkle and flaw on Susie Billie's face was visible. She looked as if she would speak at any moment. Thick layers of beads adorned Susie Billie's neck. The life casting process had captured every tiny bead perfectly.

Laura climbed into the artist chair and shifted her weight around until she felt comfortable. Camille reached over and pushed the play button on the CD player and strains from *Pachelbel's Serenade* filled the room.

"Nancy, while I get Laura's hair out of the way, would you go around to the kitchen sink and get this bucket about half full of warm water?" Nancy took the bucket and wandered back through the house to the kitchen, the point at which they had entered the house. She noticed things that she had missed before, like the drapes that hung on all the interior doors and archways. They were hung high on the wall above each doorway. The satiny fabric of the drapes puddled in the floor. Several of the door drapes were fringed and Camille had tied them back to create passageways. *Moving from room to room was rather like coming out from behind a curtain, onto a stage,* Nancy thought.

As she entered the kitchen she moved left around an enormous antique wooden table dominating the center of the room. The table contained among other things a large stuffed black bird that looked menacingly at her. Nancy bent over the circa 1940 enamel sink with large dish drains on both sides. Camille had artistically embellished the sink with an array of colorful, fruit laden vines coming out of the facet, circling around the basin of the sink and coming to rest on top of the drain. As the water splashed into the bucket Nancy looked up and noticed a small dead frog that seemed to have been mashed flat, artistically framed, hanging over the sink. There was no plaque to explain this one. *Wrong place, wrong time,* Nancy thought as she lifted the small bucket of water from the sink.

She returned to the studio taking a slightly different route than her host had led them through earlier.

Traveling alone through the old house, she was even more aware of the elaborately framed photographs, shadow boxes and castings that filled the walls. She passed through a small interior room whose walls had been painted hot pink, though no one would have noticed, not with so many other things to catch the eye. The only furniture in this small space was an ornate, oak sideboard that had been converted into a cabinet to hold a pearly white lavatory with antique brass fixtures.

One of the photos that hung near the sideboard was of a younger Camille in a Playboy Bunny outfit. In the picture her stance is a little awkward as if she'd fall were it not for the close embrace by none other than Huge Hefner. A little higher on the wall Nancy noticed an older Camille in a photo where she was apparently accepting some type of award from Andrew Young. A "twenty-ish" looking Camille preened at her from another photo. She was painting what looked to be a Totem Pole holding up a canopy over a nightclub bar area. Next to that photo Nancy recognized a signed photograph of Helen Keller. *Wonder why that's here?* Her eye fell on still another small photo showing Camille with a *hippie-grown-old hair do*, performing a life casting of Esther William's face. Nancy remembered Esther Williams as an Olympic athlete who made the top level of Hollywood stardom by performing spectacular water ballets. *Wonder how Camille met her?* Nancy's confidence in Camille's artistic abilities had risen significantly in the past few minutes.

"Where in hell is that hot water?" Camille's voice boomed so loud Nancy thought she could have probably been heard in Hell! Startled, Nancy resumed her task. As she turned to leave the pink room, her eyes fell on a plaster casting of a woman's face. Her brown hair swirled upward over three feet high and to it Camille had glued green plastic snakes and hideous plastic bugs. The brass plaque below it read "Migraine from Hell."

When Nancy returned to the studio Camille locked eyes with her, but Nancy could not read her meaning. Camille continued to eye Nancy as she took a drag off the cigarette dangling from a long Hollywood-style cigarette holder. Nancy sat the water down on the small table then stepped into a position close enough to hand Camille whatever she asked for.

Everything about this woman, Nancy thought, *is dramatic and overstated.* She thought about the life size, self-portrait that Camille had shown them earlier as they toured through her bedroom. The huge portrait hung on the wall opposite her 19th century four-poster bed. *That painting, Nancy thought, exudes clues about Camille's self-image.* In it, she sits regally atop a white stallion, ornately dressed in a period costume reminiscent of a cross between a 17th century Rubens and a Playboy Bunny centerfold. *Drama,* thought Nancy, *should be Camille's middle name. No wonder she gets along so well with Laura. Peas from the same pod!*

"What are you grinning about?" asked Laura.

"Oh, nothing" said Nancy as she handed Camille a strip of gauze to hold Laura's spiky hair away from her face—*although,* Nancy thought, *that hair is not going anywhere.*

Two hours later, Nancy and Laura slowly walked

back to the car.

"Laura," Nancy said slowly, "I thought I had seen everything." After a short pause she continued, "I thought I knew this island—I mean, this is my home turf! But today...well, I learned something entirely new. Life is... " She had no idea how to finish her comment.

"Life is art, and art is life" her twin finished her thought. Neither of them spoke on the short drive home.

Rachel's Allstate motor scooter was parked in Nancy's driveway *again*.

"She sure must love her mother a lot!" Laura grinned at Nancy.

"Yeah, right!" said Nancy. When they came in Betty was sitting watching TV with Frank and Rachel. Betty was wearing her new robe and when she saw them, she smiled. Bernie came running over to greet them. He had stopped barking when people came in. Nancy reached down and gave his ears a scratch. Nancy knew her dog's life had changed as swiftly and completely as her own.

"How about I give you an art lesson tomorrow Frank," said Laura. "I'm all enthused about painting again, after meeting Camille tonight." Frank's face brightened.

"I remember you trying to teach me to paint when I was a kid."

"So do I," she said. "You actually showed some

talent. Maybe you are an artist and just don't know it yet, Frank. She looked down at her feet for a minute, lost in a memory. "I'm on the books for three free art lessons, remember? Let's get an early start. Light might be better early, before the rain sets in. Meet you out there near the apple orchard, say around 7a.m., OK?"

"O.K.," said Frank.

"I'm going to grab a sandwich and turn in," said Laura looking at Nancy. "This time change has me a little screwed up." Laura made herself a sandwich, grabbed a glass of milk then disappeared up the steps.

"Everybody on their own tonight for dinner," Nancy shouted into the den where Frank and Rachel still sat. "Claudia sent all her left-overs - they need to be eaten," Nancy directed her voice toward the TV watchers.

Nancy turned and surveyed her kitchen. After spending several hours at *Rosewood,* everything in her home seemed so...*predictable,* in comparison. There wasn't a stuffed bird or frog to be seen anywhere. No drum major arms jutting from walls bearing the name of Jesus Christ. *And Rosewood, I completely forgot to ask Camille where that came from. I'm sure there is a story.*

"Come on Betty," let's have a turkey sandwich." Nancy spoke again into the little cluster of TV watchers. They seemed to be absorbed in some program about '*the year in review.*'

As Nancy put two sandwiches together, Betty sat on

a stool and watched. "You know, Nancy, I think I feel good enough to go home. And I could always get Sarah Clifton to come in as needed, now that I know about her and she knows me. I mean, who would have thought remission a month ago? I mean, I sure don't want to be a burden to you." Betty spoke haltingly, stopping between each sentence.

Out of the corner of her eye, Nancy saw Betty tracing an indention in the butcher block with her fingertip. "Whatever you feel is best, Betty," Nancy said turning toward her with the finished sandwiches. "But Betty, I really love you being here. And Rachel, too. I'm not sure I'd know how to be a family with Frank if you two weren't here. It gives me some..." she looked for the word, "some leverage." Nancy sat down next to Betty and pushed the sandwich-laden plate in front of her. "You know we agreed to be honest with each other right from the start Betty, and well, I honestly don't want you to leave. In the beginning I didn't have any idea how this would work, but it works, I mean, for me at least." She waited for Betty to speak.

"It works for me too, Nancy. Honestly, the thought of going back to my little house, without Kenneth there, seems down right depressing. Never a dull moment around here."

"That's settled, then," said Nancy and lifted her glass of milk in a toast to Betty. As they clinked their glasses, they heard a soft knock on the back door. Bernie started growling in a low, menacing tone and rushed toward the kitchen door.

Nancy opened the door just enough to peek out. It

was Pat Roberts. She glanced over at Betty and mouthed *the constable.* She swung the door open but did not invite him in. Instead she stepped out to meet him, closing the door behind her.

"Bernie might want to bite you," she said smiling, trying to hide her true reason for not letting him in.

"Came by to tell you and Frank that he's got a court date over in Vancouver on April 15th," he said as he handed Nancy a folded piece of paper.

"OK," she said. She didn't know why but she did not want to get into a conversation with him. Pat stood there for a moment staring up at the back door.

"How's your boy?" he asked.

"Seems fine," said Nancy, minimizing her words. Pat looked like he wanted to say something for a moment but didn't know how to get started. Nancy waited. Pat shifted his weight and touched the revolver in his holster.

"You look nervous or something." Nancy finally gave in.

"I guess I am a little rattled tonight," he said.

"Why?" Nancy really did not want to know. She feared it was more bad news regarding Frank's ten-year hiatus.

"Well," Frank glanced up at her nervously, and then continued. "You know that animal we were trying to locate -- the one we think killed Ray Phillips? You know the one we were tracking when we found Frank over in Hell Hole?"

Nancy's face brightened. Maybe this wasn't about Frank. "Yes," did you find it?" Nancy asked.

"Well, yes and no. We had some hikers come over a couple of days ago...went over to Yellow Point Park to camp and hike, and...," Pat hesitated.

Nancy could not stand the way Pat hemmed and hawed like a schoolboy! "Yes, Pat, what about them?" her impatience showed. He looked down at his feet, then said haltingly, "they had a large dog with them -- and when they woke up the next morning--they found it dead—body pretty mangled up -- 'bout half mile from where they had pitched their tent." Pat looked at Nancy, not knowing how much more he should tell.

"Come in Pat, and have a cup of tea, or maybe something stronger. You look all done in."

"No thanks," he said. "Just help me get the word out that everyone on the island needs to be on the alert. Keep an eye on your dog, too. I asked 'em to run an article in the local paper about it and I've put fliers out over at the Sleeping Pig and at the co-op. Big John's going to give the fliers to folks coming onto the island, starting tomorrow." Pat turned to leave. Nancy took a step closer.

"Pat, did you say you *thought it was* an animal or that *it was* an animal attack? Pat looked down at his feet again.

"Still not sure," he said. "For that matter I'm still not positive exactly what happened to Ray. I've got

Yellow Point corralled off as a crime scene."

Betty looked at Nancy's ashen face when she came back into the kitchen and said "What in the world?"

"Looks like another animal *murder*," Nancy said.

"An animal was *murdered*?" Betty looked stricken.

"No, a dog--some hikers camping over at Yellow Point Park--had a dog with them. They found it dead and mangled. Pat thinks it might be the same animal, bear or something big, that attacked Ray Phillips."

Betty studied Nancy's face in disbelief. "Nothing like this has ever happened on this island as long as I've lived here," she said.

Nancy walked into the den and told Rachel and Frank about Pat's visit. Nancy saw Frank's face flush as he quickly looked down at the floor. It was not how she had expected him to react. Rachel just stared at her with her mouth hanging open. *Now that, she did expect!*

Nancy got up early the next morning and was reading her Bible and having coffee when Laura came into the kitchen. "I feel good!" she said. "Slept ten hours, sound! Well except for Frank's chattering in his sleep. That boy's a regular chatter box at night!" Laura poured a cup of coffee and sat down next to Nancy.

"What does he chatter about?" asked Nancy. "Can you make any of it out?"

"As long as I have my bathroom door closed I can't hear him at all, which I make a point to do, usually. But last night, I had gone into the bathroom to pee. It was about 3 a.m. His door was open a little. I heard him yell out a name. Sounded like Adam Stanley or Standish. But it was clearly Adam something."

"Who knows?" Nancy shrugged. "Might mention it to him while you have the next Van Gogh out there painting this morning."

"I smell coffee!" Frank said coming into the kitchen.

"Ready for your art lesson?" Laura smiled.

"Will be as soon as I process a cup of mother's melted pencil lead over here."

"Melted pencil lead!" Nancy said, faking a shocked expression. "Too strong for you?'

"I had hair on my chest before I started drinking your coffee, mom. Now my chest hair is gone and my teeth are falling out." It was his first attempt at a joke. *He must be settling in a little.*

"You can always water down a strong cup but you can't do anything with a weak one," Nancy said.

"Except maybe pour it out," added Laura.

"Laura," Nancy changed her tone. She sounded serious. "Pat Roberts was here last night, after you went up, and told us to be on the alert for a dangerous animal. In addition to killing Ray Phillips, he thinks this animal might be responsible for another death. They found a mangled dead dog over at Yellow Point Park. Be on the lookout any time you are outside."

"My God!" blurted Laura, almost spilling her coffee. "What kind of place is this? Wild animals on the loose - killer wild animals! Have to take a damn ferry to the grocery store, never heard of spa..." Laura's voice trailed off as she and Frank headed out the den door and on toward the apple orchard.

The sun was just breaking over the mountains to the east, throwing streams of light through the clouds. At that exact moment a rainbow appeared above the rain soaked orchard. Nancy watched them from her office window. She saw Laura taking a picture of the rainbow with Frank standing near one of the leafless apple trees. The sun, shining through the branches, casted a crisscross pattern over Frank, making him appear to Nancy, even more like puzzle pieces all stuck together at odd angles.

Nancy got ready for her day at the hospital. After a steamy bath, she donned her usual cashmere *uniform* and went up to see if Betty was awake. She was.

"I'm going over to the Hospital today. Need anything?" Betty said, "well I would appreciate it if you could get someone to notarize this and take it by the courthouse."

Nancy was surprised. "What is it?"

"It's my last will and testament," she said. "Leaving it all to Rachel. I didn't care who got the house before, but things are different now. Do I have to be there to get it notarized?"

"I'm a notary, Betty," said Nancy. "Well, even better," Betty said. "Will you watch me sign it?" "Sure, " said Nancy. "You want this filed over at the courthouse in Comox?"

"Yes."

"Will do. Anything else?"

"That's quite enough for today," said Betty smiling.

"I do have a couple more questions about the Bible when you get a chance," said Betty.

"Tell me what's on your mind and if I need to bring in a pro I'll call Susan before I come home."

"Ah, it's nothing you can't answer, Nancy. I'm just so new with understanding the Bible."

Nancy stepped into Betty's room. She'd been standing in the hall with her head poked into the room. She wanted Betty to know that Bible study was much more important to her than a volunteer job at a hospital.

"Well, my question has to do with those poor people wandering around in the wilderness, suffering, living on whatever that stuff was that floated down every night, just wandering around, dying, people always attacking them, and then God attacks them with snakes! Nancy I'm having a hard time understanding that. It's almost like there are two different Gods, one for the Old Testament and a different one for the New Testament." She looked up at Nancy.

Nancy was once again stunned with the depth of Betty's question. "And you think I can toss you out an answer on that one! Betty, you have me figured out as someone much smarter than I actually am!" she said laughing. "In fact, I've wondered the same thing myself. The Old Testament is so--well--bloody! To me the stories seem to have main characters that are flawed, ignorant, and superstitious people that God had to force and coerce into being a nation of people. But it was through them that He intended to bring Jesus, our Savior."

"Flawed and ignorant," Betty smiled. "I resemble that remark."

"Well, it's true. And I am always tripping up on the fact that the narratives in the Old Testament were written from oral stories that evolved over hundreds of years. But, back to that snake business. Our Pastor just preached on that passage not long ago. She did an excellent job describing the context of it – you know what I mean by context?" Nancy hesitated and Betty nodded. "I owe her a dinner anyway, or at least she keeps telling me that I do!" Nancy smiled. "I think I'll see if she can come over for dinner one night soon so we can kick this around with her. It will be a much more enlightened discussion than I could give you."

Betty nodded. Nancy glanced at her watch. "I just have enough time to make the 9 o'clock ferry, Betty. I'll try to reach Susan on my way in this morning."

Betty nodded again this time with more energy and made a shooing sign with her hand.

The Stillmore's Christmas

Abigail and Brock Stillmore sat on the top step waiting for their parents to wake up. They had been sitting there since 5 a.m., whispering and occasionally giggling. Micah laughed when he saw them perched like buzzards waiting to swoop down on their prey. Micah stepped back into the bedroom for his camera and nudged the shoulder of his sleeping wife.

"*Your* children are already up," he said smiling down at the face he loved. Pam pulled a pillow back over her face and groaned, "They are not *my* children. You spawned them! Just tell them Santa didn't come--couldn't get to the island--boat broke!"

"Santa doesn't need a boat! Anybody knows that," seven-year-old Brock said from the doorway.

Micah wheeled around. "You guys!" he shouted with laughter.

"Come on Dad, just leave Mom in the bed!"

"Nothing doing! said Pam as she rolled out of the bed and slipped on her house shoes. "Let's go down," she said as she kissed her husband on the lips. "Merry Christmas" said Micah returning her kiss. The kids bounded down, taking two steps at a time. They waited in the den for what seemed like forever.

When Micah and Pam finally came into the living room the kid's hands were poised in mid-air, ready to rip open the gift they had chosen to be *first* after weeks of deliberation. For the next full hour, the camera flashed, laughter and *thank-yous* flooded the room.

Micah brought Pam a cup of tea, bent down and pushed the hair off her neck and kissed it. She smiled up at him. The truth was, Pam loved her life with Micah and the children. Living on the island had brought them all closer.

At 9 a.m. Pam looked around the room, now empty of children but filled with paper and open boxes. The kids had retreated to their rooms and were busy laying out their precious gifts on *display.* They knew their cousins would be over soon to *inspect* everything. Brunch would follow after Pete and his family arrived. Pam shoved the coffee cake and egg casserole into the oven. Sharon, her sister-in-law was bringing the Christmas ambrosia. Christmas dinner this year was at Pete and Sharon's house. Swapping back and forth each year for Christmas dinner had become the Stillmore Christmas tradition. It had all started the same year Micah's brother and his family moved to the island.

Pam and Micah sat next to each other enjoying a moment of silence. Pam pulled a small gift from the pocket of her housecoat that she had carefully placed there the night before. She handed it to Micah.

"What's this?" he said smiling.

"I think it's the best gift I have ever given to you, or

ever could."

"Sure got my attention now!" said Micah. He looked at the package carefully, turning it slowly in his hands several times. He had no idea what it could be. He removed the wrapping paper easily to reveal a small, spiral bound notebook. On the cover was a picture of Ray and Micah standing together with Tribune Bay in the background. Ray was holding his hat in one hand. His other arm was thrown around Micah's shoulders. The wind had rearranged Ray's white hair so that it stood almost straight up. The sun was high in the sky and a few white caps could be seen on the low, gentle waves lapping into the bay behind them. They were both grinning at the camera. It was a picture full of life and love. Micah ran his finger over the picture as if to touch Ray's face. Micah still missed Ray every day. His absence was so real Micah could almost touch it. Ray left a hole in Micah's life that could not be filled by anyone else. Among all the things that Ray had brought into Micah's life, the greatest gift was that he was the one who introduced Micah to the Christ.

Micah did not look at Pam. He knew if he did, he would not be able to hold back the tears that now burned at the back of his eyes. "It's not from me," Pam said. "It's from Ray to both of us," she said. "I just helped it get printed." He slowly opened the book to the first page. Centered on the sheet, the words stood there alone, like a sentinel guarding a secret:

>'As you are now, so once was I
>As I am now, so you must be
>So don't fear death and follow me.'

It was the same words that Ray had chosen for his tombstone. He had ordered it the same year Linda died and had it placed alongside hers in the small cemetery near his beloved Episcopal church. Micah risked looking at Pam. On the next page Pam had simply written Ray's full name and the dates of his life: Raymond Sinclair Phillips, December 24, 1935 - November 25, 2010. Under that appeared the title that Pam had given the book "Heaven Visited."

"I took the notes you made as Ray told you about Heaven and typed them up," Pam said. "I added a few words here and there to complete a sentence or thought. If I didn't understand what he was trying to say, I left it as he spoke it to you or as you wrote it down. I made a copy for Dr. Alice. She's getting hers this morning too." Micah sat transfixed. He had not read the journal since the day that Ray had labored so near death to speak these words to him. He feared that reading it would plunge him once again into the same shock and grief he had felt when he found Ray near death in the freezing mud. Even now his emotions threatened to overwhelm him with the pain of that loss.

Micah looked at Pam again, searching her face, his eyes pleading with her to help him.

"I think," Pam said quietly, "that you will be as amazed as I was while typing it. This is not a book of sorrow, but of incredible joy and promise. Ray has given us a glimpse into Heaven, Micah. I am now certain that there is life after death -- a place of such overwhelming peace and love and abundance that if you could, you would not call him back. Not even for a moment."

"I just don't think I'm ready to think of him as ...gone," said Micah. "I can't take it in, somehow, that he is—gone. It still hurts so much."

"Leave it then, until you are ready," said Pam, and laid her hand over his as he closed the book.

Later that night, after all the company was gone, after all the dishes were washed and his two sleepy children and their mother lay sound asleep, curled up in one bed, Micah sat down in his favorite chair. He pulled the drawer open on the coffee table and took the small book out. He sat there awhile and stared at the picture on the cover. He hadn't really thought of anything else all day. He remembered the summer day two years earlier when that picture had been taken. His fishing and tour business was going well, all thanks to Ray's encouragement and advice. Ray had met him down at the landing as he and Pete were coming in from a day's fishing. He had a six-pack with him and together they drank all of it. Pete had taken the picture.

He opened the book slowly. With deep reverence he began to read Ray's words.

****

"I dreamed I was lying in my hospital bed. I looked over and saw Linda sitting there, where you are."

Micah remembered that it had taken Ray several minutes to complete these two sentences. *Two or three words at a time—that's all he could manage at first.* He could still hear the raspy sound of Ray's voice.

She smiled so sweetly at me and said *Come on*! The way she looked at me filled me with a love so complete I cannot describe it. I told her I was too weak to come--she said *she'd help me.* I held my hand out to her—amazed I found I could stand up quiet easily."

"I felt like I was almost floating but I didn't notice myself as much as I just couldn't get over seeing her! She looked incredibly beautiful. How did you get here? I kept asking her. She smiled and said it was easy. She looked and acted so young! Just like when we first met."

Micah realized that Pam had taken his brief, staccato notes and made them into sentences. But she had done a beautiful job and with great sensitivity.

"Linda was beaming like a child—like she had a fantastic secret and was just bursting to show and tell—smiling and nodding—she kept insisting that I follow her. It made me feel like a child again, too. She led me over to that big window over there (Ray pointed to the window in his hospital room) and together we looked out at the cars in the parking lot and the people coming and going into the hospital. Then I looked over toward the Comox glacier. Suddenly I was out over the lawn in front of the hospital. I looked down and saw that I was passing over the street. For an instant I felt terrified. I wanted to go back but at the same time, I wanted to stay with Linda. I wanted to stay with her more than I felt afraid."

"She looked at me and smiled then squeezed my hand tighter. My fear left--just like that—gone. I looked back at the hospital. I could see both inside the walls and outside at the same time—hard to explain. I was above everything and in everything—at the same time—hard to explain. I could see myself lying in this hospital. I looked dead--still and grey, lifeless. But *I* wasn't there, in that body. *I* was holding Linda's hand and we were like--Wendy and Peter Pan flying along over the streets of Comox!"

"We went up and up until we passed over the glacier summit. Linda started talking to me again and I focused on her. I was one with her—her mind, her being and mine were linked, overlapped—hard to explain. I felt free as a bird. We went through some clouds but they weren't wet like I thought they might be."

"I looked back and the world was dropping away-- just like I've seen in the movies. I started to be afraid again but Linda just spoke to me--but not with words. Somehow everything she said just slipped into me--not only into my mind, but into *me*--can't explain. And every time I felt afraid, she knew it-- instantly--and would start talking again. Her mouth did not move but I could hear her speak. She told me she was taking me to someplace special. "

"The next thing I realized I was sitting with Linda in a wide open grassy place. The closest thing to it on earth would be a prairie. The vastness of the space seemed larger than the whole earth and yet I could see all of it at the same time--but be in only a tiny portion of it. Can't explain."

(Ray repeated the phrase 'can't explain' so often that Micah starting writing in 'CE'. Pam left it as she found them in Micah's notes.)

"There were no houses around, just a vast open space with beautiful, incredibly green, well watered trees along the bank of a stream. The stream broadened out in front of us and appeared quite deep, like a swimming hole I once went to as a boy. But the water in the stream was like nothing I had ever seen before (CE). I became fascinated with the water. It seemed to sparkle in response to my attention--like it was alive (CE). All along the stream's bank I saw stones that looked like they had been polished so that they reflected the light. And the light! Light filled everything. I really can't describe it. Everything got my attention but I was more overwhelmed with what I felt than what I saw--I felt *perfectly loved* and *perfectly at peace*."

"The warm sun hit my back and I lifted my hands out in front of me. Once again I noticed how rough they were and even noticed the missing digit on my right hand, a sawing mishap when I was in high school. *Let's rest here for a minute*, Linda said. And I was glad."

Ray went to sleep, Micah had written into his notes. Then he suddenly woke up about 15 minutes later and continued to talk as if he had never stopped.

"I looked down at the grass I was sitting on. I wondered if I was going to get my pajama pants wet. The grass felt moist and amazing. Every blade of it appeared perfect. I was fascinated by the grass and looked closely at it. There were no blemishes, no decay or dried out parts. And the color was so alive and vivid. (CE)"

"Linda called to me and when I looked up, she had

waded out into the stream. She was already up to her knees. And she was laughing and said *come on*! It was the same words she had used to coax me from my hospital bed. I couldn't refuse her. I rolled up my pajama pants and waded in. The water was wonderful. It felt...I don't know how to say it... it felt alive, swirling around my legs like a tender massage. It wasn't cold or warm; it was...just amazing. Linda kept telling me to *come on in a little further...a little further.* I took a couple more steps toward her and by this time she was up to her shoulders. I remembered that she had never learned to swim so I reached out to her, but then she pulled me under the water!"

"At first I was afraid the water would go up my nose or that I didn't have enough air. She pulled me under so quickly that I didn't have time to take in a breath and hold it. She spoke to me, into my mind, not in words and she told me to *breathe*! I was afraid to try. I was under the water and all of my human reflexes kicked in. Everyone knows you can't breathe under water. She just smiled and showed me how to do it. To my utter amazement I found I could breathe as easily under the water as I could out of the water. Linda took both of my hands and tugged at me gently until my feet left the bottom and we were floating. Floating like that, holding hands with our arms extended in front of us, face to face. She told me to relax and I did."

"I don't know how long we floated like that. Time meant nothing to me. Then slowly I became aware of the music. Some mystical strains of melody... I could not tell where it was coming from; it seemed to be all around us. It wasn't coming into my ears. It was coming in through my whole body. And I listened. The music was soft, it seemed to caress me and I simply drifted along with it in the swirling water. I could not tell if I was drifting in the music or drifting in the water. There was no difference. I felt completely loved, completely safe."

(Ray drifted off to sleep again, exhausted.)

"I never wanted to leave that water. It was perfect, my lovely wife holding me, the intense feeling of unconditional love filling me. But Linda again tugged at my hand and slowly we got our feet back under us and started walking toward the bank. I thought that my clothes would be all stuck to me when I came up out of the stream. I thought that my hair would be dripping down in my face, and I wondered where I would find a towel for us. But I was amazed to find that when we walked up out of the water, my hair was not wet at all. My pajamas were not wet either. In fact, I was completely dry! I also found that as I touched my hair and clothes, that they were soft and dry and had a sort of glow to them in that amazing light that was in everything, on everything."

"I looked down at my hands, the roughness was gone and the missing digit on my finger had been restored. I looked at Linda, her chestnut brown hair was perfectly dry and luxurious like the first time I had ever touched it. She looked radiantly healthy and beautiful. I reached over and touched her hair again and pulled her close to me. She whispered in my ear *Welcome, my dear. You are honored and loved here.*"

"I came to understand that the time we had spent in that marvelous water was in fact, my baptism into Heaven."

Ray slipped back into a peaceful sleep.

Micah slipped a bookmark into the book and closed it. He laid his head back on the sofa and drew his arms around the book, holding it against his chest like he was holding a beloved child. He sat there like that for a while. The house was dark and quiet. He tried to remember every detail of those last few minutes with Ray. He remembered that his hand was sore from so much writing. He thought Ray had just drifted off to sleep again, like he had done several times that afternoon. He looked over and touched Ray's hand. It was the first time he had taken a break from writing in a couple of hours. He remembered being shocked to find that Ray's hand was cold.   Micah had looked at Dr. Alice. She just smiled and slowly nodded her head. Together they had watched as Ray's breathing slowed until it seemed he only drew one breath every minute or so. And then he just stopped breathing. There was no struggle, no gasping. His mouth fell open slightly, as if he were about to speak again, but there was no other movement.

Ray was gone.

What A Gal

Carve into my life Lord signs that You have passed this way.

"Betty?" Frank whispered.

"Are you OK?" He'd heard her coughing again, gasping for air.

Betty looked stung by his question. It was early. She was sitting in the big blue chair with her lamp on, an open spiral notebook in her lap. She smiled up at him, her coughing subdued for the moment. "Did I wake you with my hacking?" she asked.

"Not really." He spoke slowly still full of sleep. "I wake up pretty easy. Still not used to sleeping in a safe place, I guess."

He was standing in the hall leaning into her room through the half opened door. She motioned for him to come in. He sat down on the foot of her bed and faced her. Betty thought how solemn he always looked. His thinning hair and receding hairline accentuated a forlorn look. She studied his serious face for a moment. He looked down at his bare feet as if to block her analysis. "I was just writing my obituary," she said with a little grin. Frank's head shot back up, "What?"

"I was just sitting here wondering what people would

say about me when I'm gone. Seemed like a good time to write down some things I probably need to work on -- you know, to give who ever writes my real obituary some material to pull from." Her smile broadened.

"Oh," said Frank in his typical flat tone. This was an area Frank obviously had not given much thought to and certainly no planning.

"Are you leaving us soon?" It was a logical question.

"Who knows?" said Betty. "Back last fall I thought I was a goner for sure. In fact I wanted to die. But then, my new favorite word came floating into my life - remission. I think all this coughing is because my lungs are trying to clear up." Betty glanced down at her notebook. "Sorry for all the racket."

"What do you want people to say about you when you're gone Frank?" Betty changed the focus. She was good at that.

"Never thought about it much. I haven't had much of a life, I guess."

"Never too late to start," Betty said. She dug her feet into the carpet and pushed her back into the chair and squirmed. After a moment she said, "I definitely see some gaps in my obituary. Want to hear what I have so far? Then you'll see what I'm against. I want to make as many of these things reality in my life --before I check out."

"Sure" Frank said feeling like he was being let in on some important secret.

Betty cleared her throat and took a sip of water before she began. "Elizabeth Barrett Bishop was found dead in her late model red convertible spots car Friday." She glanced at Frank and grinned. Then she continued. "Her death was sudden. Apparently she had been overcome with joy!" Betty glanced at Frank and grinned. She was enjoying this. "Her favorite people on earth are in charge of a party this afternoon at the beach where Betty's ashes will be spread. There will be free hot dogs and drinks for everyone." Betty stopped and looked at Frank who was grinning back at her. She continued, "Betty was a devoted mother." Betty stopped and looked at Frank. "You can see why this list will need some work?" Frank nodded slowly.

"What do you think a devoted mother means?" she asked Frank in earnest. He was not expecting the question.

"I know more about what it is *not* than what it is, I guess," he said.

"Maybe a devoted mother gets Mother's Day cards and a Christmas visit or gift or something like that?" Betty suggested.

"At least," Frank said.

"OK," said Betty, "I'll work toward that."

"You already had the Christmas visit," Frank offered. "So now you just need to work on that Mother's Day card."

"Unsolicited?" she asked and they nodded in agreement. Frank was beginning to get into this.

"...She was a child of God." Betty was reading again. "That's something I heard on the radio the other day," she said. "I was just born again, Frank. Did you know that? So I guess I'm a child of God."

Betty contemplated the darkened windows. After a long pause said, "It seems to me that adults are always trying to get back to being a child of God--all their lives. It's a funny thing but I think that's what Rachel is trying to do right now. Rachel and me – daughter and mother --. We are both the same age, spiritually speaking. That's weird isn't it?" Frank shrugged at her question. "We're both so full of shame—how do you cure shame, Frank? Can't take a pill." Her words were slow and thoughtful. "How do you cure feeling bad about who you *are*?"

Frank knew he was a paying member of the *shame club*. He suddenly felt like jumping up and running out of the room. But he didn't. He forced himself to sit still and listen. Frank, despite all the bad choices in his life, was a gifted listener.

"The key seems to be having someone you trust and respect to give you the message that you deserve to be taken seriously as a person. Kenneth gave me that message. God, I loved that man--I just didn't have him long enough." Betty's eyes filled with tears as she looked over at Kenneth's picture. Frank waited for her to continue. "I guess some folks get acceptance from their parents--you know when they are young children." She looked at Frank, "I don't think you got it there, did you?" He drew his lips into a tight line and shook his head *no*.

"If you don't get it when you are a little kid from

your family, sometimes you get it from a teacher ∣ coach, growing up--you know. But sometimes we don't even get it there." She was looking out of the darkened window again. "I watched a movie the other night that was the story of this black guy who had an awful time as a young kid--just awful—abused, you know. No parents, no one investing in him. But he went on to have a successful life—and it was because someone along the way took him in hand and believed in him. Accepted him for who he was. That's what Kenneth did for me."

"Isn't that what church is supposed to do?" asked Frank. "Accept us, forgive us for being flawed, imperfect people—take us in—believe in us?"

"Well if you find a church like that, let me know!" said Betty, "I'll join right up!" she was smiling again. "The problem is, church is made up of people just like me and you. And sometimes they forget that. You know, they get all cleaned up and start hanging out with the 'saved' bunch and forget who they were, or are--depraved people that are utterly dependent on God's Grace."

"Amen, Sister!" It was Laura. She had been standing in the doorway, unnoticed.

Surprise and annoyance battled it out in Betty's face. Laura disregarded it and said "your final art lesson starts right after I get a cup of coffee, Frank." She disappeared as suddenly as she had appeared.

Frank stood up to leave. "Betty, I'll be back a little later. I'd like to know what is next on your obituary-to-do-list." He disappeared into the dark hallway.

Betty sat quietly for a few moments. The first light of day was visible now on the horizon as she looked east from her bedroom window. After a few minutes she heard the back door close. She rose to stand by the window and look down. She watched as Laura and Frank walked slowly across the back yard toward the easels they had set up in the apple orchard. They both carried steaming cups in their hands with a small canvas tucked under their arms. Frank was holding a small box of paints and brushes. As Betty watched them she noticed the trail of footprints they left in the damp grass. It could have been a scene from some early morning rendezvous by Paul Gauguin and Vincent Van Gogh. Betty continued to watch them as they set up their canvases. They shared the box of paints but each one worked from their own pallets. Laura jabbed her brush at the horizon as if instructing Frank. Frank's head bobbed up and down, looking first at the horizon, then at his canvas, focused on translating what he saw into what he painted. Betty tried, but could not see either canvas.

Betty returned to the big blue chair and picked up the spiral notebook. She wrote *Dazzling...*she hesitated for a moment then struck through the word. She couldn't get into describing anything dazzling just at that moment. She pushed her back against the big blue chair again, trying to put pressure on the jabbing pain she felt there. At first it had been just a twinge, but now, it had turned into a sharp, jabbing, fiery pain. *Probably pulled a muscle coughing*, she thought.

****

Three hours later, Nancy slowly climbed the stairs

toward Betty's room. She had not heard Betty moving around and wondered if she might be taking a mid-morning nap. She knew Betty got up early. Frank and Laura were still in the backyard painting. It was a glorious mid-winter morning, clear and cool. Nancy had just returned from taking Bernie for a walk. Coming back to the house she retrieved the local paper from her driveway and lingered over an article Camille Carmichael had written for the editorial section. The headline was *Annual Seafood Festival and Blessing of the Fleet.*

Nancy enjoyed knowing Camille. The mystery woman at 14 Honey Bear Lane was no longer a mystery. The life casting session had been fun and enlightening. Nancy knew she would be going by to visit Camille often. And she could hardly wait to see the finished bronze busts. Nancy had told Laura the busts would have to spend 6 months on Rainman Island then 6 months in Atlanta each year. The twins had agreed that the bronze statues would not become geographically separated, as they had.

Nancy felt relaxed and happy and stopped on the stairs for a moment enjoying the silence. Just at that moment, she thought, her world seemed perfect. She took a mental snapshot of it -- Frank and Laura out there, companionably engrossed in painting and her newest best friend asleep upstairs— in remission. She felt alive and fully vested in her own life. *Whenever we give love to someone else, to share our strength for their weakness, it does not diminish us, but always gives more than it takes.*

Nancy tapped lightly on Betty's door then quietly peeped in. She saw Betty sitting in the big blue chair. Her eyes were closed and her head sagged so that her chin touched her chest. *Sound asleep* Nancy thought. She tiptoed over quietly, wondering what would be the best way to wake her. She noticed something odd about the way Betty's hands lay to her side and one of her ankles was twisted back. *Not a very comfortable looking position to sleep in,* Nancy thought. She touched Betty's shoulder. Betty did not respond. Instantly, Nancy knew something was wrong—very wrong. She shook her this time. No response. Betty's head lobbed over against the blue chair, her mouth hung open. She was unconscious.

Nancy took three long strides to the phone beside Betty's bed. She stood there for a moment in panic trying to remember Dr. Alice's number but could not. She ran down the steps and grabbed her cell phone from the charger. She fumbled the phone and dropped it twice before she finally found Dr. Alice's name in her contacts. Dr. Alice was 911 for the island. The phone rang twice before Dr. Alice answered, "Hi Nancy."

Nancy was almost screaming. "It's Betty, Alice. She's unconscious. What should I do?"

"Oh my God," said Alice. "I'm over at the clinic on Vancouver Island." Alice went silent for a moment, trying to think of all the options. Nancy started to ramble about how she looked - how she found her. "Calm down, Nancy. Get Frank to help you and get her over to the hospital in Comox, as quickly as possible. Don't panic. Call Big John and see where the launch is. I'll meet you there. Call me when you get to the landing at Comox."

Nancy hung up without saying goodbye. She quickly

found John Parker in her contact list and pressed call. He answered on the first ring. Nancy told him about Betty and asked him to come quickly. "I'm just pulling into Rainman now. Bring her to me. I'm turning the boat around." Nancy stumbled toward the back door and started screaming for Frank. Startled, Frank knocked over his easel, the wet paint smearing as his canvas slid into the tall, wet grass of the orchard. Frank came running toward the house. He slipped and fell in the wet grass, jumped up and continued to run toward the house. Nancy left the door open and ran back up the stairs. She screamed over her shoulder "It's Betty!"

Betty had not moved. Nancy put two fingers on Betty's neck feeling for a pulse. She had seen this done many times. She felt nothing. Frank entered the room and without being asked, he scooped Betty up in his arms. Her head flopped over on his shoulder. He took the steps two at a time down into the kitchen. Nancy was right behind him. Laura stood in stunned silence in the kitchen watching them hurry past her. Nancy grabbed her purse and glanced at her sister, suddenly needing her. An exchange of strength passed between them. Frank got into the front passenger seat of the car and held Betty in his lap like a child. She felt weightless to him. Nancy drove the five-minute trip to the landing in under three minutes. John was watching for them. The last car was moving off the ferry ramp onto the island. Only one car was in the ferry line in front of them. Nancy pushed the car into park, jumped out ran around to speak to the driver. She recognized Mrs. Fitzsimmons and told her briefly about Betty. Mrs. Fitzsimmons backed out of the ferry line immediately, giving Nancy's mission priority. "I'll catch the next one over - I'm in no hurry," she quickly told Nancy. Islanders knew the drill.

John brought the ferry about and headed out again at full speed. Thankfully the calm sea and bright clear day gave them no delays. Once underway, John gave controls over to his first mate and headed to Nancy's car. Frank was still holding Betty in his lap. John motioned for Frank to roll down the window near Betty's head. He reached in and tried to find a pulse in her neck. Nothing. He did not speak, he just slowly shook his head at Nancy and Frank, then removed his arm from the window.

Nancy called Alice again and gave her their E.T.A.

"Someone should call Rachel," said Frank while Nancy was still on the phone.

"Oh! And Alice, call Rachel. She'll be over at the school today."

Frank studied Betty as the boat slipped effortlessly toward Vancouver Island. "She's not breathing, Mom." The words hit Nancy with such force that she stopped breathing herself for a moment. Then she took in a deep breath as if trying to will Betty to breathe. "Maybe we should lay her on the back seat and give her CPR," Nancy said.

"I think it's too late, Mom. She feels really cool." Frank pulled Betty closer to himself as he shifted his weight and locked his arms around her tiny form as if trying to keep her from escaping.

John made the 15-minute crossing in just 12 minutes. As they approached the Comox landing,

Frank and Nancy saw Dr. Alice running toward the boat. By the time John docked and tied off, Alice was on board with her skilled fingers searching Betty's neck for a pulse. She pulled the stethoscope from around her neck and listened to Betty's heart. She pulled back her eyelids, and then took out her cell phone.

"Don't need the sirens, Jim. There's no rush." The ambulance driver acknowledged her instructions. Dr. Alice looked over at Frank and Nancy.

"Sorry folks, she has passed." Nancy heard the words in disbelief. She wanted to argue with Alice. She wanted to say mean things to her like she was just some second rate, island doctor that didn't know death from a donut! She wanted to say, Well do something! Or let's just wait until a real doctor looks at her over at Comox. But she did not say anything. She just sat there and repeated the words to herself - *"she has passed—passed—passed where?—passed what?"* The words tumbled around in her mind. She could not process them.

Nancy followed Dr. Alice's car that in turn followed the ambulance on the short trip from Buckley Bay landing to Comox General Hospital. Frank and Nancy sat in numb silence in the waiting room as Betty's lifeless body was pushed through the double doors and disappeared. A few minutes later Dr. Alice reappeared and simply said "She's gone, apparently a pulmonary embolism." She looked down at Nancy. "That's a blood clot, Nancy, in her lung."

Nancy moved her head slowly acknowledging what was being said to her. "No reason for you to stay here. She's not here anymore." Alice knew the look on Nancy's face very well --shock, disbelief, anger, and guilt. Every negative emotion you can feel would likely surface over the next few hours.

"Do you need me to help you get back home?" she offered.

Frank said, "We'll be fine. I'm a little worried about Rachel though. She'll take this hard."

"I'll come by this afternoon and check on her. Will she be at your house, Nancy?"

"Probably." Nancy did not look forward to dealing with Rachel.

"Do you have any idea of arrangements for Betty?" Alice asked.

"Not really." Nancy hesitated for a moment then said, "Send her over to Daniels, I guess. Frank and I will stop by there on our way home and give them some preliminary information. Rachel will need to get involved in the details."

Frank remembered the last conversation he had with Betty. "Speaking of details, she told me she wanted to be found dead in a late model red sports car, overwhelmed with joy."

Both Nancy and Alice shot him a look. They both thought he had suffered some sort of psychotic break at the trauma of Betty's death. "Honest, it's what she told me just this morning. I heard her coughing, went in to check on her and she was writing her obituary - seriously! I'm not making it up," he said. "Mom, I'll show it to you when we get home. It's in that little spiral notebook she writes in all the time."

"A red spots car?" Nancy looked up at Dr. Alice. Alice couldn't help it. Her hand flew to her mouth as she tried to stifle a laugh. But it didn't work. She could not contain the laughter. Nancy started laughing, too, then crying, and then laughing again. Her boiling emotional *teapot* had found a release valve.

"Rachel, it's Dr. Alice. I have some bad news," Alice's voice sounded strange to Rachel, metallic and foreign. Like someone speaking to her from far away.

"Your mom passed peacefully this morning." Alice waited for some response. She only heard a thump. Rachel had fainted. Alice disconnected the call and quickly called the school. She knew the headmistress there very well.

"Margaret, you need to go check on Rachel Hollingsworth. I'm not sure exactly where she is but I'm pretty sure she has fainted. Her mom died this morning."

"I will go immediately," said Margaret.

Rachel had come around enough to make it into a chair in the teachers lounge. That's where Margaret found her. She was not crying. Margaret thought that she just looked stunned, pale, and disheveled as usual. She was still holding the phone.

"If you'd like to make a call" the mechanical voice broke into the silence. Margaret deftly removed it from her hand and pushed the off button. Then she went over to the sink and filled a Styrofoam cup with tap water. She offered the water to Rachel. Rachel did not notice. She seemed to be concentrating on the tiny specks of color in the grey tile floor. Margaret did not speak. She pulled a chair up close to Rachel and took her hand. They sat that way in silence.

Margaret waited for Rachel to speak, to question, to cry. Margaret herself had recently lost her mother. She vividly remembered the feelings of confusion and disorientation, even though they had expected her mother's death for days. She remembered reading that the relationship between parent and child is the most complicated relationship a person will ever have, even more than between husband and wife. When a parent dies, you lose not one relationship, but several: friend, parent, and mother... There tends to be more unresolved conflicts in these multiple relationships. Margaret didn't know anything about Rachel's relationship with her mother. She didn't know much about Rachel at all, except that she was quiet and withdrawn but dependable and good with the children, especially the needy ones.

"I'll drive you home, when you're ready, Rachel. Is there someone for me to call to come and be with you?" Rachel looked at Margaret as someone would look at a stranger on a busy street. "Call Frank Hogan. See if he can come."

By 3 p.m. Rachel was sitting at home. The clear day had disappeared into thunderstorms around 2:30. She had spoken to Frank and he had promised to come to her as soon as they got back home. She felt comforted that someone cared. She felt hope. knock on the door made her jump. She hoped it was Frank. It was not. Standing there under rain soaked umbrellas was Claudia Jacobs and Susan Weaver.

"Nancy called us," Claudia said. "Everyone is shaken up by this. We came to see if we could help." Susan reached over and laid her hand on Rachel's shoulder causing Rachel to flinch a little. Susan looked directly into Rachel's eyes.

"We're going to pray you through this, Rachel," said Susan. Her confident words penetrated the fog that had crept into Rachel's mind. *Why hadn't she thought to pray*? She did not know, but just at that moment, she wanted to pray more than anything in the world.

"Everything seems strange and empty, and everything I think and do is in a fog. I feel like I'm losing my way," she said.

They stood in a circle of three in Rachel's tiny living room holding hands. Susan began to pray God's promises for Rachel. She quoted from the Psalms and from the Prophets. Scripture after scripture pushed their way Heavenward. Images of her life with and without her mother started to emerge in Rachel's mind. There had been so much disappointment between them—so much anger-- Rachel's anger. For most of her life she had felt powerless and often humiliated that her own mother would leave her. And now she had left her again. Death was the ultimate abandonment and once again, without even saying goodbye.

As Susan prayed, Rachel, for the first time that day

Tears streamed down her face, but [she did] not let go of the hands that held hers. [The]y stopped praying and went into the [kitchen. S]itting around the table, they heard the rumble of thunder moving closer and closer. Rain came down in sheets. Claudia could hardly see out of the kitchen window the rain was so heavy.

Suddenly Rachel began to cry out to God, asking Him to show her why she had never been the daughter Betty wanted and why Betty had never been the mother she wanted. Wave after wave of emotion surfaced on her pleas to God. And then she grew quiet. It was a natural quiet like a child that has finally cried itself to sleep. There was no more emotion left in Rachel. Peace filled all three of them as the rain slacked to a trickle and ran down the windows.

Susan looked at Claudia, and then they both looked at Rachel. "The Comforter has come, Rachel," said Claudia. "Can you feel Him?" Rachel nodded.

"Rachel," said Susan, "the Bible is full of characters that were good people but bad parents. There are lots of stories about people who made huge mistakes and hurt others. Why our entire Western culture is founded on people like that! We are all screwed up." She laughed a little. "You are far from alone in agonizing over the relationship you had with your mother." She hesitated and looked down at the floor thinking how she should continue. Looking up again she said, "I am thankful Rachel that none of us have to be perfect to be loved by God. Your mother is in Heaven. She has now been made complete and perfect. In other words, Rachel, she just won the lottery! Praise be to God!"

Rachel smiled weakly, "I'll try always to remember that, Dr. Weaver."

On that upbeat note they left, promising to come back by the next evening. As they pulled out onto Peterson Point Road, they passed Frank, heading toward Rachel's house, driving way too fast on the rain slick road. They both recognized him.

"What do you make of that?" Claudia asked.

"Two wounded souls trying to console each other is my guess," said Susan.

"Drop me off over at Nancy's," Claudia said. "She's home if Frank is. I'll get Jim to come over and pick me up after while."

"It's me!" announced Claudia a few minutes later as she let herself into Nancy's kitchen.

"Well, it's about time!" said Nancy getting up from the kitchen island to receive the hug she anticipated from her dearest friend.

"Pour me a cup or a glass of whatever you're having. This has been one hell of a day!"

Laura responded and quickly sat a glass of California Merlot in front of Claudia.

"We were just about to toast Betty," said Laura.

"What a gal." They lifted their glasses and chimed in together, "Yes, what a gal."

The Kiss, The Letter

Frank entered without knocking. He rushed into Rachel's living room and she ran into his arms. They stayed that way for a while, clinging to each other. Then he pulled her back and kissed her, hard on the mouth. The kiss had been a long time in coming. They had both daydreamed about it, but this was a huge step for both of them, and they knew it. Frank kissed Rachel again, then again. The heat began to rise between them. Frank pushed her away and held her at arms length. He didn't speak; he just looked at her, trying to read her mind. She stared back. A tidal wave of feelings had just emerged from her while she prayed with Claudia and Susan. Now another tidal wave of very different feelings swept over her. She floated helplessly in them.

Finally she spoke, barely above a whisper. "I have often heard people say that the worst day of their lives was also the best day of their lives." She hesitated then looked again into Frank's dark eyes. "Today, I guess I have experienced it."

He drew her back into his arms. At that moment, he never intended to let her go again. It had been a long time since either of them had felt *hope*—or wondered about a future. They only had a past. But the future suddenly seemed much more important to both of them than the past. Rachel felt shy and attractive and lovable and horrible, all at the same time. Frank was also filled with mixed emotions--feelings of being appreciated and valued along with knowing he had just lost his best friend. He felt loved. They had both stepped into that sparkling world of infatuation. Love, true, deep and committed, promised to follow. Something shifted in both of them that afternoon.

It had been dark for almost an hour when Rachel asked Frank if he was getting hungry. "I can eat any time," he said and grinned at her. "When you've been homeless as much as I have…"

She went into the kitchen and busied herself making scrambled eggs and toast. "I've got something for you," Frank said as he sat down at the kitchen table. "Your mom kept a diary or journal, not sure what you would call this. Looks like she started writing in it about the time she came to live at Mom's." He laid the spiral notebook down on the table. Rachel glared at it from across the room.

After they had eaten, she reached over and with one hand touched the notebook and with the other hand touched Frank's arm. "My future and my past, in my hands at the same time," she said.

"I only know a little of what's in there, Rachel. She read some of it to me this morning. For her funeral she wants a big, loud beach party, with beer and hot dogs."

Rachel smiled. "Sounds like her."

"I guess you will want her cremated. She said something about scattering her ashes on the beach."

Rachel's eyes suddenly filled with tears. "I hadn't really thought about that. I guess I will need to decide, won't I."

"I'm afraid so," he said tenderly. "Mom and I went ahead and had her moved to Daniels this afternoon. We told them you would call them tonight or in the morning about the arrangements." Silence filled the room. Frank waited.

"I wonder how much all of that will cost. I don't have but a little bit of savings. Under $1000."

"We went by Daniels' after we left the hospital—just to make sure we understood what was needed from you or from us. They told us that your mother had paid for her cremation right after Kenneth died. I guess she got a little money from his insurance, or something. Anyway, it's all paid for.

And there's more, Rachel. They gave us this envelope. It's addressed to you."

Tears streamed down her face as she tore open the envelope. Inside was a copy of a burial policy along with a hand written note.

My dear Rachel,

When you read this, I'll be gone. And while it is true that I have left you again, it's not like it was before. This time, you will know where I am and can talk to me anytime you want to. I'll be listening. And I'll be with Kenneth. Wherever he is, that will be heaven for me. I have been so sick these past couple of years that I no longer fear death. It is my friend. I am so glad we have had the last few months together, especially the time with Nancy and Frank. Together, we met the LORD! Together, Rachel! You met Him first then led me to Him. Child, who would have ever guessed that maybe that was the very reason we were put together in this life. I know I have been a disappointment to you - not been the mother you wanted or needed, but I always loved you and Robert.

Always. I read the other night that the greatest fear a child can have is that she is not loved, and rejection is the hell that she fears. You were not rejected Rachel, not ever. I loved you always. Always. I was an addict. I have punished myself for my failures far more than you will ever know. I pray that Robert will come to know the LORD in the days ahead, and heal. Please help him Rachel, he is as hurt by my mistakes as you have been. Forgive me, please.

Rachel still felt confused and numb. Maybe in the days to come she would find a place to tuck each word her mother had written, bandage up her wounds with them, but she wasn't ready for that just now, not today.

Rachel handed the letter to Frank to read. "There is no date on this but I bet she did this the same day we all went over to Comox for doctors appointments and shopping and stuff. She was gone about two hours. She didn't tell us where she was going—acted mysterious. We all thought it had to do with Christmas shopping."

"What's this?" Frank handed Rachel a small note that had slipped to the floor when Rachel had ripped opened the envelope. Across the letterhead was the name and address of a law firm. Betty had scribbled a note across the bottom. "The house is yours."

Rachel looked wide-eyed at Frank. "Mother left her house to me. I guess these attorneys have the papers and stuff."

"Looks like it," said Frank. "Looks like I'm going to be hanging out with an heiress!" He was smiling so big every tooth in his mouth could be seen. Rachel could not hold back the joy. A smile slowly spread across her face.

The Woes Of Wine

The wine sodden women finally turned their conversation from Betty and Rachel to the peeping Tom next door (or peeping Danny to be exact.) "Betty's solution," Nancy said with a snort of laughter, "was to put a trip wire along the back of the house, and when it was tripped, lights and sirens and stuff would come on and in her words - scare the hell out of him!" Bursts of laughter bounced around the room. "I like that idea very much," said Laura, slightly slurring her words. "I might try that myself. You know all those good-looking, intelligent, rich guys that keep hanging around my house. There are just way too many to deal with!"

"Now seriously, girls--we have to be s-e-r-i-o-u-s!" As Claudia was saying this her phone went off in her purse. The ring tone was Ray Charles "I Can't Stop Loving You." They all squealed in laughter like schoolgirls.

"That would be Jim," said Claudia. She stood weaving back and forth to the music.

"Well answer it stupid!" said Nancy.

"I Can't Stop Loving You" Claudia sang into the phone, half crocked. "Unhuh," Claudia said. She listened for a couple of minutes and then hung up the phone. "Jim's coming over. Thinks we need to go out to dinner and get something on our stomachs besides the Merlot."

When Jim arrived 10 minutes later, he took one look at the three women standing in the driveway, their arms folded around each other like a Radio City Rockettes dance line and knew what he had to do. "Just in time," he said, getting out of the car. "They arrest people for less than this public display of ..." he broke off. Not sure what to call their *condition* Jim hustled them into his car. "Next stop, the Sleeping Pig," he said. "Black coffee for everyone."

The noise level in the Sleeping Pig came up a notch or two when their party arrived. "Hi Sandy" said Jim. "I've got some adult delinquents here. Need some coffees."

"Beer all around!" shouted Laura, caught up in the moment.

Big John was sitting at the bar when they came in. He looked at them and grinned. "Quite a day these ladies have had, Jim," he said and raised his hand in a welcoming gesture.

"Come on over and join us, please," Jim said, "I can use the sobriety."

John smiled and moved his beer over to the table where Jim had settled the girls.

"John, I think the only one here you haven't met is Laura. She's Nancy's twin and visiting from Atlanta."

"Hiddy, Mam." It was John's best effort at a southern accent. He slid into the booth next to

Laura.

"Hiddy sir," Laura shot back at him. Laura didn't know if it was her inebriated condition or not but she found Big John to be very attractive. Of course, she found most any single man over 50 attractive. "Tell me, John," her words slurred, "whatever happened to that peeping Tom that lives with you?"

The table went silent. Claudia, Nancy and Jim all knew that Laura had just landed a punch in John's gut with her words.

John looked at Laura, heat rising in his cheeks, "He went back east to live with his grandmother for awhile. I thought it was best."

Laura felt the tension at the table. She was not accustomed to being ostracized. She had more often been in the company of people where the wilder your comments, the more you fit in. This was not her crowd and she knew it. Even her twin sister looked disgusted with her at that moment.

Their sandwiches and coffee arrived and they ate mostly in silence. Jim used his most effervescent personality and tried to engage John in talking about the upcoming Seafood Festival and the annual pre-festival party at Camille Carmichael's house. All the local artists and business owners were invited and it was usually a great turnout and lots of fun. John talked a little but as soon as he had finished his dinner, he excused himself. Said he was "all in" and left.

The drive back to Nancy's house was quiet. Laura and Nancy went immediately up to bed. Frank came in sometime later, surprised that no one was up. He had a lot of news to share for a change and wanted a listener or two.

Wednesday broke grey and rainy. Laura had retrieved Frank's canvas from the grass and sat it on an easel in Nancy's office to dry. Hers was sitting on a nearby chair, unfinished. Frank rose before daylight as usual and was on his second cup of coffee when Laura made it downstairs.

"This is going home day for you isn't it Aunt Laura?"

"Sure is, Son," she said. Her southern accent seemed stronger to Frank this morning. He groped for something to say. Small talk was not his forte.

"Had a good time?—well except for Betty dying yesterday, and all," Frank sounded awkward.

"Yes, I've had a very interesting time." She seemed distracted, nervous.

"Ah, Frank, what time do you think John next door has to get up and go to the Ferry?"

"Why, Aunt Laura? You don't have to go until this afternoon. Mom told me."

"Because I owe him an apology and I want to go over there—and I don't know if he is still home." She hesitated searching for the words to continue. "I shot my mouth off last night and made a fool of myself and well, I just don't want to leave Rainman Island with *that* hanging over me."

"Oh," Frank said without really understanding. "I

think this is his day off, Aunt Laura. Wednesday. He runs only twice today, one morning and one afternoon on Wednesdays in the winter. Nobody seems to complain. I think his first mate runs those for him, but I'm not sure. You want me to go over and knock and see if he's home?"

"No! I need to do that myself," Laura snapped. She rummaged around in one of the lower cabinets until she pulled out two Styrofoam cups with lids. She filled them with freshly brewed coffee. She stuck two of the Danishes Nancy had taken out of the freezer the day before into a plastic bag and headed out the door. Frank watched without saying a word.

"Oh!" said Laura, turning toward Frank. "The painting you did is excellent, and I'm not just being nice. I mean it. You should look into doing some more. You are gifted, Frank. Seriously." With that, she was out the door and heading across the driveway with her peace offering.

Frank was stunned by Laura's compliment. He had always loved to paint and draw, but never thought he was any good at it. He walked into the office and looked carefully at both of the canvases Laura had put there. He could see where Laura had tried to fix the grass smears on his. He sat down at his mother's desk and pulled out a pencil and piece of paper. He began to sketch Rachel's face. She was constantly on his mind and he wished he could see her right that minute. He was so engrossed in sketching he did not hear his mother moving toward the kitchen. It was only when she dropped the bottle of aspirin all over the floor and groaned, that he shot to his feet to see if she was OK. Nancy stood there leaning up against the counter looking at the aspirin all over the floor. Bernie stood near her feet looking confused.

"Those aren't for you Bernie," said Frank quietly pushing the dog away. He went for the broom with a smile on his face. "Need help, Mom?" he said over his shoulder with a grin. She looked at him and scowled. "It's nice to see you do something human, Mom," he said as he swept the aspirin up into a dustpan.

"Too much wine last night. Where is my sister?"

"She's over at Big John's apologizing." Frank headed toward the trashcan with the aspirin.

"Give me a couple of those before you throw them away, would you?" she said frowning. He did.

Two cups of coffee later, Nancy began to feel a little more comfortable. "Frank, I don't know what came over me last night. Three glasses of wine and I was looped! I guess it was a whiplash effect of losing Betty—not eating anything all day--just running on adrenaline. I really felt lousy when I came home. The house is sure going to seem empty without her. And now I'm going to lose Laura, too." Frank nodded.

"You know, Betty only lived here for a little over two months, but—I came to honestly love her. She helped me change. I'll never be the same."

"Me neither," said Frank. Nancy moved into the living room to try and make herself a little more comfortable. Frank followed her. He plopped down on the floor near the fireplace and started slowly poking at the lumps of cold ashes with the poker.

"What do you mean, Frank--that she helped you change?" Nancy asked quietly, gently rubbing her temples. "Can you put it into words?" She was always trying to draw him out, to piece together the missing years.

"Ah, you know I'm no good with a lot of words, Mom." He hesitated, seemingly absorbed in watching the small particles of dust rising from the disturbed ash. Light filtered into the room through the large front windows. The clock on the mantel ticked. "But when I first came here, there she stood in that pink bathrobe." He smiled at the memory. "She sure was a tiny little thing." Silence again. Nancy waited. "She looked like I felt, I guess—lost or out of place or something like that." *Tick, tick, tick.*

"She seemed to know how I felt. She could look right into me--you know--like inside me." Frank poked gently into another lump of ash. "She talked to me, treated me like I was important." Frank glanced up at his mother and saw the expression on her face change. He sensed he had said enough, but pushed on a little further. "I guess I thought, ah... I thought *you had to take me in*--but she didn't." Nancy did not speak.

She let the heavy silence surround her and it felt good. *Yes, it felt good to sit there in the silence with him. She could reach over and touch his arm if she wanted to. Only a few weeks ago seeing him again was something she thought would never happen.*

Nancy got up from her chair and sat in the floor next

to Frank. They sat there in the floor together for a while. Nancy watched as Frank poked at the little heaps of ash. *Tick, tick, tick.*

"Can I talk to you about Rachel?" His question caught her off guard. An image of Rachel's face popped into Nancy's mind; her big eyes glaring at both of them sitting there. "Sure." Nancy thought she already knew what he was going to say.

"I like her," he said simply.

Nancy smiled a motherly smile at him. A picture of Rachel driving down the road on her scooter like a bat out of hell popped into Nancy's mind. She wondered what on earth Frank saw in Rachel. She surely did not see it! Stringy hair, overweight, clothes that looked like she had slept in them. Nancy caught herself. She reminded herself that it was usually better to ask a question than to give advice – and she was full of advice! She tried to think of a question that would help Frank -- throw him a line so to speak. She sensed he felt awkward. She prayed silently to the God of love to help her.

"I mean" Frank looked down at the floor, a slight blush rose in his cheeks. "With her mother dying and all, I guess it's not the right time to…ah…get into a…relationship, is it?"

Please dear Lord, let me answer this right, she continued to pray. She waited for an answer. Frank looked over at her. He shifted himself uneasily on the floor. He had laid the poker down against the hearth and was looking straight at her. He knew she had heard him. And then it came to her. Something Betty had said just a few days earlier.

Nancy spoke slowly, almost in a whisper. "Frank, Betty and I were talking the other day and she told me something that I think is good to remember, always. Maybe this applies to your question." *Nancy thought how ironic it was that she was about to quote the worst mother on earth, while trying to be the best.* Well, at least, that's what Betty called herself whenever motherhood came up in conversation between them.

"She said," Nancy continued, "I can almost hear her scratchy, smoker's voice--she said that--" Nancy slowed down, pronouncing each word emphatically. "Life is short. Life is fragile. Loving someone is always the right thing to do. Always. Because love is from God. And when we give our love to someone, we honor God -- reflect His light. When our love is unselfish, that is." Nancy's mind searched her own heart and she continued. "Find ways to love her and help her become the woman she was meant to be. That's what I mean by unselfish love. She'll love you back for that. And you know Frank, you might just be God's man for the job."

Frank's solemn face contorted into a lopsided smile. Nancy felt relieved. For once, she thought she had said the right thing, at the right time.

Laura banged the door shut. "We're in here," Nancy said, lifting her voice toward the back door.

Laura appeared in the doorway looking a little odd--disheveled.

"What!" Laura almost shouted as Nancy looked her

up and down.

"Nothing" Nancy blurted back.

"How's John? Did you apologize?" Frank asked his aunt in a soft, monotone voice.

"I did, but he, well, ah—he's a nice man, and well-- he and I... ah...ah...I am forgiven, let's just leave it at that!" She seemed nervous or excited or something. Frank and Nancy looked at each other mystified. "I'm going upstairs to shower and pack. Time I went back to civilization." Laura quickly turned and disappeared up the steps.

Frank and Nancy looked at each other. "No clue" Nancy said shrugging her shoulders. "I'll pull it out of her on the way to the Duke's Point Ferry this afternoon." *But she forgot to ask.*

Tommy

March blew in like a lion. Rain storms had hit the island almost every day and left the earth saturated. The creeks and rivers of Rainman Island were raging full. Toppled trees could be seen here and there. Spring seemed to have hurled herself at the small island. Nancy spent Valentine's evening with Jim and Claudia at a fundraiser for the local theater group. Many people had asked about Betty. Nancy had begun to summarize the time she had spent with Betty into a small paragraph and dispensed it when asked. *People were mostly just curious. They did not really want to hear about the transformation that had taken place in both of them. The pain of loss simply cannot be communicated.* Nancy still missed Betty every day.

Laura's daily letters had resumed. Little stickers covered the envelopes. A hand written note was scrawled across the bottom of today's letter:

Got dirt fever yet? I've fallen under the spring spell again. I've been to the Garden Shop three times this week and it's only Tuesday!

Nancy laid the letter down on the kitchen island. "What happened to February?" she asked Bernie, who made no comment. Camille Carmichael had called to say the bronze busts would be in around March 15th. Nancy was eager to see them. While Camille had Nancy on the phone she mentioned getting a call from Laura.

"Your sister thinks your son has some significant artistic talent. She wanted me to take a look at some of his work. Maybe he'd like to have a booth at this year's Seafood Festival. Could give him some visibility." Nancy thought about what to say to her. She hadn't seen much of Frank since Betty died. He was spending most of his time at Rachel's house -- day and night. So far as she knew, Frank hadn't painted anything other than the small smeared canvas now hanging on the wall in her office.

"I'll let him know about the Seafood Festival option," she said.

As she hung up the phone, she rehearsed the conversation in her mind. She wondered what Frank would choose to do with his life. He had not asked her for any money. She had no idea how he was living. She assumed Rachel was feeding him.

"We're back on our own, Bernie," Nancy said wistfully. " *Dear Lord,*" prayer drifted in and out of her thoughts like clouds moving through a summer sky. *What else do you have for me to do? I feel more alone now than ever. You gave me Betty then you took her home. Frank is on a revolving door basis. But I sure do thank you for the time I have had with both of them. Is there someone else like Betty that can*--she smiled, *come and help me?* Her thoughts drifted away from prayer again and into the day that lay ahead of her. Ferry, hospital, grocers, ferry, and home -- same as last week and the week before. She sighed deeply then busied herself getting ready for her day. Bernie watched with interest.

At 6 p.m. that evening Nancy turned again onto Honey Bear Lane. The day had turned out warmer than usual and a light fog was beginning to rise from the cool, rain soaked earth. Nancy loved every season on 'her' island, but early spring always brought to her a sense of awe. Forsythia bushes had just started to flower. *In another week or so they would shout their spring message loud and clear. The proud daffodils, with their yellow and white trumpets would sound off at the front of the spring parade. They would selfishly grab all of the attention if it were not for the tulips. They rode in next like beauty queens on a parade float bobbing and nodding their heads as onlookers reveled at their beauty.* Nancy smiled as the images of a 'spring parade' played in her thoughts. *Bringing up the rear*, she amused herself sounding like a radio announcer at the Rose Bowl Parade, *were the azaleas and dogwoods!* Dogwoods always made her think of Easter. She reminded herself to look up the legend of the dogwood tree when she got home. Easter was coming early this year. *I need to make some plans,* she thought. *Invite some people over, have a cook out or something.*

March 14

Dear Laura,

Seems to me that I've been attending a lot of funerals lately.

Nancy looked through the dark windows of her office. She felt tired and lonely. She wondered what her own funeral would be like. She pushed the thoughts from her mind and continued to write.

Laid to my rest sounds pretty good to me at this moment. I was thinking...we never really know when our time is up, so, I was thinking... maybe we need to make some funeral arrangements...you know, what songs we want sung—how we want it done --things like that. You told me once that you want your ashes put in a giant firecracker and shot off over your backyard. I think I'll have jugglers. Now don't laugh. As I understand it, juggling first made an appearance in ancient Egypt at funerals. The juggler's balls were used to represent birth, life, death and the afterlife. I want the afterlife one painted gold. I don't really care what colors the others are. And on my tombstone, or whatever marker may be handy, please have inscribed:

"End of construction, thanks for your patience."

Camille Carmichael called today and said the bronze busts should be here tomorrow. You've got to come back to the island and see them. Obviously I will have custody for the remainder of this year... and possession is nine tenths of the law!

The house lay quietly around her as she tried to think of where to take this "conversation" with her sister. She tried to write Laura something every week. She knew Laura loved to get mail. She'd tried several times to interest her in email, but Laura refused to touch a computer. More often, she just picked up the phone.

The familiar sound of Rachel's motor scooter broke the silence. Nancy listened. From the sound of it, she was pulling into her driveway. Bernie barked a couple of friendly barks as they made their way to the kitchen door. She opened the door expecting to see Rachel but was a little surprised to see Frank.

"Where's Rachel?" She asked as he walked in. "I half expected to see you two together."

"She thought I should talk to you about—this-- alone." Frank's voice, the way he hesitated and beat around the bush when he spoke, had become familiar to Nancy over the past few months. But she couldn't shake the feeling when she was with him that something bad was about to happen, again. *Maybe it's just the same old feelings from years of disappointments with him*, she thought. Nancy had no idea what Frank was about to say but she wondered if it was about money.

"You got my attention," she said. "Want a sandwich or anything?" She asked him suddenly realizing that *making food was an activity that helped her feel in control.*

"No thanks. Rachel is cooking me something."

"Oh." A negative image of Rachel standing over a big black pot stirring something bubbling and green, with her hair hanging down in her face started to form in Nancy's mind. She mentally tried to block it.

"By the way Frank, Dr. Davis' office has called me again saying that you never followed up with the appointments and testing he recommended. What's up with that? Why aren't you following up?"

"Ah...you know...stuff gets in the way." It was an excuse.

"What stuff?" Nancy asked and then waved her hand as if to erase the question and said "never mind." She really did not know what her role was in Frank's life now. She knew he needed ongoing medical evaluation but he was an adult, and theoretically at least, capable of making his own decisions, including health decisions. She earnestly did not want to fall into the category of mothers who continuously come along behind their adult children and rescue them.

Frank quickly changed the subject. "Do you remember that kid I told you about over in Vancouver...Tommy, Tommy Johnson?"

Nancy nodded yes.

"Well Pat came by Rachel's last night. I don't know how he knew I'd be there - guess everyone on the island knows everything, huh?" He managed a slight grin. "Anyway, he said he'd gotten a call--said that the kid had been placed in protective custody. His mom was arrested for drugs. They couldn't find any other relative of hers. And I guess it was because Pat had located me recently, they called him to see if he still knew where I was. Tommy was asking for me." Frank's face looked earnest, like the time he told her that he had not lied to her about something. He had wanted her to believe in him. She had not.

"She's going to jail, Mom. This time, she'll be gone a long time—said the kid was trying to find me. He asked them to try and find me." Frank was repeating himself. He stopped and looked down at the floor, then back at Nancy. All the blood seemed to have drained out of his face. "Mom, it just broke my heart. He's a good kid. He's the reason I'm sober. I just want to find a way to help him." Frank hesitated. "They won't let me take him because I don't have a job or a house, or anything, but...*you could.*"

The words crashed down on Nancy like a wave. She could not even think of what to say. "Ah..." silence. *Talk about rescuing an adult child!*

Excuses started to flood into her mind. It started with the 'I'm toos'-- *I'm too old, I'm too busy, this island is too isolated.* Then she switched to the 'what ifs' -- *What if he got sick, ran away, didn't like me.*

Silence lingered between them for a moment as Nancy studied Frank's solemn face. "He wants *you*, Frank, not me. He knows *you*, not me."

Suddenly it dropped into Nancy's mind that this child might be another answer to her prayers, like Betty had been. It sure didn't feel like it. Then again, neither had Betty. A 5 year old abused kid. The thought of it made her sit down at the kitchen island. Frank continued to stare at her without speaking.

"I just don't know, Frank. I..." She closed her eyes, trying to focus her thoughts, hoping to hear from God. *Yes,* she thought, *some loud voice telling me what to do right here would be nice, Lord!*

Frank waited, looking first at her then down at the floor.

"I guess..., I guess I would be willing to try, but only under one condition." She raised her voice for emphasis. "You must understand that *you-are-responsible-for-him,* NOT ME. And what I mean by that Frank is that you ..." She dropped off into silence again. She did not trust Frank. He had never acted responsibly for anything. It had been so long since she had cared for a child that she could not even think of where to start. *What would he need*? She prayed, *Father if this child is not from You, for us, then please do not let him come.* She felt overwhelmed. Then these words came into her mind...*You are a vessel, Nancy, perfectly formed to hold My Spirit. I never intended for you to live by your own power or strength. You do not walk alone.*

Frank waited for her answer. "I guess I just need a little time to think it over," she said. Slowly Frank rose and walked toward the door. He stood there holding the doorknob in his hand, looking down at the floor.

"Frank," Nancy said. "I have often been tempted to fix things for people, especially for you." Nancy spoke slowly as if finding each word in her heart before she said it. "I used to think I could rescue people...you...and that..." Frank turned and looked at her. "But then Betty came along and through her God taught me that fixing people and their situations is not up to me. That's His job. Somewhere along the way I have learned that God meets people exactly at the point of their obedience to Him -- and often that seems like the point when things are at their worst – you know when things seem impossible." Frank nodded. Nancy paused for a moment the continued.

"I guess what I'm saying is that I have learned that God is able to take what looks like failure, or some impossible situation and offer it to us -- as an opportunity. He seems to love *second chances.* You and I are living in one of those *second chance* places right now." Frank looked steadily at Nancy.

"What does Rachel think about Tommy coming to the island?"

"She's reserved, hasn't said much. Pat just told us about him last night. I guess she's thinking it over, too."

"Well, I need to think it over, too," Nancy said. Frank opened the door and a gush of cool spring air flowed into the kitchen.

"We'll talk tomorrow, then?" Frank said, his eyebrows rose in a question.

"Tomorrow," said Nancy nodding her head.

She heard Frank grind the gears on Rachel's motor scooter before he backed out of the drive and rode away. "Come on, Bernie, we need a walk, rainy and cold, or not!"

Bernie strained at his leash as they walked along Honey Bear Lane. A light mist quickly covered her hat and jacket, but she didn't care. There was something cleansing, even joyful about walking in the rain. It was staying light longer now, Nancy thought as she sidestepped a puddle. Bernie growled at his own reflection in the next puddle, and Nancy had to laugh out loud. The heavy mist collected on her hat and began to drip off the brim. She prayed again, *Drench me Father, in Your love. Cover me in Your Grace until it fills every part of me. Help me to be yielded to every good thing you are doing around me. Is Tommy to be part of our family somehow? Is he Lord?* Nancy fell silent, waiting for some new insight, some word from her Father. Frank's face came to her. She thought about how he looked when he told her about Tommy. His eyes were pleading. Frank wanted this very much.
There's just so much I don't know. I should find out all I can about Tommy, his situation, and my liability, IF I should take this on, she thought, and then

caught herself. *Typical Nancy,* she told herself. *Research, get the facts.* Her left-brain was kicking in.

Nancy dreamed that night that she was sitting on a giant conveyor belt that stopped periodically so that a message or a gift could be *deposited* in her. She heard loud noises like hissing steam engines all around her. More than once she heard the loud cries of a child. The overall sense of the dream was that she was under construction. The conveyor belt loomed out in front of her, curving out of sight. Likewise looking backward she could only see where she had been. In her dream she knew that she was not able to control or even predict where the next *filling station* would be on her conveyor belt--or what would to be deposited -- joy or sorrow?

She woke feeling tired and restless. Even two cups of strong, gourmet coffee had failed to bring her around. *Is that what dreams do,* she wondered, *deposit their message or their gift in you then drop you off at the corner, abruptly. And most of the time you don't even remember what was 'deposited.'* She called Claudia but got no answer. She left a message. "I really need to talk to you. It's important, call me back—TODAY!"

"Hello Pat, it's Nancy Hogan calling. She spoke into Pat's voice mail. "I wanted to talk with you about Tommy Johnson, the boy you told Frank about last night. I wondered what is involved in bringing him to the Island." She made no indication that Frank had asked that Tommy live with her. "You know...I want to understand both the court process and any personal pros and cons that you might offer." She left her number.

She called Susan Weaver. "Not able to take your call just now. Please leave a message and have a blessed day." *Was everyone on the entire island gone?* She left another message then wandered into the empty living room. She looked out on a greening world. Leaves that had not been there yesterday now blocked her view. Life was literally bursting forth again. She grabbed her purse and she and Bernie climbed into her car. She was determined to beat the feelings of despair that were pushing in on her. Slowly she backed out of the driveway and headed toward Peterson Point.

A few minutes later she arrived at the cliffs. The walk along the top of these cliffs was magnificent in any kind of weather. The views were unique--not found anywhere else on earth, and they were only a few minutes from her home! The sheer beauty of this place was one of the reasons she stayed on the island—with all its inconveniences.

Bernie ran ahead, stopping every few seconds to either sniff or pee. There was no need to leash him. Few people even knew about this trail and those that did know, seldom came in March. She threw Bernie a stick. It arched over his head and he bounded toward it then clenched it in his teeth. He never retrieved anything, just grabbed whatever she threw and tried to play keep away. "You silly dog" she shouted at him, her feelings lifting rapidly. She walked to the edge of the cliffs and looked down at the ocean gently lapping 500 feet below. It's constant slapping against the volcanic rock of the cliffs did not seem to have changed anything since her very first visit more than 15 years earlier.

She stood there for a while letting the air push against her, taking deep breathes. Bernie's sudden sharp barking startled her from her thoughts and she wheeled around to see Pat Roberts walking quickly up the trail toward her. He was smiling broadly. She waited. Bernie ran over to him and started sniffing the leg of his pants.

"Supposed to have your animals on a leash out here in the park, Mrs. Hogan."

"Am I under arrest, officer?" She quizzed, returning his smile.

"Well, I guess I can let it go this time," he said playfully.

"Did you get my message?"

"Yeah. I was driving over toward the co-op and saw your car parked out here. Decided to take in a little of this beautiful spring day myself and walk up and talk to you about Tommy Johnson."

"Thank you, Pat," she said and meant it. "What do you think?"

Pat was quiet at first as he fell into walking beside Nancy. "I don't know if you know this or not--but I was a foster kid."

"My dad took off right after I was born apparently, and my mother..." Pat looked out at the open water. "She just couldn't handle me, I guess. When I was about 3 years old, she took me to an orphanage and left. I never heard from her again. The only reason I know even that much about where I came from is because the Sisters at the orphanage told me--when I was about 5. That's when they sent me to my first foster home." Pat hesitated and stared out at the blue outline of mountains on the horizon.

"I don't even know if I have brothers and sisters." Nancy was deeply touched. "The first foster family they sent me to was nice enough people, I guess, but I never felt at home there. I remember they made me eat everything on my plate and I hated a lot of it. Sometimes I would gag on that food and throw up.

I got passed around a lot after that. I remember the first thing I would do when I got to a new foster home was to find the telephone. I used to think that when that phone would ring, I would be moved to another home. Funny how kids imagine things." Nancy didn't speak. This was an experience of life in which she had no frame of reference. They walked on for a few minutes in silence.

"Mrs. Hogan, I don't know anything about Frank but I do know a little about you. I heard how you helped Betty Bishop. I knew her but I knew her husband Kenneth -- pretty well. I talked to her a couple of times after she came to live with you. Did you know that?" Nancy shook her head no.

"What are you trying to get at, Pat?" Nancy asked.

"I guess I'm saying that I believe every kid needs a fighting chance, but it takes more than food and a clean place to sleep. It takes an equal measure of love and discipline and a kid knows when that's offered and when it is not. I think that's the question you need answering before you check into what the court process is all about."

"Pat," Nancy said, "I'm still not sure what you are trying to tell me."

"Ok," Pat said, his voice taking on more of an authoritative tone. "Why don't you get Tommy over here for a visit. See how it goes. See if he likes you. I know he likes Frank, but Frank just strikes me as a little, well... Nancy finished his sentence for him "self-absorbed?"

"Maybe that's it," said Pat. "But someone like Frank, well, I mean someone that has dropped out of life for so long, you know, they very rarely find their way back, *entirely*. At least that's been my experience."

Pat stopped walking and looked at Nancy. "I've got to start back, but let me know what you decide. If you decide to be a foster parent for Tommy, you'll have to go through a certification process, background check, some training, that sort of thing. It'll take a few days, that's all. They are begging for foster parents everywhere. They'll even pay you a little each month for his room and board." Nancy still didn't speak.

Pat bid her goodbye and briskly walked away. Nancy turned and kept walking. After a few minutes the phone in her pocket rang. It was Claudia. "What's up?" she said.

"Pray with me Claudia. I think there's about to be a new man in my life. Got anything over at the shop in a size 5?"

April

Tommy sat securely strapped into the car seat Claudia found for him at a Salvation Army Thrift Store. Nancy's car inched along through the outbound ferry traffic at Horseshoe Bay on the mainland. She glanced up in her rear view mirror at the child sitting in the back seat. She thought he looked small for a 5 year old. Tommy was a handsome, mixed race child. Nancy thought he had gotten the best of both races: a mass of dark brown curly hair and big blue eyes, which were now closed.

The two days of court hearings and then meeting Tommy had not gone as badly as Nancy had feared. Actually Frank's court date on April 15th had gone exceedingly well, all things considered. It turned out that the Bench Warrant was for a "no show" on an old DUI traffic ticket Frank had managed to forget. It was resolved quickly with the very large check Nancy wrote. Frank learned that his driver's license had been suspended for years.

The judge laid out the process he'd have to go through to get it back, including DUI School. And while the back child support Tommy's mother said Frank owed was easily within Nancy's financial reach, she didn't have to pay it because the person bringing the case for child support was now in prison. And, to Nancy's surprise, since it was the same judge that had just given her temporary foster custody of Tommy, the back child support payments were waived. Except of course, for the court fees, which required another substantial check from Nancy.

With that behind them, early the next morning, Frank and Nancy had waited in the lobby of a large red brick building in downtown Vancouver for almost two hours while Tommy was brought to them. Frank immersed himself in an old copy of National Geographic magazine and was flipping through it when Tommy suddenly appeared in a doorway.

Nancy watched as a smile spread across Tommy's face and he shouted Frank's name. He jerked his hand from the woman that was escorting him and ran across the tile floor, leaping into Franks waiting arms. The black woman came up behind them and handed Nancy a small suitcase, a form to sign--and that was it. And, *That Was It!*

Nancy had easily worked through the foster parent certification program, and now...here she was...a foster parent, a foster grandmother, or... something to this child. She had no idea how this chapter of her life would play out. But she knew God was in it. And as she looked at Tommy's sleeping face in the rear view mirror, she silently repeated Philippians 2:13, the verse that God had used to answer her as she had prayed, asking Him what to do about Tommy. *For God is working in you, giving you the desire to obey Him and the power to do what pleases Him.*

The man in the car behind Nancy blew his horn! She looked in front of her and realized that the line of cars had moved up and she needed to roll forward. Tommy was startled awake by the blasted horn. She looked up at Tommy again in the mirror as she slowly moved forward. The dark circles under his eyes intensified their color. Bright blue. He had not smiled much at her so far. Every time she made eye contact with him, he just looked away. He needed time to adjust, they all did. With all her heart she believed that Christ was able to redeem even the most difficult situation. His plan for Tommy was perfect. She could relax.

For weeks she had immersed herself in reading all she could about the childhood fear of abandonment. It had changed the way she responded to Rachel and Frank. She realized that little Tommy's perspective of what was happening to him was very different from hers.

Frank pulled out the magazine he'd lifted from the waiting room and starting reading an article about Mt. Everest.

"Where is Mt. Everest, Mom?" he asked her. Nancy looked at him and shrugged. She had no idea.

A tiny voice from the back seat said, "That's in Nepal, isn't it?" Nancy looked wide-eyed at Frank. He returned the shocked look.

He turned to Tommy and said, "How'd you know that, buddy?" Tommy did not answer. Silence.

"Did you see it on TV?"

"I guess so," he said.

"Did you watch a lot of TV back there, Tommy?" Frank asked.

"It's all we had to do in that place. They wouldn't let us go outside," Tommy said. Nancy felt a shudder go up her spine.

Frank changed the subject. "When we get on board that big old boat over there," Frank pointed, "How about you and me taking a walk around -- see what's on that big ole' boat and maybe get some ice cream?" Tommy nodded but did not smile. It was impossible to know what he had lived through in the year since Frank left.

"Vanilla," Tommy said. "Make that two," Frank said. "Make that three," Nancy said. That got a little smile out of Tommy. And that was enough for now.

****

Betty's room had been transformed into what Nancy hoped would become Tommy's 'safe place,' a room that he would learn to call *his*. Nancy imagined 'keep out' signs appearing on the door at some point and sleep overs with his friends.

Nancy had felt like a young mother again as she and Claudia worked for days designing, painting and buying things for Tommy's room. Claudia's grandchildren had been called in a couple of times for consultation. Nancy replaced the twin beds with stackable bunk beds, assuming Tommy would want to sleep on the top. The big blue chair was replaced with a navy blue futon, which was turned to face a built in game and TV center. Shelves were installed to hold a multitude of action figures. Nancy and Claudia had practically cleaned out the action figure aisle at the Comox Wal-Mart. Even Tommy's bathroom had a fresh coat of paint. A boy friendly stool was placed in front of the sink and Claudia had come in laughing one night displaying an action figure that dispensed toothpaste! "I got Jim one, too!" she said, laughing.

The "dreaded" blue toile room that connected with Tommy's room through the adjoining bath had been transformed into Frank's new bedroom. The walls were now a masculine beige and every trace of blue toile had been removed.

When it was all finished, Nancy had stood in the middle of the new room for Tommy one night in her nightgown looking around, pleased with the outcome. *What else, Father, does this room need besides a little boy?* she prayed.

Like the slow rise of tidewaters, a thought developed in her mind. She sat down on the futon and opened the Bible she had placed on a table near the bunk beds. It was a child's Bible with lots of pictures. She remembered the passage in Deuteronomy about how we are to teach our children God's word. She found it in chapter 11 and began to read by the light of a small action figure lamp. Verse 19, *Teach [these words] to your children. Talk about them when you are at home and when you are away on a journey.* "Ah ha," she said, throwing her head back a little as if finally comprehending something.

Down stairs she flipped on the light in her office and fumbled around in a stack of printer paper until she found several sheets of paper that looked like parchment. With a felt tip pen she wrote out the verse that she hoped would become Tommy's life verse, that bit of scripture he would use all through his life to guide him. A simple verse he could center his life on, no matter what. It was the one that the Lord had used to affirm Nancy to this new assignment: *For God is working in you, giving you the desire to obey Him and the power to do what pleases Him. Phil. 2:13.*

Using the stool from Tommy's bathroom, Nancy stood on her tiptoes and taped the handwritten note above the door jam in his room. *I'll pick up a frame later,* she thought as she stood back and surveyed her work. *Now for the blessing. Father, Your will be done in this room, in this house and in all who dwell here. Amen.*

****

"Here we go" Nancy said as she opened the kitchen door for Frank and Tommy to enter. It had taken most of the day for them to get home. Lunch at McDonald's and a stretch on the playground had suited Tommy just fine. Bernie was barking and straining at his tether in the back yard. Nancy knew that Bernie had heard them and wanted to be a part of the action.

Nancy quickly disappeared into her room and busied herself unpacking from their trip, leaving Frank to show Tommy around. She hoped it would all seem a little less strange to him if he and Frank were alone for a while. After all, he was familiar with Frank, but he had never laid eyes on her before that morning.

After a few minutes Nancy realized how quiet the house was and stepped into her office, looking out the back windows. She watched Frank throwing a stick for Bernie and Bernie playing keep away with Tommy. Tommy chased after Bernie and Bernie allowed himself to be 'almost' caught, again and again. Tommy was laughing! The sound of it thrilled Nancy. She had not expected that a child's laughter could evoke such a strong feeling.

"Thank you *again*, Bernie," she whispered. She continued to watch them for a while, unobserved. *I'm a peeping Nancy.* She thought of Danny and Big John. Frank and Tommy settled down in the tall grass of the orchard. The apple trees had leafed out and the late afternoon sun sprinkled little patches of light everywhere. She had no idea what they were talking about. She assumed Frank was trying to explain to Tommy about the house, and her, and maybe himself and how it all fit together. She watched transfixed. Frank sitting shoulder to shoulder beside Tommy. A grown man, a little boy. A flawed, talented, loving man who had squandered most of his life was now reaching out to another human being—one who was just starting out in his life.

What could Frank teach Tommy? What could she, for that matter? She knew something important was happening out there. Dots were being connected. And something else began to dawn on her. This child could be Frank's doorway to maturity, to a responsible productive life. She was just a catalyst, a sideliner. But she felt good about it. "Let's see what love can do," she said out loud to herself.

Nancy retrieved her camera from the shelf in her office and headed to the foyer. She had placed the bronze busts of herself and Laura on two matching pedestal tables she'd purchased especially to hold them. She started to take shots of them from every angle. She was heading to the main island for work and shopping tomorrow and wanted to get pictures printed to send to her sister. Camille had done a wonderful job. Nancy had called and thanked her profusely.

Supper that night was toasted cheese sandwiches and cream of tomato soup. Nancy was somewhat grieved by the absence of fruit and vegetables from Tommy's diet. *All in good time* she consoled herself. When Tommy was shown up to his room, he didn't say anything he just looked around a little and then climbed up into the top bunk. He fell asleep quickly. Nancy felt a little disappointed.

"I guess I was expecting a Christmas morning response," she told Claudia on the phone, "but he just didn't say anything."

"Maybe he didn't know it was all his, Nancy!" Claudia said laughing. "And he was probably overly tired. This has been a big day for him, Nancy. Just give him some time."

****

The phone rang early. "I'm looking for Frank," the voice said.

"He's still asleep," said Nancy. She had never heard the voice before.

"Wake him up! It's important. Tell 'em it's Adam."

Nancy stepped on something sharp as she walked through the darkness in Frank's room. "Ouch!"

Frank rolled over and looked at her bewildered,

forcing himself awake. Nancy bent down and rubbed her aching foot. An action figure lay in her path, looking pleased.

"Frank you have a phone call--said his name was Adam, or something. Sounded weird and insisted that I wake you up." These last words were spoken to Frank's back. When he heard the name *Adam* he jumped up and went out of the room like the house was on fire.

"I'll take it in Aunt Laura's room" he said and quickly closed the hall door behind him. Nancy peeped into Tommy's room. Still sound asleep. One foot dangling off the top bunk.

A few minutes later, Frank joined Nancy in the kitchen. Nancy watched as Frank went to the coffee pot and poured himself a cup. Frank turned and looked at her.

"Guess you wonder who Adam is, huh?"

"Who is he?"

"Bad news, that's who."

"Well, who is he?" Nancy's voice showed a slight irritation. Frank looked down at the floor, obviously trying to collect his thoughts.

"I met him about two years ago. He's a *druggie*, but...mean...turned up at our house one day...jerked Cathy around a little, told me he was Tommy's daddy and that I had no right to *his* boy. You know, just stirring up trouble. What I remember most about him was how--." Frank hesitated and tried to think of a word, "evil, I guess, ...yeah, evil he was. He's worse than mean. He struck me as somebody who'd hurt you just for the fun of it." Frank paused again fumbling for words in that way that Nancy had grown accustomed to over the past few months. "Not long after that, Cathy took off. I don't know if it was with him or somebody else. That's when I took care of Tommy on my own for awhile." Frank looked drained. Long explanations seem to exhaust him.

Little by little, Nancy thought, *I'm getting a picture of Frank's life for the past few years* "It's good to know a little more about that time in your life Frank," she said. "You think he's on the island to stir up trouble?"

"Mom, you can count on it. He just told me he wants money for Tommy. Said he walked by this big old fancy house last night and knew you were loaded. Said a buddy of his had been in court the day we were and heard everything that went on about Tommy."

Nancy nodded her head. Some questions were getting answered before she could ask them.

They both heard him at the same time. Tommy was standing behind them in the kitchen wearing his new action figure pajamas. He had heard everything.

****

"Susan! I've stepped in it again! Need advice." Nancy phoned her pastor and told her the whole story about Tommy. "Figured you might have had some experience that would help us all out here," she finished and waited for a response.

"Two things come immediately to mind, Nancy. Pray and call Pat Roberts."

"Right," said Nancy. "She hadn't even thought about Pat."

"I'll start praying, you call Pat! - Now! Nancy." Her pastor sounded urgent.

"Hello Pat..." He answered on the first ring. "We got trouble in River City!" It was a stupid thing to say and she instantly regretted it. Nancy often said stupid things when she was nervous. Wasting no time, she told Pat about the phone call and the history Frank and Tommy had with Adam. "He may be dangerous, just don't know," Nancy finished.

"What's Adam's last name?" she shouted into the den over the noise of Sesame Street. "Stanley," the answer came back quickly.

"Nancy," Pat said, "keep a constant eye on Tommy. This guy may try to snatch him, you know, hold him for ransom or something."

Nancy had not even thought of that. "Will do" she assured him.

"Let me know immediately if he makes any further contact. I'll pick him up and hold him for questioning if I can find him. And Nancy, I still have this dangerous animal alert going on. I need a little help from Frank. Is he there?"

"Yes, just a minute."

Frank listened while Pat talked. "Nine o'clock, then," said Frank and hung up. "Pat's getting together everybody he can on the island - every body that can carry a gun that is. He's going through Peterson Point Park, shoulder to shoulder if he has enough people, until he finds that bear, or whatever he finds. He's worried that the summer season is about to start up and Pat said that this dangerous animal thing just couldn't go unresolved any longer. He and Bill have been calling everybody on the island, getting together a posse. The 'hunt' starts at 9 a.m. in the morning. Can I leave Tommy with you?" Nancy nodded yes.

"We're supposed to meet in that parking lot over near Hell's Hole." Frank glanced down at the floor, as if trying to think. Looking back up at Nancy he said, "do you still have dad's shotgun?"

It was the first time Frank had been into Nancy's bedroom in years. He looked around as she went into the closet and found the gun and shells.

"I kept it just in case..." she said.

"I don't see any pictures of dear 'ole' dad in here Mom." Nancy didn't answer.

Tommy woofed down his pancakes and bacon like an escaped convict on the run. He ignored the fruit. "Tommy, can you bath yourself or do you need Aunt Nancy to help you?" *Where did that Aunt thing come from,* she wondered?

Feeling awkward she said, "ah...Tommy, what would you like to call me?" She thought this was a better question. He shrugged, turning his little hands out.

He didn't know.

"Why don't you just call me Nancy--everybody else does."

"OK."

"Bath, Tommy! Now!" barked Frank. Nancy watched Tommy turn away from the TV and walk obediently toward the stairs in his baggy pajamas. Something stirred in her and a smile spread across her face.

****

Around 9:15 a.m. the next morning Pat and Bill jumped up and stood in the back of Bill's pickup truck. 35 or 40 people were milling around in the parking lot, most of them carrying a gun with some still in their cases. It wasn't the first time a posse had been pulled together on Rainman Island, but, Pat thought, this may be the first time they have been armed. Pat felt nervous. He knew accidents happen when people carry guns. The crowd began to move in a little closer to the truck when they saw the constable and his deputy jump up into the truck bed.

"Alright, listen up everyone!" Pat jerked the bullhorn away from his mouth and turned the volume down a little. A few smiles scattered through the crowd. "I appreciate all you folks coming out today. Before we start, I must ask anyone that has not been certified in a gun safety class to please leave your guns in your cars. I sure don't want anybody getting hurt out here today."

Several people started walking back to their cars.

Frank was one of them. He put his father's shotgun back in Nancy's car. Pat waited until everyone regrouped. "We're looking for a bear, and I think it's a Grizzly, and I think it's a big one, probably over 6 feet tall and weighing as much as 500 or 600 pounds. A few of us," Pat nodded at three men who stood at the front of the crowd closest to the truck, "have been out here looking for this bear a number of times in the last 5 months. So far we've found no trace. We think it went into hibernation before Christmas, maybe way back in one of the caves on the island. The paw print I found over at Ray Phillips place helps us to sort of guess what his feeding range may be, but now that the salmon are running, he could be just about anywhere there's a stream with fish in it.

I want everyone to hear this next part real good." Pat paused for affect. "Grizzly bears are top-of-the-food chain predators. They are fast and they are dangerous, especially if you walk in between a bear and his food or if it's a female between her and her cub." A few heads nodded an understanding of what Pat was trying to stress.

"Those of you who don't have a gun, I want you to partner up with somebody that does. Always walk in groups of at least two through the park - got it?" Heads moved up and down and folks started to form small groups of two or three. "Everybody got a time piece - a watch or a phone with the time on it?" Heads moved. "I want everyone" Pat hesitated, "I mean everyone." Pat sounded almost angry as he anticipated all the things that might happen, "Everyone!" he said it again, "to meet back here at noon for an update - if we don't find it, that is.

These three guys up front here - hold up your hands boys, have walkie-talkies and are going to walk in the three different sections we've mapped out. If you see anything - a print, a recent scratch mark - anything, find one of these guys or me and let them know." Pat pointed to the map he had taped up on the side of his truck and asked everyone to come over and look at it.

On the map he had divided the park up into three sections, drawing a red line between the sections. After everyone had a chance to glance at the map, Pat divided the group up, assigning each of them to one of the sections. Each section had a captain. The detailed instructions continued for another 5 minutes or so and then Pat jumped back up on the tailgate of the truck and asked if there were any questions.

"What about that dead dog thing - the one that belonged to those hikers? Did the bear get him too?" someone from the back of the crowd shouted it out.

All eyes turned toward Pat. "I think that's a good bet, but we have no real way of knowing." Pat's voice was getting raspy.

"Any more questions?"

"Yeah!" someone shouted.

"Did you ever find out if it was the bear that killed Ray?"

Pat nodded. "Yes. After he died, an autopsy was performed on Ray. The coroner said he could not be completely certain but it was his educated guess that

Ray died from wounds inflicted by an animal. Ray told us before he died that he had not seen what hit him." Pat looked around the group.

"Any more questions?" No one said anything else. "Remember, meet back here at noon - no excuses!" Pat and Bill jumped down off the tailgate and reached inside the truck for their rifles.

Bill looked at Pat and said, "you didn't tell them what to do if they found the bear!" Pat glanced over at Bill and said, "guess they can figure that out on their own."

Around noon small groups of the posse started appearing back in the parking lot at Hell's Hole. Some ladies from the Episcopal Church had brought over sandwiches, coffee and water for the searchers. They had spread the food out on the tailgate of Bill's truck.

The tired searchers weren't saying much. Some of them shook their heads at their friends who had been in a different section, signaling that they hadn't turned up anything either.

Pat's voice came back over the blow horn. This time he just stood in the middle of the parking lot. "This afternoon we're going to search over at Yellow Point. If nothing turns up over there, we'll search the campgrounds over by Tribune Bay. I plan to keep doing this in two and three hour shifts until every square inch of this island has been covered--*again*," his voice trailed off.

Most of the people gathered didn't hear that last word. The truth was that Pat and a small group of men had searched the island many times since the attack that killed Ray. They had turned up nothing. Not a trace. Bill started to count the posse. Within a few minutes all 'heads' were accounted for.

Frank had just finished his sandwich and was walking back to Nancy's car when Pat touched him on the arm. Frank jerked around, apparently still a little uncomfortable around cops.

Pat said, "Need to talk with you a minute Frank." Frank didn't answer, just looked down at his feet.

"That guy--Adam Stanley. The one your mom called me about yesterday." Frank glanced up at him.

"Yeah, what about him?"

"Found out that he has a record over on the mainland and they're looking for him too. He's a pretty screwed up guy, implicated in at least two murders." Pat watched for some reaction from Frank, but saw none.

"He was last seen heading our way. That was before Christmas. We think he may have been on Rainman Island for a while. He might have even followed you here." Frank shot Pat a look that showed his surprise.

"Who's we?" Frank snarled.

"The RCMP major crime unit got called in on this one."

"Look Pat," Frank said, "If you think I had anything to do with Adam Stanley coming to this island – well

– I didn't!" Frank was almost shouting. Pat let him calm down a minute. He studied Frank's face. He saw Franks' mouth twitch in anger, his lips were pulled into a tight line. Nothing else changed on his face except his eyes, which were now looking directly into Pat's. "I told you I don't know anything about that guy - he knows me, not the other way around. I married his ex-wife. I didn't know anything about him...until...I think she ran off with him...she was gone for awhile...then she came back to give me hell. That's when I left Vancouver. I was tired of that shit."

Again, Pat waited. "Frank, we think he is somewhere on this island. We think he might try and contact either you, Nancy or Tommy. He's probably broke and needs money to get out of here. If he does make contact," Pat hesitated and looked directly at Frank, "give him the money - don't try anything heroic--tell your mother the same thing. Don't forget to tell Rachel, too. I have no idea how he might try to get money. He's probably been watching you for awhile-- probably knows exactly where you go and who you see." Frank looked pale.

"Well what are you doing about that? Out here looking for a bear! Shouldn't you be looking for Adam?" Frank was indignant.

"The RCMP has had three plain clothes detectives assigned here since right before Christmas. For awhile it looked like he had left the island, but yesterday, when your mom called me...you know, after he called you, I notified them and they came back to the island, immediately. They had been looking for him up around Comox and Campbell River areas on the main island."

"Oh" said Frank. It was almost a whisper.

"I'm asking you and your family to be on high alert. The RCMP put your mother's home and Rachel's under surveillance late yesterday."

Frank looked at Pat questioningly. "I hadn't seen anybody snooping around."

"That's their job, Frank. They blend in."

The conversation with Pat left Frank feeling threatened and a little angry. Things had not been going well with Rachel lately either. She seemed withdrawn and critical. Frank wasn't sure why and he didn't know how to ask. He thought maybe she was grieving for her mother or something. Her pain and her loss was all she wanted to talk about. That plus how much she loved Jesus! He didn't feel connected to her the way he had at first, while Betty was around. Betty understood him, he thought. Rachel didn't. On his way home Frank drove past the Sleeping Pig and noticed it was open. He went in and asked for a beer.

One beer can't hurt anybody he told himself.

Adam

The headline in the small local newspaper read "Dangerous Bear Found Dead." There was a fuzzy picture of Micah and Pat looking down at what was described in the short article as the remains of a large bear. The article said that it been discovered in Yellow Point Park by one of the posse members late the day before in a cave. It was believed to be the bear that attacked and killed Ray Phillips. The article also said that samples from the carcass were being sent to the FBI for further testing...that Pat Roberts was hopeful that the DNA test results from the samples might help in solving the Ray Phillips case. Apparently the bear had died of natural causes.

Nancy read it and thought the writer of the article needed to go back to school and get at least his high school diploma! The sloppiness with which many of the articles in the local newspaper were written often brought up more questions than answers.

Maybe I'll go down and volunteer as their new columnist, she thought. *Better not* was her second thought. *Then I wouldn't have anything to gripe about!*

She and Tommy had just returned from a trip to the big island for groceries. She glanced at Tommy, sitting at the kitchen island playing with two of his action figures. *He was an unusually quiet child.* He acted shy around her especially when Frank was nearby. Tommy had been living with them for almost two weeks. From the day they had brought Tommy home, Frank had completely stopped going to Rachel's house. And Rachel had not been over to her house either. Nancy wondered what was up with that relationship but when she had asked Frank, he'd just looked down and said, "I guess we're giving it a rest."

After daily contact with Tommy for almost two weeks, they had both relaxed. A few days earlier Tommy had fallen and skinned his knee. Tommy had come running up to Nancy crying and needing help and comfort. Frank was at home -- up in his room. Nancy wondered why he had not come down when he heard Tommy crying. Nancy did comfort Tommy, patched up his knee and knew that a little tender thread of trust had grown between them.

Nancy could tell that Tommy had never been the center of anybody's attention. He accepted Nancy's smiles and words of comfort, but Nancy thought, he was still holding something back.

Since the day of the big bear hunt, Nancy was aware that Frank had started going out more and more, alone. He told her he was looking for a job but Nancy knew there were very few jobs on the island this time of year. Trying to stay positive, she thought Frank might just want her to have some 'bonding' time with Tommy. When Frank was around Tommy did act differently toward her. He seemed to cling to Frank -- didn't want Frank out of his sight.

Nancy hoped that time would change his behavior

toward her -- normalize it somehow. She had researched and read all she could find about the impact of abuse in young children, in their formative years. Her research had led her to the definition of childhood amnesia. Tommy had certainly had a rough start in life. She hoped, in fact felt committed, to help him grow into a well rounded, balanced person. But her interest went beyond Tommy; it was personal. She felt like she'd missed the mark in raising her own son and now, maybe God was going to give her a second chance. She was grateful that God, in His infinite kindness, designed us all with childhood amnesia. And with Tommy, she saw the value of it.

Tommy was just finishing his lunch when Nancy finished putting away the groceries. She sat down with him at the kitchen island. The library books they had picked out together lay spread out in front of them. She'd been describing the upcoming Seafood and Art festival to him, what fun it was for children, when she heard a light knock at her back door. She peeked out through curtain over the back door window to see who it was and saw a handsome, young man smiling at her. He was holding up a badge.

"I'm Inspector Tom Meyers, Mam, RCMP." Nancy nodded, acknowledging that she understood.

"We have Adam Stanley in custody." He glanced over his shoulder down the driveway toward a parked car. Nancy opened the door wider and also looked toward the parked car. Tommy walked over and stood near her when he heard the name Adam Stanley.

Nancy instinctively reached down and pulled Tommy close to her leg. Tommy didn't resist.

"Is your son here, Mam? We'd like to speak to him."

"No he isn't. I'm not sure exactly where he is or when he'll be back."

"I see," said Inspector Meyers. He handed Nancy a business card and asked that Frank call him as soon as possible.

"Is he in some sort of trouble?" Nancy asked. This was also an instinctive response. Frank had always walked a thin line with trouble.

"No Mam--just some questions. I'd appreciate him calling us as soon as possible." And then he was gone.

Nancy and Tommy took a few steps out onto the driveway and watched the car pull slowly away.

The dark skinned man sitting in the back seat did not look at them.

Rosewood

"It is my one great regret in life that I cannot carry a tune," whispered Nancy to Claudia. Claudia turned and looked at her.

"You have a great deal more than *that* to regret, my dear friend," Claudia said putting her hand in front of her mouth to stifle a giggle.

"Oh! I suppose you mean that brownie ala mode, last night?" Nancy grinned.

"Well--that, too," said Claudia looking away to prevent a giggle from escaping.

"Shall we pray?" Dr. Weaver's voice boomed out over the congregation, which numbered 25 that morning. Nancy thought Susan was an excellent speaker. She kept her sermons short, to the point and her style was that of a storyteller. This Lord's day, Susan had told the story of Peter healing the lame man outside the temple. She said she was going to start at the end of the story and work backwards.

"Peter had not always been able to heal a lame man by just speaking the name of Jesus, had he?"

Susan focused the congregation on the power of the Holy Spirit by telling a story about a little boy. His father was trying to move a very large, heavy desk.

It was so bulky and difficult that after several futile attempts to move it he noticed the legs were getting stuck in the carpet. So he flipped the desk over so that the legs were up in the air. With the legs out of the way, the heavy desk began to move slowly across the carpet.

It was about this time that his little boy entered the room. Seeing the tough job his father was having, the child asked if he could help. With great patience for his son, the father let the little boy stand in front of him, between his arms and together they pushed. The desk began to move again, slowly. After a few moments of extreme effort, the little boy looked up at his dad and said, "*you're in my way, Daddy!*"

A ripple of laughter went around the chapel.

"Peter wanted to help Jesus, didn't he? But Peter had his own agenda about *how* Jesus should move the Kingdom along. But when the Holy Spirit put His arms around Peter and said *push*, Son, things began to move in the right direction.

"We can't do it on our own, folks. The Spirit is able to do more in 60 seconds than we can do on our own in 60 years."

Susan's words sank deeply into Nancy's thoughts. It was a sermon she would remember again and again in the coming days. On her way home, she stopped at Camille Carmichael's house.

Maybe I can do some good here, she thought. Over the past couple of months she had learned that Camille often had flare-ups of Rheumatoid Arthritis. During those times it was difficult for her to stand up long enough to cook herself a meal. So Nancy had started bringing a casserole by now and then. Today, Nancy brought homemade yeast rolls, ready for Camille to pop in the oven, and a small poppy seed chicken casserole.

"Toss a salad, and you're there!" Nancy said, sitting the disposable foil containers on the kitchen table. The stuffed black bird scowled at her. Camille turned to put the food in the refrigerator and Nancy stuck her tongue out at the bird.

The day had turned warm. Camille had been sitting on the back porch with the kitchen door open when Nancy arrived. Camille invited Nancy to join her for a few minutes on the porch and enjoy the beautiful spring weather. Nancy gladly accepted.

Camille looked regal wearing a floor length, brightly colored caftan and puffing on a long cigarette holder. Camille settled herself comfortably in a large padded chair and was resting one foot on a low stool pulled close for that purpose.

"I've been meaning to ask you something for a long time--since that very first day I met you," Nancy said.

"And what would that be?" Camille asked, sincerely interested.

"Why did you name this place *Rosewood*?"

"Oh!" said Camille. She had expected another question from this 'church lady' -- something to do with her rebellion against organized religion maybe.

"It's been awhile since anyone asked me that." She put her other foot up on the stool. Nancy took this gesture as a signal saying, *relax, this may take awhile!*

"Did you know that I am originally from Georgia, Nancy?"

She did not. "That's amazing," said Nancy, thinking this was another one of those *'small world' moments. Like the time she found out that she and Betty Bishop had exactly the same birthday.* "I am, too." Nancy said. Camille nodded.

"Well", Camille said slowly as if looking for a place to start. She flicked the ashes from her cigarette into a nearby ashtray. Nancy noticed Camille's face and tone changed. She spoke softly, slowly.

"Being from the South you may know more about this than you think--coming from the segregated south and all. But by segregation I mean I grew up in the Jim Crow South, back in the 40's and 50's. I lived with segregation all through my childhood. Somehow I always knew it was wrong, even before I really understood why or could express it in my own words. All of my childhood memories are of having white friends and black housekeepers."

Camille stopped and looked at Nancy. Nancy nodded her understanding. Camille continued. "I knew our housekeeper had children, but my brother and sister and I never saw them. About our only exposure to black people was through our granddaddy. He owned a couple of rental houses in what some people called *Nigger Town.*

Sometimes granddaddy would let me go with him to collect the rent. That's the only time, as a child, I was ever allowed to go into a black person's house. And you know, I didn't think anything of it. It's just the way things were. I often saw drinking fountains labeled *white only*--bathrooms were the same way. Even the public buses were segregated. I always thought it would be fun to ride in the back seat of the bus. But once..." Camille hesitated to pull back the memory. "When I tried it," Camille bit down on the long cigarette holder in her mouth and took a deep draw. "My mother saw me sitting back there and jerked my arm so hard it hurt for the rest of the day." Camille blew the smoke out of her mouth hard. "She dragged me to the front of that bus." She paused as if remembering every detail. "With my feet barely touching the floor. She made me sit up there—up front--with her. She didn't explain anything to me—didn't tell me what I had done wrong. I don't think she could have." Camille took another long draw on her cigarette. A light gust of wind carried the cigarette smoke away from Nancy. She was grateful.

"Back in the 20's," Camille continued, "Rosewood was a quiet little whistle stop of a place in rural Florida. It wasn't a very big place, just a little community, mostly of black people. And they pretty much stayed to themselves...you know -- supported themselves on what they could grow, raise or sell. A few of them worked outside the community, I guess, but the residents were close knit, many were relatives.

During the first week of 1923, in the dead of winter, some white woman in a nearby county said that she had been beaten and raped by a black drifter. I don't know who she told, but almost immediately some white men got together and marched over to the community of Rosewood and lynched a man. The blacks living there were terrified and tried to defend themselves from further attacks by whites. Many of them ran into the nearby swamps and tried to hide. When word of it got out, several hundred whites started combing the woods around Rosewood and hunting down the blacks and killing them, for no reason! It was in every sense a massacre. Then the white men burned down every home in Rosewood. Only a few escaped, mostly by rail. The entire town was abandoned right after the massacre and no one ever returned.

And here is the worst part," Camille took the butt of the cigarette from its holder and snuffed it out with force. "The local authorities were aware of the violence but they never made a single arrest. THEY DID NOTHING!" Camille mumbled something under her breath that Nancy did not quite make out but there was little doubt what she meant.

"In fact," she continued, "they didn't even write it up! I HATE RACISM! I HATE IT!" Camille looked pale and her mouth was drawn into a tight line. Both of her feet were on the floor now, as if she were ready to jump up in anger.

"Sixty years went by. SIXTY! Finally, some of the survivors and descendants from people who lived in Rosewood got together and sued the state of Florida for failing to protect them. They won their case, thank God! I was outraged when I heard about it, and how it was all covered up." I didn't know what to do with my anger. Eventually it came to me—something I could do. It's a little thing I know, but I decided to name my home *Rosewood,* in honor of those who died or were chased away."

Nancy was stunned. She had never heard the story before. Her mind raced back to Susan's message that morning about evil. The atrocities Camille had described were evil. Unspeakable evil. "There's a movie about it if you're interested in that sort of thing," Camille said. "I've seen the movie. Not sure they got it right. Hollywood doesn't let the facts stand in the way of what they want to say about anything."

Nancy's phone rang. It was Frank asking when she would be home.

"What's up?"

"Well," said Frank, "I need to go out for awhile."

Do people ever really change, she wondered again as she slid into her car, heading for home.

For Lease

The small sign in the yard of 64 Honey Bear Lane said, *For Lease.* Rachel had scrubbed Betty's house clean and hired someone to help move most of Betty's furniture over to the big island to Claudia's Closet. "Whatever you can get for it is fine," Rachel had told Claudia.

As Claudia unpacked the boxes she once again thought of how *things last longer than people.* An antique bed from Betty and Kenneth's bedroom now stood in the front window of her shop. Claudia looked up at it. The eight foot high headboard had barely made it into their tiny cottage. The face of an angel, carved into the heavy, dark oak gazed down on all who lay on it.

What have you seen? Claudia wondered as she looked up into the face of the smiling cherub. *Did you see people being born? People dying? People in distress or maybe simply resting. Ahhh, and the lovemaking! I bet there was a lot of that in this fine old bed!* Claudia was smiling at her daydream when she heard the tiny bell on the front door tinkle, alerting her that someone had entered the shop. Two white-headed women stood just inside the door looking around. They were sisters and came almost every Tuesday--the senior discount day at Claudia's

Closet.

Claudia turned and smiled but did not move away from the front window. Immediately the sisters were *upon* her with questions about the bed. "I don't know, maybe 19th century -- definitely Victorian. This kind of furniture deserves to be in a room with a high ceiling, you know -- to show it off." Claudia closed her sales monologue as she glanced back up at the smiling angel.

And that's all there was to it. The sisters, well known around the big island as two of it's wealthiest residents, gladly wrote a check for $1950 and told Claudia that they would send *their man* around later to pick it up.

Claudia was so excited she called Rachel after the sisters had gone and told her she had sold the bed. "My commission is 25% but you'll get $1712.50! Isn't that great?" Claudia exclaimed.

"Thank you" said Rachel sounding a little flat.

"Thought you'd be pleased. Maybe you can buy yourself a new motor scooter - stop terrorizing the neighbors with the backfires from the old one." Claudia was trying hard to get a more cheerful response from Rachel. Nothing. "What's up?" Silence. Claudia waited. The shop was empty.

"Men." Rachel finally said. "Are they all just plain screwed up?"

 "That's been my experience," soothed Claudia. "Except Jim of course, but I'm still working on him." Claudia laughed a little at her own joke trying to lighten Rachel's mood. It didn't work. "Rachel, can I help you?" she asked.

"Maybe. Maybe I need to talk to you. I really don't want to talk to Nancy, you know, Frank's mother and all."

"Want me to come by tonight or maybe just call?" Claudia offered. "I can also bring the money for the bed."

"I'll see you after supper if that's o.k. -- and thanks Claudia. Thanks for everything."

****

Nancy walked west along Honey Bear Lane with Bernie. The sun was low and cast long slanting rays through the spring evening. It was early April and the trees overhead had already started to leaf out. She noticed a dirt road leading into a pasture. It wasn't so much a road as it was two dirt tracks packed down hard by the frequent use of farm equipment. A light mist had started to fall. The smell of rain mixed with the packed earth created a fragrance that only nature can produce. A light breeze pushed at Nancy's wet hair. She felt alive, empowered and free.

Branches from the trees arched over the small dirt road creating a green tunnel. Nancy stopped for a moment and studied it. The parallel tracks of the dirt road sloped down, then turned sharply out of sight. *Where does it go? What is beyond the bend?* The mystery of it seemed to summon her.

She stood in the misting rain and was once again

caught up in the magical beauty of *her* island. *Life is like an untraveled road -- it leads us onward – always to where we have not been before. We cannot see around the bend any more than we can know what is next in life -- every turn is filled with unknowns.*

She thought of Tommy and Frank Jr. She thought of Betty and Rachel. *An untraveled road is like a birth canal -- a place we slip into and move through when our time has come to be born. We have no knowledge of what lies ahead – but we are compelled – drawn along -- with no will of our own.*

She turned onto the dirt road and imagined herself stepping into the 'green tunnel.' *Where would lead?* She had no idea.

She was sheltered from the mist under the heavy green canopy and giggled when she realized she was walking through mud. *Just like when Laura and I were kids.* It was then that she remembered the letter from Laura. She had stuck it in her pocket as she and Bernie had walked past her mailbox. She lifted it out now and studied the stamps and artwork on the envelope. *Heart shaped balloons, now what could that mean?*

She stuffed the envelope back into her pocket, smiled and walked on. The 'road' took a sharp turn and suddenly Nancy found herself standing in a sea of emerald green grass. On the horizon, she saw a few cows grazing in the late afternoon sun. The word *tranquility* came into her mind. She felt she had entered a great cathedral with a soaring ceiling of lemony blue. Lush green carpet encircled her feet. She stood still and quietly prayed. *Thank you,*

Lord, for this place, this time, this beauty. Open my eyes and ears to You, dear Heavenly One. I want to remember this moment forever.

An hour later, happily tired and thoroughly wet, Nancy and Bernie arrived back at 354 Honey Bear Lane. After toweling Bernie off, she headed down the hall for a hot shower. She was just coming back into the kitchen with her hair wrapped in a towel, wearing her favorite pajamas, when the phone rang. She glanced at the caller ID -- it was Laura. She smiled and answered as she filled up the coffee pot and turned it on.

"Did you read my letter yet?"

"You mean the one with the heart balloons?"

"Yeah, did you?"

"Not yet, I was saving it until after supper. You know, on the Island we have to space out our entertainments."

"Oh. Well, read it and call me back."

"Why don't you just tell me what's in it and then I won't have to call you back."

"Read it and call me back, but...be sitting down when you read it, OK?"

"Now you've gotten my interest up. What's going on?" Click. Laura had hung up.

Dear Sisterwoman,

I'm not sure where to start but if you aren't sitting down, you soon will be (don't hurt yourself). Big John and I are going to get married. That means I will be your next door neighbor."

Nancy read those sentences over several times. She sat down. Then she stood up again, got herself a cup of coffee and sat down again. She read the lines again. They had not changed.

"I thought they hated each other," Nancy said to no one. She knew she was frowning.

Nancy glanced through the rest of the letter as she pulled up Laura's number and pressed call.

"I'm listening," she said. "You have my complete attention."

An hour later, she stared in the bathroom mirror at her own reflection. Her hair had dried into little ringlets all over her head and her sun blotched skin was dry and wrinkled around her eyes. She wondered what Laura saw when she looked in the mirror. They shared the same face, the same hair. When they blinked their eyes closed the same way. "We're twins" she said to no one. But they were as different as two people can be. Nancy's mind could not capture or explain exactly how she was feeling at that moment.

She ran through the conversation again in her mind. Laura had told her about the passionate way she and John connected when Laura had gone over to apologize to him for her rude comments about

Danny. Since that day, Laura said, they had talked to each other often—flirting at first...then something more serious started to take shape.

Laura told her that John had even flown down to Georgia and spent a couple of weeks with her. All this happened without a word from either Laura or John! For a second she felt betrayed, irritated, left out. She wished Betty were up there in her room so she could talk out her feelings. As she creamed her face and brushed out her hair she kept repeating 'Laura and Big John, Laura and Big John.' It simply would not sink in.

She headed for the kitchen and noticed the clock beside her bed. It was 7:30 p.m. *Guess Frank and Tommy will be home soon,* she thought. Frank had taken Tommy to watch softball game. She figured they would be hungry by the time they came home. She retrieved frozen veggies for a stir-fry and was going into the pantry for rice when she heard a light tapping on the back door.

Nancy cracked the door open a bit and there stood Big John, grinning at her. "Laura told me I'd better get over here with the smelling salts," he said.

Nancy opened the door wider and said "I might need something a little stronger."

"Well, we can make that happen too," he said, coming into the warm light of her kitchen.

"John, I—I'm in shock!" she said it in almost a whisper.

"Of all the things that I could have ever imagined

happening--this was not even on the list!"

"I know," he said. "It wasn't on my list either."

"Let me start at the end and work back toward the beginning" Nancy said. "How did you talk Laura into living on the island? She's always said she hated the Island, the remoteness."

"I told her about all the artists who live here. Why, hell, she knew half of 'em!"

The door flew open and Tommy came in. Frank followed closely behind. Nancy took one look at the mud covered boy and said "stop!" "Frank, help Tommy out of those clothes in the laundry room and hose him down in the sink in there."

"Tommy, did you slide into all the bases, too?" Tommy looked at Nancy and Big John then down at the floor, shyly.

Frank lifted him and they disappeared into the laundry room. "When you finish cleaning up that dirty boy, you'd better come back in here. There is some pretty big news breaking in the kitchen," John said smiling.

Two hours later breadcrumbs were strewn across the table along with crumpled napkins and empty wine glasses. The candles that Nancy had lit all around the dining room were burning low. Claudia and Jim had been summoned along with Laura via the speakerphone. Tommy had fallen asleep on Frank's shoulder and had been gently carried upstairs. Frank had not returned to the impromptu dinner party.

The wedding was planned for June, on Rainman Island. Laura was moving into John's house late next month. "Three months doesn't seem like enough time to get to know someone—well enough to marry," Nancy mildly protested.

Laura snorted from 3000 miles away and said "Nancy, we've known each other for 57 years and we are still surprising each other! That line might work when two people are 18 or 20 or such, but when you're our age, well, you know who you are and what you like."

"That's right," responded John emphatically. His inhibitions momentarily subdued with wine. "And I like you Laura!--a lot!"

Nancy thought she had never seen Big John so animated and happy. She wondered how they would be as a couple. *Laura was her twin*. She thought she knew every nuance of her person, her moods, and her preferences, even her thoughts. But this engagement to Big John had come as a complete shock. Not a word. Not a tiny shred of evidence. How can you know someone your whole life and fail to see something like this coming?

Nancy felt the coolness of the sheets on her skin as she finally slid between them. She wiggled around and got into her 'nest.' She lay there in the still darkness until she felt her body begin to relax. Prayer came easy tonight--she had so many questions.

Seafood Festival

The terrible, tragic fallacy is that down through the ages we have been duped into thinking that all man's troubles are due to his environment, and that to change the man you have nothing to do but to change his environment. That is a tragic fallacy. It overlooks the fact that it was in Paradise that man fell.
D. Martyn Lloyd-Jones

May 24th arrived on schedule. So did several thousand Seafood Festival attendees. Every B&B and Campground on the Island was full to overflowing. Many island residents joined in the action by advertising their homes for rent for the weekend. Friends piled in with friends to free up their homes to be rented for the weekend. The price the local residents asked for and got for their often humble accommodations was enough to pay the mortgage for a month! The festival was a huge financial boost for all the island's residents, especially the *'starving artists'* and fishermen.

Many local artists hosted other artists who traveled to the Seafood Festival from all over Canada and the U.S. Traffic on Ferries from the main island was packed on every crossing for the weekend event. No vehicles other than registered campers and vendors were permitted. Small buses had been brought over to Rainman Island and used as *people movers*. Camille and her committee had tried to think of everything, but mass confusion seemed to break out every few minutes.

One source of confusion involved vendors trying to get their 'stuff' over to Rainman. This particular logjam occurred two days before the festival actually got started. The ferry captain finally reached Camille on the phone and within a few seconds wished that he had not called. She was in rare form with her expletives and declared that all of the extra ferries Big John had engaged "had crews of *&@!!! Imbeciles that couldn't find their %$@@@!!!! in a snow storm." After thus condemning all of them and their ancestors, she told them that registered vendors were allowed to bring their cars, vans and trucks onto the island. "Idiots!" was her final salutation as she hung up on the caller.

Rainman Island had been transformed. Colorful streamers hung around the island to mark the many areas of interest or to guide visitors to participating vendors and events. At least 50 local residents had been hired just to walk around the island and offer information. They were walking information booths, easy to spot with their colorful hats and sandwich boards. Numerous porta-potties lined each crossroad all over the island. Concession areas were adorned with an array of trashcans, each with different colored plastic liners. The green liners were labeled recyclables for glass and cans. The red ones where to be used for food waste. Paper, Camille's committee had hoped, would find its way into the barrels with white liners. Did any of this happen? Well, it seems that people on holiday cannot read and most of them appear to have also been born colorblind!

Three separate event tents had been set up along

Honey Bear Lane near the ferry docks. Music streamed from all three tents from 10 a.m. till 10 p.m. all weekend. As in years past, Sandy Blackstead had planned to keep the "Sleeping Pig" open until 2 a.m. Friday and Saturday nights. Sunday morning Sandy always hosted a free pancake breakfast for the vendors and artists participating in the festival. Members of the island churches helped with the cooking, serving and clean up of the breakfast event. Dr. Susan Weaver was usually on hand and offered a short devotional.

Nancy planned to stay home. "This weekend is for freshmen, not seniors," she told Claudia.

"You ole' stick in the mud" Claudia argued. "You've got to at least come out and see some of the art displays--say hello to the convicts--you know, do your civic duty."

In the end, Claudia had convinced her that she should at least accompany Tommy and Frank to the sail-past procession and the Blessing of the Fleet.

It was nearly time for Claudia and Jim to pick them up. Nancy called out into the backyard where Tommy was playing with Bernie. "Come on in. They'll be picking us up soon," she said and waited on the deck. Tommy responded enthusiastically, racing Bernie to the deck. Nancy looked at his beautiful, upturned face. "Better go wash your hands—and that dirty face," she said as she tousled his hair.

She went in to search for Frank. She had not seen him all morning, which was not all that unusual these days. But she was surprised when she found him still asleep in his room. It was 1:00 in the afternoon! She bent down to gently nudge him awake, thinking he might be sick.

That's when she smelled the booze. He was not asleep. He was out cold!

A thousand fears launched inside Nancy. *When had this happened? How could it happen? Why did it happen?* The questions flew through her mind. *What about Tommy? What about Rachel? What about her?* She felt angry -- insulted.

She jerked back away from Frank's bed like she had seen a coiled snake lying there. Memories of those terrible years with Frank and his abusive, destructive behavior filled her thoughts.

She stumbled down the steps, tears brimming, mind racing. The back door swung open. Tommy let the barking dog in. Bernie ran over to Nancy and she automatically bent down and stroked his fur. As she straightened up she looked at Tommy. His expression changed when he saw the look on Nancy's face.

Nancy looked away before Tommy did. Tommy just stood there, looking confused, waiting, and not knowing what to do.

"Where's Frank?" he finally said in his 5 year old voice.

"He's, ah, he's...not...ah...feeling well," she lied.

"I'll go see him," Tommy said and started off toward

the stairs.

"Just a minute, Tommy" Nancy managed.

"Claudia wants you and I to go with her to the festival. She'll be here in a few minutes. Why don't you just...ah...let your--Frank sleep until he's feeling better?" She stumbled through the words.

"OK," he said and turned toward the refrigerator.

"Need a snack before we go?" Nancy thought again how the familiarity of fixing food always seemed to make her feel in control again. *When you don't know what to do, do something familiar*, she thought.

A few minutes later Jim and Tommy sat on the front seat of Jim's golf cart as they made their way to the ferry landing. Claudia and Nancy were on the back seat facing the rear. Tommy loved riding with Jim in his golf cart.

"I need to talk to you about Frank," Nancy whispered to Claudia.

"Speak, my friend!" Claudia said as she waved hello to some festivalgoers.

Nancy spoke in almost a whisper, hoping Tommy would not hear her. "He's passed out at home, drunk."

Claudia slowly turned her head to look at Nancy. At that exact moment the golf cart hit a hole in the road almost tossing them both out of their seats. They grabbed at the canopy support and held on.

"Sorry girls!" said Jim with a wide grin then turned and winked at Tommy.

Claudia looked at Nancy. Her eyes were wide with expression. "I am so sorry, Nancy."

Nancy nodded. "Me too. I was so full of hope. I thought things had really changed--you know? Tommy and all--even Rachel, although I don't know where that stands now."

Claudia listened.

Tears welled up in Nancy's eyes again. "What about Tommy? He has no one now!" Nancy's voice cracked.

"He has you," Claudia said. Nancy looked down at her lap thinking about Tommy, how his young life had been filled with chaos and neglect.

Jim parked on the grass near the ferry. "Come on girls!" he said, as he hoisted Tommy up on his shoulders. "It's already starting!"

"We'll catch up...you go on ahead!" Claudia smiled at him. Jim walked quickly into the crowd with Tommy's legs hooked around his neck.

"Rehab, again?"

"Guess so."

"Need an interventionist?"

"Maybe...probably."

"Long term?"

"I guess. 12 months maybe - don't know."

"Keep Tommy in school on the island?"

"If I can."

The short phrases went back and forth between the old friends as they walked slowly through the crowd toward the ferry landing. They both knew the process of recovery all too well.

"He's an addict, Nancy. He'll always be."

"He forgot...I forgot...guess he thought he could handle it."

"That's what they all think--the unlucky ones."

"Do people ever really change?"

"Only our Creator knows for sure," Claudia said.

They found Jim and Tommy in the crowd and stood next to them. They faced west, out into the bay. The procession of boats had already started. It was a beautiful day. The cool breeze floated through the crowd scattering the fragrance of evergreen everywhere.

Nancy held her hand up over her eyes to shield them from the bright sun. She saw Micah and Pam and their kids standing close to Susan Weaver, up on the podium. Micah was holding his guitar, smiling at someone. Every time she saw Micah, she thought of

Ray and how close they had been.

Dr. Alice shouted something up at Pam and she grinned down at her and waved. Nancy scanned the crowd for other familiar faces and thought she saw Rachel, but wasn't sure.

Nancy looked up, wondering what God saw. She thought of Betty and remembered something she had read recently that *everyone dies twice. The first death is physical. Our bodies die. The second death comes when the last person to ever know us dies. Then the memory of us dies. This is the second death. You are still alive in my memory, Betty,* she thought.

The sun's slanting rays sparkled across the water casting shimmering diamonds in its path. For a moment, Nancy thought of herself standing almost in this same spot last year, waving as the boats went by. *Last year she had not yet met Betty. She had no knowledge of Tommy or Rachel. Laura had never met Big John and now they were going to be married! And live next door to her! Incredible. Last year at this time, Frank was still missing. And now—* her mind darted to Frank, lying in his bed, drunk. A deep sense of dread began to grip her. The sun went behind a cloud and for a moment everything went grey.

Nancy looked up again. A jumble of phrases swirled through her mind: *Stay in the present, Nancy. I made you free to choose what you will do. But remember as you choose, you are forgiven. You can forgive others. Feed my sheep.* The words dropped into her mind, clear and precise. She knew who was speaking to her. The voice continued, as it always did, with scripture. *My Grace is sufficient for you; My power is made perfect in weakness.* Nancy smiled and turned the palm of her right hand up slightly in thanksgiving for God's presence. It was a small, secret gesture. No one noticed.

Nancy looked over at Tommy, still sitting on Jim's shoulders—watching in rapt attention as the fleet moved passed them.

Nancy prayed: *Lord, I guess I don't have to go looking for what the future holds--it always comes rushing at me.* Nancy noticed the dark curls around Tommy's ears while she was still speaking to God. *It is easy for me to think that I have all the answers, but in reality, only You, Father, know exactly why things happen the way they do. And as for my part, Father, please give me the courage -- the strength I will need to bear not only my own suffering but my son's as well, or anyone else you may bring into my life. Please love them through me. May I be able to enter into their lives so completely that I laugh when they laugh and cry when they cry. And in my laughter and tears may they hear Your joy and know Your compassion. Thy will, not mine, be done.*

Epilogue

Some say Heaven has streets of gold and angels flying around playing harps. Others say Heaven is not real--that it exists only in the weak minds of people brainwashed into thinking that there is life after death. Still others say they believe life goes on after death, but they honestly don't have a clue what that life might be like. I am among the latter. I believe in the integrity of the Bible and the principles and insights for living that I find there. I am nurtured and inspired by the writings of men and women who down through the centuries have written of their endeavors in seeking The One That Has No Equal. And I believe that those who seek, find.

While writing this book, my second child, a son, died, after a long illness. He was 50 years old. My daughter died suddenly 8 years earlier. She was 43. I've been thinking about meeting them again -- in Heaven. What would it be like? I can only imagine.

So if you wish, please read on and imagine with me a little more of Ray's encounter with Heaven, as he told it to Micah. A tiny fragment is all I can offer, for you see, I believe...there is no end.

For those who, near death have experienced Heaven and returned to tell us about it, I am indebted. They say that human language is completely inadequate to describe the beauty, love and Presence they found there. May it be so for each of us.

Ray's encounter in Heaven

I (Ray) stood there stunned with the realization that I was actually *in* Heaven. *Come, I have many things to show you*, said Linda in that way she spoke into my mind. *Becky is just about to burst with excitement to see you. Becky! our precious daughter - here!* I said. *Yes, of course,* assured Linda, *and your mom and dad and ...* she just listed them off. She told me names I had forgotten long ago--names of the people who were the dearest on earth to me.

Together, Linda and I went along a path beside that lovely river eventually coming over a small rise. Stretching out before us, in the greenest valley I have ever seen, was a village. It seemed to beckon to me, respond to me, like the water had. Almost immediately we were in the village, walking or flying I--I can't explain.

We went down a narrow street that ran near the river. I saw small cottages made of stone with thatched roofs—no two were alike. Everything was so beautiful. The river at this point grew wider, more shallow and rushed swiftly over large flat stones creating a low waterfall. As the water hit the rocks, I could hear the music again, almost like it leaped out into the air as the water collided with the stones.

Some of the houses were grand and some were small and cozy. Almost all of them had gardens with young plants springing up everywhere. The colors of everything were so vivid, so unlike anything I have ever seen! *It was exactly what I had dreamed*

Heaven would be like. The streets were definitely not gold! Somehow I recognized everything, but I certainly had never been there before. I can't explain...it was not like looking at it, more like being inside everything, looking out and looking in at the same time. *I was part of it.*

I had fallen behind Linda's pace. I kept gazing everywhere with my mouth hanging open. Linda turned and excitedly told me that she was taking me to our home. She said they had all been working on it for years. There is no way I can describe to you the utter and complete joy, the unconditional love that took over me as I caught up with her again and walked beside her.

I saw some teenagers coming our way. My heart rose even higher. I thought one of them looked familiar. She stepped out from the others and ran toward me, smiling. *Hello, Deddy.* That's what Becky always called me. Then, she was in my arms. It was as if no time at all had lapsed since I had last seen her.

After awhile, I cannot tell you how long, I held her at arms length and took in the beautiful face she lifted toward mine. She looked more like me than Linda, I thought, but in a beautiful, girl way. Complete joy swept over me. I felt...completed. After several minutes with Becky...I cannot tell you how, but our minds...connected, there was no need for words. Becky stepped back and motioned for her friends to come and meet her Deddy. They approached us, a more radiant, beautiful group of young people, I had never seen. One of the boys held a large bunch of long stemmed flowers of every imaginable color and shape. There must have been several hundred of them. The tallest boy spoke. *We'd like to put these in your home* he said. His smile penetrated me somehow. Becky cut in with a high-pitched voice, full of excitement. *We've been picking them for hours. We knew you were coming today and that you'd love them!* *Sure,* I remember saying, still not understanding exactly how we 'spoke' to each other.

Linda came up close to where we were standing. I don't know how she moved about. It seemed to me that when I thought of her, she was just—there. I didn't see her coming or going. *You'll need to pick a room for them*, she spoke into my mind. Not really understanding, for I had not yet seen my home, I suggested the dining room. They all giggled in delight and were gone as quickly as they had come. For a second I wanted them to linger. I wanted more time with Becky, but Linda's words again calmed me.

Eternity, my darling, you will be here for eternity.

Ray again fell asleep and slept long enough for Micah to get a cup of coffee. As before, when Ray woke up he continued as if he had never stopped.

They were all waiting for me when we turned down a small lane lined with flowers and large trees. At the end of the lane was a two-story house made of stone and wood. From the outside it was similar to the others in the village, but instantly I knew this one was mine. The house itself seemed alive and welcoming. The back of the house faced the river and a perfect lawn dotted with fruit trees swept down to its banks. Along the front of the house was a wide, deep porch covered by a copper roof that gleamed when a ray of sun struck it.

My mother rushed out of the house and right behind her was my precious dad. My legs no longer supported me and I sank to my knees. They laid their hands on my head. Their blessing and joy spread through my entire being. They looked radiant and young. Intense, penetrating love passed from them to me. These were faces I barely remembered on earth but *here* all my memories were alive and accessible. I not only knew them, *I instantly knew their parents and the ones that came before them.* My mind was no longer limited, Micah. *I could see both the future and the past with ease.* I was so amazed I turned to find Linda who was standing close to me. I needed her explanation.

Answers to my questions were instant and had a structure to them that revealed even more answers. I instantly had answers to unformed questions and in all of this, I understood that Linda was to be my guide. She explained that with time, I would learn to read other people's memories, both their pasts and futures as easily as I could read my own.

We are all connected, she said. *There is much for you to learn here, much that I myself have not yet learned,* she said, without speaking.

After what seemed like many days of greeting my beloved family and friends, for time has no meaning in Heaven, Linda came to me and said it was time to rest. She told me that resting was not only a pleasure in Heaven, it was required--but Micah, she didn't say required, it wasn't a hard word like that, it was...she meant...well, I can't explain it."

Micah had made a note that Ray had started to

cough. He gave him some water and after a sip or two, Ray rushed on with his story as excited as a schoolboy. He had gained amazing control of his weakened voice.

"So, this is the best part," Micah, Ray said. "Naw, I take that back," he smiled faintly as if remembering something far away. "There are too many best parts to say that." My mother and father started to take me toward the stairs showing me the way up to my room so I could rest. For a moment I thought it must be getting late - you know, night. But when I looked out--there were windows everywhere--it was still light. There were no shadows in the house, no lamps or candles or light switches--there was no night! No darkness at all.

On the way, we passed what must have been the dining room. Becky was in there, with her friends. They were "installing" the flowers I had seen them with earlier. And what I mean by installing them is that somehow they sort of threw the flowers onto the walls--then they started working on each perfect petal and stem. They used small tools like stonecutter's chisels, but smaller. It looked like they cut into the smooth surface of the stone walls and pushed each flower into the chiseled out places so that each flower was held perfectly in place, perfectly alive and vivid with color. They had finished one of the walls and it was so beautiful; indescribable. Becky told me that everyone had a job in Heaven. And just now, she said, this was her work. She smiled for she knew I loved it.

Mother and Father did not come into my room with me. They just held the door open for me, smiled, and then quietly closed it. I was alone for the first time. I stood there trying to take it in. The room was large with a high vaulted ceiling supported by sturdy wooden beams. The floor was a dark wood, honed to a luster that was unequal to anything I have ever seen. I love to work with wood, so there were many familiar things around the room made of wood. *Some of which seemed to be copies of things I had made as gifts for others along the way.*

I turned to face a row of French doors that completely covered one wall of the room. They stood open and I could see out to the balcony, which overlooked the river below. I saw some birds perched in a nearby tree peeking in at me. Their song was so merry and bright I had to laugh out loud. A large four-poster bed dominated one wall. Each massive post of the bed had been intricately carved and embellished with hints of gold. There was so much to see in my room I decided to study the carvings on my bed, later. I noticed the bed was covered with a soft grey quilt, that looked so inviting and soft I almost climbed in immediately.

The walls were a light color that reflected the glorious light that seemed to come from everywhere. The walls in my room seemed to almost shimmer with it. Everything seemed alive. I walked over and touched one of the walls for I could not understand what it was made of. As I touched it I realized that the walls in my room were covered, from ceiling to floor with Mother of Pearl.

A dark blue sofa faced the fireplace, which was directly opposite the wall of French doors leading outside. The sofa seemed to beckon me. I had not yet grown accustomed to how everything seemed to be a part of me, or me of it. The closest I can describe it was like I was magnetically drawn to things - I can't explain this feeling - no words. But before I could sit down on the sofa, I heard something or saw it - the way you hear things and see things and know things in Heaven is so different than earth. They enter you all over, at the same time, you are connected to everything.

And it was in that way that I heard or saw a man sitting, relaxing I thought, down by the river at the back of my house. He seemed to want me to come to him, and I just went. I do not know how. As I approached him I wondered who it could be. I thought of Peter or maybe Paul, the two men I often told Linda I wanted to meet in Heaven. When I looked at him his face was unfamiliar. He was tossing a few small stones into the water. Suddenly all my attention went to the water, the ripples that were formed and spread out as each stone entered the living water. The water sparkled and again I could hear the faint music that seemed to be part of the water. I looked at the man sitting there to find that he was looking at me. His eyes were the color of a clear October sky.

Come and sit with me awhile? he said. *Of course*, I said, thinking it was Paul, the apostle. I was not yet accustomed to how people come and go in Heaven. I sat down next to him in that marvelous grass. *Can I answer any questions for you?* he asked. His smile was so warm and welcoming, so filled with unconditional love that I asked him about the water and the ripples spreading out from the stones. I knew that he wanted me to ask about it and as instantly as the question was formed in my mind, the answer was also formed.

I understood that the stones represented my earthly life and that the ripples in the living water were where my life had impacted others. I was somehow aware of who they were (can't explain). *I understood that time and distance really have no meaning, no meaning at all.* Sitting there with him, the limitations of my earthly mind were gone. In less than a second I saw the meaning of entire lifetimes, every aspect of them. Each time he finished *speaking,* I quickly asked him something else for I just wanted to *hear* the sound of his voice inside me.

Later as I looked back on that moment, I remembered the birds that had surrounded my balcony and chirped so merrily at my arrival had stopped their singing while he spoke to me. I could hear nothing but His voice. I didn't think about it at the time. It just all felt so… natural, so completely filled with love. I do not know how long we talked. It could have been minutes or years. I cannot tell you. I only know that he answered every question I ever had. He filled me with insight and wisdom that would have taken me lifetimes to learn and know on earth. I have never known anything that came even close to such complete love and wisdom. After a time, he rose to leave. I did not want him to go, but he promised we would meet again and soon.

It was only after he left that the veil in my mind was lifted and I realized my visitor was not Paul. I had just been talking with the living Christ.

(Micah noted in his journal that Ray apparently slipped into a coma at this point. Micah shook him gently twice but Ray gave no response.)

Almost an hour passed. Ray suddenly opened both eyes wide and said "Did you see that!" "What!" said Micah startled at Ray's presence back in the room. "I can fly!" A boyish grin spread across Ray's face. Micah couldn't help but grin back. "Well, that must be fun!" said Micah. "Unbelievable! People travel here by thought or if you choose, you can fly."

Ray continued. I walked down by the river again today. I began to wonder where it went, what other villages were like and what work God might give me to do once I got *established.* I turned to go up to the house and find Linda and ask her my questions, and instantly she was standing before me. *You wanted to see me*, she said, without words. I wonder if I'll ever get use to how just thinking about something can bring it to me in Heaven? Linda smiled. She knew what I was thinking. She said *Only if they want to come to you my dear, and I always do. You have so much to discover,* her smile entered me as she spoke.

"I would like to follow the river for a ways today," I said out loud, for I had not yet mastered *speaking* to others without words. "I'd like to see where it goes. Would you like to come with me?" *I have some work to do just now, but Becky may enjoy taking you. She often goes to the Crystal Sea.* Linda had no more than spoken these words when they both saw Becky coming down the lane. She was alone and smiling. *Hey, Deddy,* she said cheerfully. "Should we fly or walk to the Crystal Sea?" asked Ray. *Let's do both,* Becky answered.

And that's the way we went. Becky was a wonderful guide. One of the first things to get my attention was the trees. I love wood, you know and I was wondering what kind of wood they use to make things and build with in Heaven. Then I noticed a particular tree, growing near the river. Becky saw me looking at it and said *the leaves of that tree are used for medicine on earth. There is a cure for every disease that affects humans and animals growing on that tree.* I wanted to understand more but Becky just smiled and touched my arm. Together we began to fly over many small villages like the one my home is in. We flew over rolling hills, covered with an exquisite green carpeting of grass. I saw many things I cannot describe. "Micah, you'll just have to wait until you get here, son."

Several times we stopped flying and walked by the river, enjoying the feel of the soft earth and grass along its banks. As we walked along Becky stopped to talk to someone and I continued on alone. Thoughts of living on Rainman Island, alone after Linda's death came hurtling into my mind. Suddenly I was back on earth, in this bed! I felt utterly alone and vulnerable. I can't explain the sudden depth of loss I felt. The memory of grief and fear was so real I could almost taste them. What was happening to me! My mind raced, my heart thumped. Just as suddenly as I had been swept out of Heaven I was taken into a vision. A divine vision. It was like I was watching myself from far away. *I was in two places at once.*

In the vision my feelings of fear and sadness were quickly replaced with feelings of utter safety. I felt joyful. I saw myself draped in a long, royal robe. The robe was amazing, exquisitely made of purple velvet edged with black and white fur. The robe flowed out behind me, so that it seemed to float down the road behind me for miles. I began to walk forward. As I walked the robe grew longer and longer behind me. It grew until it crowded the road behind me, filling the road up from side to side - fold upon fold of the thick, luxurious purple; as purple and deep as the night sky. "What does this mean," I asked. A scripture from the prophet Isaiah dropped into my mind *I am overwhelmed with joy in the Lord my God! For he has dressed me with the clothing of salvation and draped me in a robe of righteousness.*

Then Christ whispered in my ear. I now knew His voice! He told me in that incredible way that His words entered me, that the robe illustrated how completely He had covered me while I was on earth. And it was a robe of royalty, Micah! He told me he always had my back - or something like that! In this dual person vision I watched myself leap with joy, laughing out loud. I understood that there had never been anything in my past or future to fear. And there had never been any need, whatsoever, to worry. And Oh, Micah, at the hours and days that I spent looking back while I lived on earth. Grieving Becky. Grieving Linda.

But what about the future, I heard myself say; *cover that, too, with this beautiful robe of your Presence! Please!* I spoke to Jesus with my mind. He was everywhere. He told me that what lies ahead involves choice. *It must be so*, He said, *both on earth and in Heaven*. He saw the questions forming in my mind. *Focus on Me*, He said, *Focus on Me, always.* "And remember, His voice had turned playful, *I always have your back.*

I longed to see Him there behind me. I saw myself playfully jump up in the air and quickly whirl around, hoping to get a glimpse of Him. I did it again and again, jump up and whirl around. And just as playfully, the Lord said *Nothing doing!* The robe, which I understood in this vision to be His love and protection, was still behind me--always it lay behind me. And then, in my vision, the robe began to grow again. It grew longer and longer until it flooded out and draped over the entire world. "What does that mean," I asked Him. I began to understand how His love and provision was everywhere on earth and how it clung to His children like a royal robe, flowing out from them and touching His world.

Suddenly I was swept back up into Heaven. "That's the way it is Micah! I'm here talking to you then I'm suddenly in Heaven, or I'm somewhere in between! I want to be there with all my heart...In Heaven."

Becky called to me and at the same time joined me. We resumed walking beside the river. We never lost sight of the river. People could be seen everywhere. Some of them waved and greeted me. I saw my aunt, my father's sister. I had not thought of her for years. Aunt Ruth waved us over and hugged me. I promised I would come back and spend time with her soon. What a joy to see her.

And angels Micah! I haven't even told you about the angels!

And then suddenly, there it was, the Crystal Sea. It loomed up in front of us without warning. The river that we had followed rushed into the sea as a lover would rush into the arms of its beloved. We walked along the bank and I could hear the music that seemed to always be a part of the water. The shore was lined with the precious stones I had seen on my first day -- sapphire, agate, emeralds and onyx. I saw amethyst and topaz and jasper and many others. Becky motioned for me to come into the water. She was already halfway in herself. At first I walked carefully into the Crystal Sea, but then, in total joyful abandon I did a belly flop. I rolled over and floated on top for a while, resting from the journey, enjoying the music of the water and the fragrance. *And God will wash away each tear from our eyes.* I heard the words rise slowly in my mind, then repeat. The words and the music were one thing, not separate. I floated in the perfectly calm sea.

I noticed a bright light radiating from what appeared to be the outline of a great domed city on the horizon. It seemed very far away on the other side of the sea. While I was curious about it, I was at the same time perfectly content to be where I was.

That's the way it is there, Micah. Curiosity merges with perfect peace and contentment. Desire merges with deep satisfaction...

(Ray turned to look at Micah and said with emphasis: *Micah it's real different from the earth.* I really can't explain it. Then he closed his eyes. Micah thought he was dozing off again but Ray continued with his eyes closed, his words slowed and he could only manage a whisper.)

I went under the water and found Becky floating there, relaxing. She was talking with some friends who had suddenly joined her. I asked her about the city I had seen. She simply said that it was the *City of God. These living waters*, she said, *flow directly from the throne of God and of the Lamb.* "Can we go there?" I asked. I felt deep joy surge up in me at the thought of it. She smiled and said *God invites us there as He wills. You will go many times, Deddy. I have not yet been, but Mother has. I have often met and talked with Jesus, but maturity is needed to stand in the throne room of God. And maturity here has nothing to do with age.* She smiled. She was finished with her explanation.

I thought of the scriptures that I had relied on so much while in my earthly life. All of them, Micah--all of them, Ray repeated slowly, came instantly to my mind without limitation but with full explanation. I no longer looked through a dark glass. God is Spirit, pure and Holy Spirit, and I understood that maturity meant that some day I would finally grow out of my need for the familiar things of earth like my home, my family or even my body. At that time there would be something...more. I understood that there are other *levels or dimensions* of this place called Heaven--infinite dimensions.

Yes, I have much to learn before I would be brought before the Holy God. But I will have all of eternity to learn and grow.

Made in the USA
Lexington, KY
30 January 2016